To Achieve Security and Wealth

Symposium on the Qing Imperial State and the Economy
History Department
The University of Akron, Akron, Ohio
22-23 February 1991

Sponsored by a grant from the Ohio Board of Regents'
Academic Challenge Program

To Achieve Security and Wealth

The Qing Imperial State and the Economy
1644–1911

Edited by
Jane Kate Leonard and John R. Watt

East Asia Program
Cornell University
Ithaca, New York 14853

The *Cornell East Asia Series* publishes manuscripts on a wide variety of scholarly topics pertaining to East Asia. Manuscripts are published on the basis of camera-ready copy provided by the volume author or editor.

Inquiries should be addressed to Editorial Board, Cornell East Asia Series, East Asia Program, Cornell University, 140 Uris Hall, Ithaca, New York 14853.

ISSN 1050-2955
ISBN 0-939657-56-2

Contents

Illustrations and Tables

Acknowledgments

The success of the Qing symposium held at The University of Akron on 22-23 February 1991 resulted from the collective efforts of sponsors, organizers, editorial assistants, typists, colleagues and graduate students, as well as the scholars who presented their research findings. I would like to express my sincere thanks to the Board of Regents of the State of Ohio for the award to the History Department of the Academic Challenge grant that funded the symposium. Thanks also are due to Claibourne E. Griffin, Dean of Buchtel College of Arts and Sciences, for his generous support of the project. I also thank my colleagues in the History Department for their help and advice, particularly Keith Bryant, head of the History Department, and Jerome Mushkat, chairperson of the departmental Colloquium Committee.

As symposium organizer, I am greatly indebted to the wonderful group of friends and scholars who participated in the program, not only for the quality of their research papers, but because they met the deadlines for submitting their papers and making revisions, and were generous and helpful with their criticisms and suggestions for fellow participants. John Watt's overall contributions as gadfly and critic were invaluable. His insightful and demanding critiques of all the papers before, during, and after the symposium helped to focus the analysis in individual papers and to tie each paper to the symposium theme. Bill Rowe's keynote lecture on Chen Hongmou and his discussions during the symposium raised important issues and provided helpful critical suggestions. Bob Gardella was characteristically generous with his time in helping out with editorial work on several of the papers.

Special thanks are also due to Joseph W. Stoll (Department of Geography) for cartographic work; to Nancy Clem (Continuing Education: Outreach Coordinator) for arrangements during the symposium; to B. P. Leonard, Jacci Baker, Anita Pfouts, and Anne Csete for editorial assistance; Edie Richeson for secretarial assistance; and David L. Bird for final preparation of camera-ready copy.

Akron, Ohio
September 1, 1992   JKL

About the Contributors

Dorothy V. Borei, Ph.D. (University of Pennsylvania) is Associate Professor of East Asian History at Guilford College and a specialist in Qing history. She is the author of several studies on Qing control and administration of Inner Asia, and is co-editor with Charles Le Blanc of *Studies in Chinese Thought and Institutions* (Princeton, 1981).

Robert P. Gardella, Ph.D. (University of Washington) is Professor of History at the U.S. Merchant Marine Academy and a specialist in Qing economic and business history. He has authored numerous studies on the Qing tea trade and Chinese bookkeeping and accounting practices, including "Sitting on Mountains and Facing the Sea," Southeast China and the World Market: The Fujian Tea Trade, 1757-1937.

Chi-kong Lai is completing his doctorate in history at the University of California-Davis and is specializing in modern Chinese business history. In the spring, 1992, he held the position of Visiting Professor of History at the University of Utah, and recently began a research fellowship at the Institute for the Study of Economic Culture, Boston University.

Jane Kate Leonard, Ph.D. (Cornell University) is Associate Professor of History at the University of Akron and a specialist in late Qing history. She has authored studies on Chinese foreign relations, including *Wei Yuan and China's Rediscovery of the Maritime World* (Harvard 1984) and recently completed a study of Qing administration of the Grand Canal.

Andrea McElderry, Ph.D. (University of Michigan) is Professor of History at the University of Louisville and a specialist in modern Chinese economic and business history. She has authored several studies on late Qing and Republican history, including *Shanghai Old-style Banks (Ch'ien-chuang) 1800-1935* (Center for Chinese Studies, University of Michigan, 1976) and currently edits the newsletter: *Chinese Business History*.

Susan Mann, Ph.D. (Stanford University) is Professor of History at the University of California-Davis. She is a specialist in modern Chinese social and economic history and is the author of *Local Merchants and the Chinese Bureaucracy, 1750-1950* (Stanford University Press, 1987). Recently, she has written numerous articles on Chinese women's history and is currently completing a cultural history of women during the Qing period.

E-tu Zen Sun, Ph.D. (Radcliffe College) is Professor Emerita of Chinese History at The Pennsylvania State University after a long and distinguished scholarly career in the Qing field. Her scholarly contributions include studies of late imperial Chinese social, economic, and administrative history as well as the history of science and technology. She compiled *Ch'ing Administrative Terms* (Harvard University Press, 1961); she co-edited *T'ien-kung k'ai-wu: Chinese Technology in the Seventeenth Century*, with Shiou-chuan Sun (Pennsylvania State University Press, 1966); and she wrote "The Growth of the Academic Community, 1912-1949" in the *Cambridge History of China*, Vol. 13 (1986).

Louis T. Sigel, Ph.D. (Harvard University) has held university-level teaching and research positions in Australia; was a visiting scholar in the Department of Economics and School of Management at Zhongshan University in Guangzhou in the People's Republic; and is currently Assistant Professor of History, Eastern Kentucky State University. He is a specialist in modern Chinese foreign relations and economic history, and has written numerous articles on late Qing foreign policy and the Chinese commercial community as well as studies of recent economic reforms in the PRC.

John R. Watt, Ph.D. (Columbia University) is executive secretary of the Committee on International Relations Studies with the PRC and former editor of the *American Asian Review*. He is a specialist in Qing political-administrative history and has written studies of district-level government, including: *The District Magistrate in Late Imperial China* (Columbia University Press, 1972). He also has written extensively on aspects of health care and medical technology in contemporary China.

1

Introduction

Jane Kate Leonard and John R. Watt

The relationship between the Qing state and the economy has perplexed scholars for decades. Conscious of China's struggle to survive in the twentieth century and caught in the often rancorous debates about its modern fate, many scholars have been harshly critical of the Qing state's inability to foster and support modern economic development in the late nineteenth and early twentieth centuries. They consider its backward-looking administrative practices, its exploitive approach to the private economy, and its corrupt management of the fiscal system to have been the major obstacles to rational economic development (Balazs 1964; Feuer-werker 1958; Kennedy 1974; Perkins 1967). Other scholars, especially those investigating aspects of Qing administrative, fiscal, and business history, have tended to approach the question of the Qing state's relationship to the private economy more broadly (Chan 1980; Hao 1986; King 1965; Perdue 1987; McElderry 1976; Quan and Kraus 1975; Wang 1973; Will 1990; Vogel 1983). They have examined the nature and operation of administrative, fiscal, and business institutions and have judged their practical achievements in terms of Qing goals. These studies generally succeed in conveying the internal logic of Qing institutions and administrative patterns, and they show how the state's commitment to an agricultural economy and economic stability was linked to what modern economic historians would consider to be non-economic issues, such as social stability, internal security, and strategic-logistical control of the empire.

The studies in the present volume explore various facets of the Qing state's approach to the economy, its goals, functions, and the manner of its interface with private economic organizations through which it worked to achieve many of its fiscal and strategic objectives. They cover a range of topics, but central to each is an attempt to define and explain security and economic issues in Qing terms and to sharpen the conceptual foci to express Qing realities. Their search for meaningful interpretive categories draws attention to the fact that such terms as "state," "security," and "economy" often do not have precise correlates in the Qing experience, and it highlights the daunting problems that Qing scholars face as they struggle to find appropriate analytical and descriptive language to convey culturally specific historical phenomena.

The Qing state—call it imperium or government (*guan*)—performed a mix of fiscal, security, and ideological functions. Taken together, these functions defined the government's "strategic sphere" of operations, a sphere whose ultimate goal was the achievement of a more perfect moral-political order. For the Qing, the term "state" conveys both less and more than the Western referent. While its bureaucratic functions, centering narrowly on tax collection and security, were more limited than those of modern governments, its overarching moral-cosmic functions far exceeded those of the secular state in the West.

The notion of "security" in the Qing context is equally problematic. While scholars use the term to refer to a range of practical political and military issues connected to internal pacification and the defense of the borderlands, the Qing leadership explicitly included pivotal economic issues in their discussion of security. They took for granted the Mencian dictum that economic ordering necessarily precedes political and moral ordering, and they therefore linked problems associated with the "people's livelihood" (*minsheng*) directly to questions of security. The management of both was intimately related to their moral mission and comprised the central tasks of the state's strategic sphere of operations.

Though economic issues bore significantly on the state's strategic sphere, Qing participation in and control over the practical operations of the economy were extremely limited. This dependence on, yet distance from, the practical operations of the economy defined the Qing state's relationship to the private economy, and this lies at the heart of interpretive issues that seek to explain the seemingly contradictory elements of Qing policy toward the people's livelihood and the semi-autonomous "productive sphere" at the sub-district level. The people, not the state, dominated the productive sphere, or economy, and its operations were driven by the people in their quest for economic security and survival. In this context, the term "economy" refers to those wealth-producing activities, closely bound to sub-district social structures, that generated "the state's resources and the people's livelihood" (*guoji minsheng*) and supported the family, the community, and the state. This Qing view of the economy as a sub-district phenomenon, outside the direction and control of the government, yet supporting the latter's strategic mission, conveys the separateness and autonomy of the people's productive sphere while underscoring its intimate connection with the state's strategic sphere and the integrality of both to the whole of the civilization.

Within these general conceptual boundaries, the following studies explore various aspects of the Qing imperium's stewardship of the economy, its deep concern over the strategic-moral implications of the people's livelihood, and its multiplicity of approaches to enhancing the state's resources and the people's livelihood.

E-tu Sun examines the state's relationship to the economy by analyzing the Finance Ministry's (Hubu) links with private economic interests. Drawing on her earlier studies of Qing economic and administrative history, she defines three basic modes of operation that this central ministry undertook to carry out its long-established normative functions: the "regulatory," "participatory," and "command" (*zhaoshang*) modes. She gives extensive treatment to the last and shows how the Hubu recruited private capital and managerial resources for investment in enterprises that the state considered important to its goals, but because of its own capital and bureaucratic limitations, sought to enlist private organizations and resources to achieve them. The study reveals the limited means at the Hubu's disposal to regulate, intervene, and direct private sectors of the economy, and it suggests that perhaps the Hubu's limited institutional resources shaped its cooperative and conciliatory approach to enterprises in which the state had a strategic stake.

Dorothy Borei analyzes the Qing imperial program for agricultural development in Xinjiang that was designed to achieve agricultural self-sufficiency after the conquest of this region in the mid-eighteenth century. She shows how the Qing state undertook the direct funding and management of "start-up" initiatives in Xinjiang that were similar to those used to restore agriculture in China proper during the early Qing period. These initiatives included experimentation with seed varieties and new agricultural techniques, the construction of water conservancy infrastructure, tax incentives, and the recruitment of agriculturalists from outside the region. She argues that these measures were undertaken in order to cover the costs of the Qing political-military presence in the region and to guarantee the long-term political integration of this volatile and ethnically diverse area into the Qing empire. Her study underscores the creativity of Qing agricultural policy and the purpose with which it was pursued. Both demonstrate the Qing regime's assumption that political security was a function of economic order and prosperity, especially in the border regions. Jane Leonard considers the Qing imperium's strategic concern over economic issues that bore on the security of the canal zone during the Grand Canal crisis in the mid-1820s. She examines the controversy over the plan to use grain tax commutation in 1826 to fund large-scale repairs of the Grand Canal in northern Jiangsu. She argues that the Qing leadership rejected the commutation plan because its implementation threatened to disrupt local monetary and market conditions, causing conflict and unrest in the canal zone. Instead, the leadership adopted two temporary schemes for grain transport in 1826: canal lighterage and sea transport, both of which relied on private shippers. These findings highlight the Qing leadership's assumption that economic disorder breeds political disorder, and they also provide an important example of the government's willingness to work with, indeed to rely on, private economic groups to perform important strategic-logistical functions.

Susan Mann brings a gender perspective to the study of Qing policy towards home handicrafts, especially female production of textiles. She shows how the Qing leadership used a variety of ritual-political measures to promote a system of agricultural and craft production that centered in the household and insured household self-sufficiency and stability. She contends that this policy fostered a gender division of labor and that it bound craft production and female labor to the household unit. Her study raises tantalizing questions about the implications of this household-based economy for modern economic development and women's roles in that development. It also shows how Qing ritual, myth, custom, and law all combined to reinforce the family-based system of production and to make it a founding pillar of the Qing political-moral order.

Robert Gardella's study of the Qing tea trade analyzes changing marketing patterns in four different regional contexts: Mongolia, Fujian-Guangdong, Inner Asia-Russia, and Sichuan-Tibet. He documents the enormous expansion of the tea trade during the Qing period, in comparison to the Ming, especially in the Inner Asian borderlands; and in each of the four cases, he carefully delineates the factors that contributed to its unique region-specific character. He argues that the reason for its spectacular growth and expansion was the flexibility of Qing regulatory policy toward this trade in each of its regional contexts. These findings draw attention to the creativity of Qing policy toward the tea trade, and they demonstrate the way the Qing regime used commercial policy to enhance its strategic goals in the border regions.

Andrea McElderry looks at state-private interactions from the bottom up and focuses broadly on the institution of guarantorship and its use in working out the practical aspects of state-private ventures. She shows how the principle of guarantorship shaped the terms by which the state worked with and through private groups and individuals to perform important functions connected with customs administration, grain marketing, the ginseng and salt monopolies, and the accumulation of monetary copper; and she also suggests how these usages, particularly those connected with brokerage and licensing, changed and evolved over time. Her focus on guarantorship highlights the pivotal role that this key institution played in facilitating joint ventures between the state and private economic organizations.

Chi-kong Lai re-examines the problem of state involvement in the development of modern enterprises in the late nineteenth century as he looks anew at the rise and decline of the China Merchants' Steam Navigation Company, China's first joint-stock company, from 1872 to 1902. He analyzes and contrasts the specific features of "government supervision and merchant management" (*guandu-shangban*) during the first thirteen years of the company's operation with those of the last seventeen years. He argues that the company flourished in the first period because officials did not interfere with the practical aspects of the firm's management. It floundered and failed, however, during the last period when the company was subject to official interference. The study reveals the adaptability and innovativeness of officials, like Li Hongzhang, who helped found and shepherd the company in its early stages, and it shows how changing economic and political conditions in the late nineteenth century sparked changes in long-established patterns of state-merchant enterprise.

Finally, Louis Sigel considers the partnership between the Qing state and merchant interests in confronting "foreign" problems in Korea in the nineteenth century. He shows how Chinese merchants, working closely with Li Hongzhang, shaped and carried out policies that succeeded in blocking and reversing Japanese commercial and political penetration of Korea in the 1870s and 1880s. He contends that these merchant initiatives, motivated by both economic goals and nationalistic sentiment, worked successfully against the Japanese until the latter resorted to war in the 1890s. The study draws attention to the importance of threats to the maritime frontier and of the new role of nationalism in the late nineteenth century, and it shows how these two factors reshaped old patterns of state relations with private merchant groups and extended their reach to the conduct of foreign relations and trade in foreign places.

Taken together, these studies show a rich and varied pattern of Qing interactions with the private economy that served to stabilize the imperial state, while at the same time encouraging the development of private economic interests and expanding the options available to the people as they worked to establish a secure livelihood. The legalist character of the state notwithstanding, the pattern of interaction suggests a kind of mutuality that is reflected in the phrase, "the state's resources and the people's livelihood," and it underscores both the separateness and the connectedness of the state's strategic sphere and the people's productive sphere. The diverse threads of this pattern were shaped by the Qing leadership's emphasis on economic prosperity as a means to achieve security in the early years of the dynasty and their continuing efforts to create an environment within which economic growth and prosperity could flourish. Later, when growth and change created new problems and placed intense pressure on the lower levels of government and on customary institutions at the sub-district level, the state and private economic groups continued to work out new mechanisms to guide their interactions. These mechanisms gradually changed the nature of the relationship itself and altered the balance between the two, paving the way for dramatic innovations in sub-district institutions in the modern period.

References

Balazs, Étienne. 1964. *Chinese Civilization and Bureaucracy*. New Haven: Yale University Press.

Chan, Wellington K. K. 1980. "Government, Merchants and Industry to 1911." In *Cambridge History of China* 11, ed. John K. Fairbank and Kwang-ching Liu, 416-62. Cambridge: Cambridge University Press.

Feuerwerker, Albert. 1958. *China's Early Industrialization: Sheng Hsuan-huai (1844-1916) and Mandarin Enterprise*. Cambridge, Mass.: Harvard University Press.

Hao, Yen-p'ing. 1986. *The Commercial Revolution in Nineteenth-Century China. The Rise of Sino-Western Mercantile Capitalism* Berkeley: University of California Press.

Kennedy, Thomas L. 1974. Self-Strengthening: An Analysis Based on Some Recent Writings. *Ch'ing-shih wen-t'i* 3, 1:3-35.

King, F.H.H. 1965. *Money and Monetary Policy in China*. Cambridge, Mass.: Harvard University Press.

Lai, Chikong. 1990. Lunchuan zhaoshangju jingyin guanli wenti, 1872-1901 (Enterprise management of the China Merchants' Steam Navigation Company, 1872-1901). *Bulletin of the Institute of Modern History, Academia Sinica* (Taibei) 19:67-108.

McElderry, Andrea. 1976. *Shanghai Old-Style Banks (Ch'ien-chuang), 1800-1937.* Michigan Papers in Chinese Studies. Ann Arbor: Center for Chinese Studies, University of Michigan.

Perdue, Peter. 1987. *Exhausting the Earth. State and Peasant in Hunan, 1500-1850.* Cambridge, Mass.: Council on East Asian Studies, Harvard University.

Perkins, Dwight H. 1967. The Government as an Obstacle to Industrialization: The Case of Nineteenth-Century China. *Journal of Economic History* 27, 7:478-92.

_____, ed. 1975. *China's Modern Economy in Historical Perspective.* Stanford: Stanford University Press.

Quan, Hansheng and Richard Kraus. 1975. *Mid-Ch'ing Rice Markets and Trade: An Essay in Price History.* Cambridge, Mass.: East Asian Research Center, Harvard University.

Vogel, Hans Ulrich. 1983. Chinese Central Monetary Policy and Yunnan Copper Mining in the Early Qing (1644-1800). Ph.D. diss., University of Zurich.

Wang, Yeh-chien. 1973. *Land Taxation in Imperial China, 1750-1911.* Cambridge, Mass.: Harvard University Press.

Will, Pierre-Étienne. 1990. *Bureaucracy and Famine in Eighteenth-Century China*, trans. Elborg Forster. Rev. ed. Stanford: Stanford University Press.

2

The Finance Ministry (Hubu) and Its Relationship to the Private Economy in Qing Times

E-tu Zen Sun

Introduction

The Qing state's relationship to the private economy is a theme that raises important questions about the state's presence and actual involvement in the daily lives of its people. While it is generally recognized that the Confucian state provided an all-encompassing ideological and strategic framework for the empire, its concrete interactions were as limited as its administrative structure was thinly spread. The Hubu, or Finance Ministry, exemplifies the government's overarching supervisory role, while simultaneously revealing its limited means for achieving its narrowly defined normative goals. Yet, within those limited means, certain patterns and practices are discernible that reveal the nature of the state's interactions with the private economy and with its subjects' quest for a secure livelihood.

In the Qing imperium, the Hubu was a key branch of the central bureaucracy that oversaw a multitude of activities pertinent to the economic life of the people and of the well-being of the empire. These activities ranged from population census, taxation of all types, and regulation of trade, to the administration of such government-controlled enterprises as salt, tea, coinage, and mining. The Hubu operated on two levels to perform these tasks. At the central level, it acted as the treasury, the

9

accounting office, and the paymaster-general for the Banners and other organs of state close to the court. At the provincial level, the Hubu's role was that of central superviser. The fourteen administrative departments, each named after a different province, but whose functions had little to do with its provincial label, received tax records and reports on economic and financial matters from all the provincial and territorial governments throughout the empire. Finally, the Hubu compiled economic data and provided important technical information that was used to inform the central-regional decision-making process (Sun [1964] 3).

It is important to note, however, that, like the other central ministries, the Hubu possessed no sub-offices of its own in the provinces. In order to attain its stated objectives, therefore, it had to depend upon a close intermeshing of its goals and policies with the bureaucratic apparatus of the provincial and county administrations. While the Hubu was not in a position within the bureaucratic hierarchy to issue direct orders to the governor or the governor-general of a province, there were channels within the government structure that held those in charge of financial and economic affairs in the provinces accountable to the central government via the Hubu. The financial commissioner of each province, the customs superintendents, and the circuit intendants were answerable to the Hubu which had overall responsibility for supervising all financial and economic matters for the country (Sun [1964] 18-22).

An overview of the Hubu's role in the Qing economy, therefore, serves to identify the practical operations of the state behind the ideals, and it also reveals the distinctive features of the Hubu's normative interactions with the larger economy. These features stand in direct contrast, in many cases, to the kinds of discrete interactions explored in the other studies in this volume. In terms of official goals and methods and their impact on the economic communities involved, the Hubu's principal interactions with the private economy can be described as falling into three categories, identified here as regulatory, participatory, and command.

Regulatory Acts

Regulatory acts were those that the Hubu undertook to assist in maintaining social and political stability and included matters relating to trade and customs collection. In matters of this kind, the Qing emperors always explained the necessity of customs taxes in ideological terms and maintained that social stability was more significant than simple fiscal yield. The Qing emperors also warned Hubu officials to eliminate abuses and show judicious restraint in the collection of duties at customs stations, reminding them that "customs duties were instituted by the state to facilitate trade, not to obstruct it" (HDSL 239:4-5, 24-25). In 1686, for example, the Hubu, after consultation with other metropolitan officials, received an edict that customs duties should be levied only on sea-going ships and not on boats and carts used in local business, so as to conform to the emperor's desire "to protect commerce" (HDSL 239:3).

Manipulation of customs duties to achieve price stabilization could also be used to ward off potential social unrest. In 1737 the Hubu ordered high provincial officials in areas stricken by natural disasters to see to it that grain prices were kept from rising, and this was to be accomplished by the import of duty-free grain shipments to offset local shortages. This temporary suspension of customs collection was justified because grain was the people's basic food supply and was "different from other commodities." Grain tax therefore was not to be collected mechanically without regard to the state of the harvest (HDSL 239:16). Examples abound of this sort of use of customs levies as a tool of social regulation. In fact, procedural rules of implementation were sometimes made flexible in order to facilitate the conveyance of grain to needy areas. Nor was famine relief the only cause for the temporary remission of customs duties. It was recorded that during the second and third year of the Qianlong reign, the duties on food grains and fuel were suspended at the Huai'an customs station to prevent sharp price rises for these goods at nearby sites on the Grand Canal where "hundreds of thousands" of laborers were at work dredging the Grand Canal (Wang 1901, 6:4b-5).

The state also restricted specific areas of commerce in order to manipulate and stabilize commodity prices. In response to complaints from domestic textile producers that increased exports of raw silk, primarily to Britain, had led to a sharp rise in the price of silk, the Qianlong Emperor ordered a ban on all silk exports. However, in 1762 this policy was, for the most part, reversed because the attempt at price stabilization through curbing exports had failed to lower the market price of raw silk; and it appeared, instead, that high prices had resulted from increases in population. Therefore, when British merchants petitioned for a resumption of silk exports in order to ease the plight of British textile workers who had lost their livelihood when deprived of Chinese silk supplies, new regulations in 1762 restored silk exports. These regulations imposed clearly stated quantitative limits on each shipload, the maximum being eight thousand *catties* per ship, including any silk fabrics which could be converted at a 20 percent discount in weight (HDSL 239:25-26). Here was a case where administrative measures were ineffective as a means to achieve economic goals.

Participatory Acts

In the participatory approach, the state asserted its authority over selected industries that produced goods considered essential to the government. Copper production in Yunnan was an enterprise of this type. As copper was absolutely essential to the bimetallic monetary system, the Qing government assumed the responsibility for ensuring a reliable supply of this metal. Beginning in the first decade of the eighteenth century, the central government through the Hubu regularly allocated one million *taels* each year as subsidy to copper mines in Yunnan. As a result, copper production reached unprecedented levels during the remainder of the eighteenth and early nineteenth centuries. On the surface, the state had achieved its objective over this long period. The government purchased approximately 80 percent of the refined copper at an official fixed price and then delivered it to the government mints for coinage, while another 10 percent was levied as tax, with the remaining portion sold by the producer on the commercial market. Other mining and smelting enterprises, such as those producing lead and silver, were also relevant to the monetary system. These enterprises were placed under similar government control. At each of these mining sites, which normally included smelting furnaces as well, local officials were stationed to supervise the production. An official's ability to meet the quota set for the mine under his charge would be a part of his performance record and used to evaluate his work (HBZL 35:2).

Command Acts

More than the participatory mode, the command approach was the preferred approach to direct government involvement in economic activities. This approach encouraged the use of private human and material resources to realize specific public policy goals. The word "command" (*zhaoshang*) is used here in its purist sense to portray the ideational assumption underlying state economic activism and the way by which the impartial bureaucracy sought to assert its power and influence in the use of the country's resources. In this case, the state attempted to "recruit merchant capital" or simply "recruit investment" as a means of funding government projects. This approach was somewhat like issuing government bonds in order to raise money for specific government objectives, only without the bonds or any formula for recouping the investment by the investors. Private interests were simply asked to use their resources to fund projects the government needed to develop, especially when official funds were in short supply. Although the *zhaoshang* approach was not a regular feature of routine economic administration, when it was proposed as a way to get an enterprise started, the government rarely showed any objections to it on either philosophical or practical grounds. Many critically important ventures were undertaken on the basis of *zhaoshang*, such as the large-scale importation of Japanese copper in the early Qing. Since the Qianlong period, the *hong* merchants of Guangzhou were certainly a prime example of the *zhaoshang* principle in action.

This command principle manifested itself in smaller enterprises closer to home as well. As early as 1682, rich merchants were called to invest in Yunnan mines. Later in high Qing, as government mints continued to search for the ingredients needed in coinage, a case emerged in Shaanxi where the effectiveness of "recruiting investment" was put to the test (SZ 1744, 4:3-8). Faced with the problem of having to put more coins into circulation in order to correct the high exchange rate of copper cash to silver, the governor of Shaanxi in 1749 had copper mines and smelters opened in Lonan county of Shangzhou prefecture, using "recruited" capital as the means of operation. After several changes in investors over eight years and with very little copper produced, the Hubu in 1757 concluded that circumstances warranted closing down the project. By this time, those who had put their money into this venture, either singly or in partnership, had used all available funds with negligible return.

Somewhat more flexible measures in the command mode were adopted toward the iron industry in Jiaying, Guangdong province, where the chief aim of the government was to obtain tax revenues rather than procure material. From the eighteenth to the early nineteenth centuries, a combination of "recruiting investment" and tax contracts was in force. First, the local authorities enlisted an investor to "fill the position" (*chengchung*) of iron-master at a designated iron furnace; then the investor-cum-operator agreed to a contract with the authorities that contained standard terms for such enterprises. The agreement normally required the iron producer to pay a tax of approximately fifty *taels* for each furnace in production, which was to be collected by local officials and forwarded along with the annual land tax. The purpose of this assessment, however, was for military provisions and was so earmarked in the Hubu reports (SGYS 1:309-10). When a smelter declined and production diminished below economically practical levels, the operation would normally be permitted by the Hubu to close down (SGYS 1:312-13). But such was not always the case. In 1815, political concerns at a time of popular unrest prompted the Jiaqing Emperor to forbid the shutting down of two iron furnaces in Jiaying for fear that the workers who thus would be unemployed would turn into bandits and rebels (SGYS 1:311).

The *zhaoshang* principle was applied to enterprises other than the mineral industries. It is well known, for example, that the merchant ships that went to Japan to purchase copper for the official mints belonged to private entrepreneurs on government mission who had responded to the government's call. As an inducement, these merchants received permission to trade on their own account. In another context, there is evidence that at times local officials used the *zhaoshang* method to help them cope with the problem of bringing food to famine areas. In 1794, an edict ordered officials in Fujian to handle the work of transporting food supplies themselves and not to "recruit merchants" so as to prevent malfeasance (HDSL 239:21).

On a much higher fiscal level than the iron furnaces of Guangdong were the *hong* merchants of Guangzhou, the most visible examples of the *zhaoshang* principle in action. Originally "recruited" on the basis of their considerable mercantile wealth, these entrepreneurs as a group came to play a significant role in both an economic and political sense. In the eighty years or so of their monopoly of Qing-European trade, while large fortunes were made and lost, these merchants functioned as an extension of state authority in foreign relations. What is interesting to note here is that the central authorities constantly scrutinized the actions of this group. The *hongs'* internal organization especially was discussed often by the Hubu and other metropolitan officials, and they were also the subject of imperial queries, such as how to recruit new merchants into the group and whether it was advisable to have a head merchant to be held accountable (HDSL 240:8-9). The pace of official acts in these respects accelerated toward the early nineteenth century as the system's weaknesses became evident.

Other Aspects

The interaction between the Hubu and the Qing economy was, therefore, multifaceted. Over time, government presence in many important areas of economic activity appeared to be a given. This presence, however, was not universal, as certain types of industries were largely left to private endeavors. The sizable lumber industry in Jiuzhi, Shaanxi, was a case in point. Timbering had had a long history in this mountainous area. In the

Daoguang period, it was noted that to start a lumber camp here, one needed to make a substantial investment and hire a large labor force. The government, however, did not appear to have acted either as a funding source, nor did it regard lumber as an administratively crucial commodity that required the recruitment of private capital for its development or of private managers for its supervision. Government authorities confined their attention in this industry to periodic check-ups and the updating of tax records (SGYS 1:306-309).

On the other hand, if we wish to understand the activist stance of the Hubu in the national economy, we come inevitably face to face with the political-cultural assumption that the organized power of the state did indeed have an important part to play in guiding and shaping the economy. This assumption was linked to an ideological framework that affected all levels of the bureaucracy. An activist Hubu could find its counterparts in many other branches of government. In the Daoguang period, Yan Ruyi, governor-general of Shaanxi, spoke in a heavily didactic voice to the peasants of that province on the virtues of hard work and frugality, and he opened his long colloquial poem addressed to them with these lines:

> Industry and frugality are essential to livelihood,
> But ignorant hill farmers know this not.
> How frightful to see land gone to waste!
> So listen to my rhymes to instruct the farmers.
> (SN 12:609)

The Hubu did not exist in a separate world when carrying out command acts in the government's interaction with the private sector. The concept of the state's primacy in the use of private resources permeated the entire bureaucracy, particularly, it seems, at the policy-making levels. The following episode, as recounted by a county magistrate, illustrates the preponderance of state authority that, as the empire progressed toward high Qing, showed just how the common citizen fitted into the overall system.

While serving as magistrate of Tancheng in the 1670s, Huang Liu-hong received an order from the Ministry of Military Affairs (Bingbu) to supply it with lumber for the construction of gun carriages. Huang immediately summoned "the members of the gentry and local elders" to a meeting at the Temple of the City God. To start off the project, forty *taels* from the county treasury were distributed among these local leaders for purchase of the lumber and its delivery to Beijing. Any additional expenses that might be incurred would be credited against these persons' future tax payments, provided this was approved by the Hubu. The total expenditures amounted to one hundred *taels* when the lumber was finally delivered to Beijing, accompanied by four of the local leaders. The Bingbu, however, refused to accept their lumber, saying it was sub-standard. Instead, the four Tancheng men were given two options: either buy the necessary lumber from the government stockpile or go back to Tancheng and do the project all over again. The men chose the first alternative, which cost them an additional two hundred *taels*, making the total cost of the lumber project three hundred *taels*. The government sent down seven *taels* as reimbursement. Appeals for a larger amount fell on deaf ears in Beijing, and Magistrate Huang and the several rural leaders were compelled to absorb this big loss as best they could (Huang 1984, 602-603).

One could multiply the countless times that the state failed to recompense private interests that had undertaken projects for the state. This was particularly evident in situations where provincial and local government had a somewhat greater role to play than the central government, for example, in public works projects of a highly localized nature. Dike reconstruction in Shunde county in the Pearl River delta was a case in point. Following a major flood in the late Qianlong period, as much as thirty thousand *taels* were needed to repair serious breaches in the dikes that protected poldered farm land. The county magistrate urged an obviously reluctant group of leading landowners in the affected areas to contribute their share according to their ability to pay: "Let the reasonably well-off pay according to the acreage they own, and the wealthy ones contribute generously" (SD 4:9-10).

Contributions for public works projects could become a major financial obligation for wealthy households in the delta region. Between 1760 and 1829, the Wu family made three large donations toward dike building that totaled 133,000 *taels*, mainly because new construction techniques were so costly that local government was unable to finance it (Sun 1981, 196-97). Unlike the wealthy magnates who received a government grant of land for draining the fens in East Anglia from the sixteenth to the eighteenth centuries (Gough 1969, Chap. 12), the Guangdong landlords apparently received no direct material compensation in return for financing these public projects. They were simply fulfilling a role expected of them under the operating tenets of state-private economic relationships in Qing times.

At the same time, the state, as initiator and exerciser of economic authority, continued to be the prevalent framework. In the late nineteenth century, when economic reform and modernization became national imperatives, it was hardly surprising to see the government take upon itself an activist role in the introduction of modern improvements. When the provincial government of Henan established a silk textile bureau in 1881, for instance, it simultaneously performed a range of related functions, from recruiting accomplished artisans from the prime silk-producing areas of the lower Yangzi, setting up classes to teach local apprentices, and fixing the monthly wages, material costs, and production quotas for the textile workshop, to evaluating the quality of instruction by the artisans and the progress of the pupils (SGYS 2:20-22).

Fallibilities in the Pattern

One must pause and ask, how did all those Hubu-state modes work? Did the various types of interactions indicate a general consensus on economic norms, or were differences in perspectives a significant problem? From the instances cited above, it is clear that under the surface of all three modes lurked the potential for conflict between state priorities and private interests. A few examples will suffice to illustrate what was, in fact, an endemic state of tension whether the government's strategy was regulatory, participatory, or command. When customs remission was used as a means of stabilizing food prices, the customs officials were, at the same time, ordered to ensure that duty-free grain boats were indeed destined for famine relief and not for private profiteering. Traders who violated this rule and the officials in charge were all to be penalized in the event that this occurred (HDSL 239:17).

As an example of the actual operation of the participatory mode, the Yunnan copper industry generated persistent disputes between the producers and the Hubu respecting what the former regarded as artificially low official prices paid for refined copper. Because of the importance of this metal to the monetary system of the empire, the government was compelled to adjust its policy, not only in raising the official procurement prices slightly, but also in permitting a larger proportion of the copper to enter the commercial market (Sun 1968).

Under the command mode, the recruitment of private capital for the pursuit of state objectives led to recurrent friction. In some instances, private investors adopted the tactic of passive resistance by asserting, for example, that the enterprise—mine and/or smelter—should be closed because the ore had been exhausted. Another way to resist the government's call was simply to ignore it. In just such a case, the local government of Jiaying, Guangdong, had to make up a shortfall in iron furnace taxes because it was unable to attract enough investors to operate the iron smelters (SGYS 1:311). Nevertheless, *zhaoshang* retained its hold on the thinking of policy makers as a viable option even in the latter part of the nineteenth century. An obvious case was the China Merchants' Steam Navigation Company that utilized private capital, merchant management, and general government supervision. It is significant that the term *zhaoshang* was in the Chinese name of this firm. In 1874, Li Hongzhang urged the recruitment of Tianjin merchants to ship government grain tribute from the Yangzi River to North China via the coastal route (LHC 1:12).

Li Hongzhang's persistence in resorting to the *zhaoshang* method, at a time when it seemed to be less than productive, throws interesting light on the mind-set of late-Qing officials. They were prepared to make necessary modifications to the *zhaoshang* ideal in order to adjust to new practical imperatives. At the inception of the China Merchants' Steam Navigation Company, Li, as the major initiator and promoter, was keenly aware of the intertwining of the needs of the state, such as establishing a Chinese navigation firm, with the question of the method of funding the enterprise. Li, at first, was optimistic that the *zhaoshang* approach would provide just the right answer: private capital was to be recruited to enable the government to set up a company in order to compete with foreign companies in the carrying trade, and the operation should be supervised by the government. Lack of private investment in the early years of the company and mistakes in official management gave the enterprise a precarious start. It was the commercial wealth and business expertise of Tang Jingxing and Xu Run that succeeded in putting the company on a solid financial and managerial foundation; and, for a number of years, the private sector appeared to have gained a strong, almost controlling, role in the enterprise. Eventually, however, the private side proved unable to overcome the weight of traditional state power (Lai 1990, 17 ff.).

Yet, the very fact that the Tang and Xu groups were able to gain enough influence within the China Merchants' Company so as to be largely responsible for its development for some two decades, was indicative of the fallibility of the perceived traditional ideals and methods. In the last quarter of the nineteenth century, non-traditional configurations of resources and thought patterns were increasingly being felt, which demanded more reflection and adjustment from the side of the Qing state. As William McNeill once said, "Any theory about human life, if widely believed, will alter actual behavior, usually by inducing people to act as if the theory were true. Ideas and ideals thus become self-validating within remarkably elastic limits" (McNeill 1986, 2). The intermeshing of state goals and private economic interests, despite tensions and conflicts, had worked reasonably well over a long period under the Qing. What is significant for the historian is the legacy of the activist state in terms of economic decisions.

It seems clear that the ideals and ideas concerning the role of the state have outlived the traditional imperial system itself.

References

AAAS. 1990. Conference Report: Workshop on Confucian Humanism. *Bulletin of the American Academy of Arts and Sciences* 43, 9 (March).

Gough, J. W. 1969. *The Rise of the Entrepreneur*. New York: Schocken Books.

HBZL. [1865] 1968. *Qinding Hubu Zeli* (Imperial Qing laws and regulations of the Finance Ministry). Reprint. Taibei.

HDSL. [1899] 1963. *Da Qing huidian shili* (Imperial Qing statutes and precedents). Reprint. Taibei.

Huang, Liu-hung. 1984. *A Complete Book Concerning Happiness and Benevolence*. Trans. Djang Chu. Tucson: University of Arizona Press.

Huang, Philip C. C. 1990. *The Peasant Family and Rural Development in the Yangzi Delta, 1350-1988*. Stanford: Stanford University Press.

Lai, Chi-kong. 1990. Lunchuan zhaoshangju jingyin guanli wenti 1872-1901 (Enterprise management of the China Steam Navigation Company 1872-1901). *Bulletin of the Institute of Modern History, Academia Sinica* (Taibei) 19:67-108 (June).

LHC. [N.d.] 1962. *Li Wenzhong Gong chuanji* (Collected writings of Li Hongzhang). Reprint. Taibei.

McNeill, William H. 1986. Mythistory, or Truth, Myth, History, and Historians. *American Historical Review* 91, 1 (February).

SD. [1929] 1966. *Shunde xian zhi* (Gazetteer of Shunde county, Guangdong province). Reprint. Taibei.

SGYS. 1957. *Zhongguo jindai shougongye shi ziliao* (Source material on modern Chinese labor history). 2 vols. Beijing: Sanlian.

SN. N.d. *Shaanxi Shangnan xian zhi* (Gazetteer of Shangnan county, Shaanxi province). N.p.

Sun, E-tu Zen. [1964] 1981. The Board of Revenue in Nineteenth-Century China. (*Harvard Journal of Asiatic Studies*). Reprinted in *Selected Essays in Chinese Economic History*. Taibei.

_____. 1968. Ch'ing Government and the Mineral Industries before 1800. *Journal of Asian Studies* 27, 4 (August).

_____. 1981. "Changing Landscape of the Canton Delta in the Ch'ing Period." In *Selected Essays in Chinese Economic History*. Institute of Advanced Chinese Studies and Research, New Asia College, Hong Kong. Taibei: Student Book Co.

SZ. 1744. *Xu Shangzhou zhi* (Supplemental gazetteer of Shangzhou prefecture, Shaanxi province). N.p.

Wang, Qingyun. 1901. *Xichao jizheng* (Political records of the glorious dynasty). Shanghai: Tianzhang.

3

Beyond the Great Wall: Agricultural Development in Northern Xinjiang, 1760-1820

Dorothy V. Borei

Introduction

A combination of unprecedented population growth, vast territorial expansion, and rapid development of the commercial economy made the Qing, particularly in the eighteenth century, one of China's most dynamic periods. The burgeoning of the population in China proper was augmented by the incorporation of non-Han peoples on the frontiers of Manchuria, Mongolia, Taiwan, southwest China, Tibet, and Xinjiang. Large-scale migrations followed military conquests as Han Chinese from the densely populated areas moved, at times with government sponsorship and at other times illegally, to border regions where land was more abundant and economic opportunities greater. These processes stimulated the further development of the agricultural and commercial economies as the empire gradually proceeded towards greater political and economic integration.

The emergence of a sprawling, multicultural state during the Qing raises questions about the causes of such expansion, the nature of central rule over the new territories, and the effect of this vast empire on Manchu fortunes. For several reasons an examination of Xinjiang, the largest of these new acquisitions, offers a significant case-study for understanding the processes involved in Qing empire-building. First, located on the Inner Asian frontier, Xinjiang in the eighteenth century was still the focal point of Chinese foreign policy. The major threat to Manchu hegemony in the mid-Qing came from the Zunghars, a Mongol confederation whose homeland in northern Xinjiang had provided the base for territorial expansion. Moreover, the geographic and ethnic complexity of Xinjiang provides an excellent example of the diverse approaches—some traditional, some innovative—the central government adopted to rule the enlarged realm. Third, Xinjiang is, as it was in the Qing, one of China's most rebellious provinces. Several major uprisings in the nineteenth century almost led to China's loss of Xinjiang; the province is still politically suspect in Beijing's eyes because of its large number of minorities, many with ties to ethnic groups in the Central Asian states that were formerly a part of the Soviet Union. We need to examine more closely the exact nature of the relationship between state policy and frontier disorder. Finally, a study of Qing Xinjiang helps us understand the role played by the central government in opening the northwestern border. From the perspective of the Manchus, Xinjiang's strategic value to the defense of China proper demanded its vigorous development by the state.

This paper analyzes the role of the Qing government in promoting the colonization (*tuntian*) and agricultural development (*kenwu*) of northern Xinjiang from 1760 until 1820. Once the conquest of Xinjiang was completed in 1759, Manchu rulers initially allowed the more densely populated southern cities more autonomy and focused their attentions instead on the underpopulated northern steppelands that had spawned Zunghar power. This study focuses on the period before 1820 because in that decade the rebellion of Jahangir forced the court to reevaluate and ultimately alter its policies in Xinjiang, particularly towards the southern oases. It is my contention that early and decisive initiatives by the central government to open northern Xinjiang were a prerequisite to China's continued hold on this distant border.

The Setting

Xinjiang, located in the remote northwest of China, lies about three hundred kilometers beyond the western terminus of the Great Wall (Drew 1968, 206). In the Qing it bordered Kazakh tribes and Russia in the north and northwest, Mongolia in the northeast, Gansu and Qinghai in the east, Tibet in the south, and the Central Asian khanate of Kokand in the west. Mountains surround nearly the entire region: the Altai range divides the northwestern frontier with Mongolia, the Kunlun mountains separate

Xinjiang and Tibet in the south, and the Pamirs protect the southwestern flank. The Tianshan range bisects Xinjiang into the Zungharian Basin in the north and the Tarim in the south. The larger Tarim Basin contains one of the world's driest deserts, the Taklamakan, as well as oases cities inhabited by Uighurs, a Turkic-speaking, agricultural people who adhere to the Muslim faith (Liu 1985). North of the Tianshan, the triangular Zungharian Basin is open on both the east and west and has traditionally been a passageway connecting northern Mongolia with the west. Prior to the Qing conquest, this northern region was populated by Zunghars, nomadic tribes of the Lama Buddhist faith. The geographical and ethnic contrasts between northern and southern Xinjiang induced the Qing court to adopt very different policies toward the two regions after imperial troops conquered the entire territory.[1]

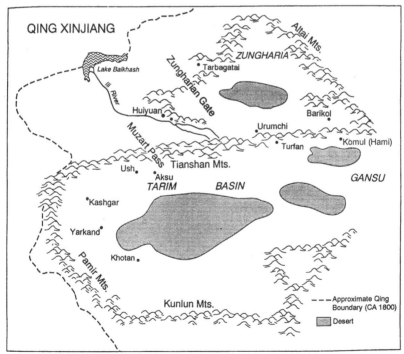

Map 1. Qing Xinjiang.

Military Administration

Military Security

During the early seventeenth century, while the Manchus were developing into a major power in the east, the Zunghars organized the Khoshotes, Torguts, Derbets, and Khoits into a strong military confederation that quickly came to dominate Inner Asia.[2] By the end of the century, the Zunghars had succeeded in controlling all of the territory that later became Xinjiang, attacked the Khalkhas in Outer Mongolia, and extended their influence in Tibet (Lee 1979, 55). The Zunghar coalition thus posed a serious threat to the newly consolidated Manchu empire in both the north and the west. Furthermore, the growing Russian presence on the northern border and early contacts between the Russians and Zunghars compounded Manchu fears since an alliance between the two powers would certainly imperil Manchu hegemony in East Asia. Finally, the Qing rulers feared that traditional divide-and-rule methods of controlling Inner Asian peoples might be undermined by religious unity. Although Inner Asians were a politically and ethnically diverse people, Tibetan Buddhism, practiced by a large percentage of the people in Tibet, Xinjiang, and Mongolia, could become a link unifying the region against the Manchus (Hambly 1969, 250; Barfield 1989, 284). From Beijing's perspective, all these security considerations dictated the subjugation of the Zunghars, a task that occupied the foreign affairs of three Manchu rulers—Kangxi (1662-1722), Yongzheng (1723-1735), and Qianlong (1736-1795). Not until 1759 were the Zunghars finally crushed and imperial troops in full control of the "new territories" of Xinjiang. In order to prevent a resurgence of Mongol power in the northwest and protect China proper, the court decided to govern the new territory as a military colony.

Administrative Structure

Divided into two major districts, known as the Tianshan northern and southern circuits (Tianshan beilu, Tianshan nanlu), Xinjiang came under the jurisdiction of both the Court of Colonial Affairs (Lifan yuan) and the Grand Council (Junjichu) in Beijing. The latter set major policy for the colony while the former handled diplomatic relations with the Muslims and Mongols.[3] In Xinjiang a military-governor (*jiangjun*), usually a Manchu bannerman of the first rank, ruled in Ili with the aid of other officers and troops stationed in strategic locations throughout the colony. The powers granted to the military-governor were broad, but ill-defined, making his position comparable to that of provincial governors-general and governors (Ding [1944], 89). His military duties included the maintenance of internal order, the surveillance of exiles, and the training and provisioning of troops. He also managed economic projects, such as land reclamation and mining, supervised trade and taxation, reviewed judicial matters, and oversaw the various civilian administrative systems of Xinjiang.

In recognition of the vastness and diversity of Xinjiang's geography and cultures, the court developed three patterns of civilian rule to govern those not directly under the authority of the military commander. First, the court permitted Muslims in Xinjiang to be ruled by *"begs"* (*boke*), indigenous administrators who had existed prior to the Qing conquest. There were thirty-five different positions, including local governors, their assistants, tax collectors, and agricultural managers. Unlike the earlier *begs*, however, these officials were no longer hereditary; the Qing government reserved the right to appoint politically reliable Muslims to these posts, to station them outside their native districts, and to dismiss them for malfeasance in office. In return for their cooperation with the Manchus, the *begs* were given rank in the Chinese bureaucratic hierarchy, land grants, servants, and cash awards (Fletcher 1978, 78-79).

A second method of indirect rule was employed to control the residents of Hami and Turfan as well as the Mongol tribes. These people were governed by *"jasaks"* (*zhasako*), hereditary nobles in control of the Mongol banners. The *jasaks* acknowledged Beijing's supremacy by presenting annual tribute to the emperor, but were allowed considerable autonomy over their banners. A final system of civilian rule, the *junxian*, emerged as a result of the influx of migrants from China proper to the Urumchi area (Cai 1986; Lin 1972b). Attached to Gansu for administrative purposes, the Shaan-Gan governor-general supervised civilian affairs while the Ili military-governor retained jurisdiction over military operations (Lo 1983, 52).

Xinjiang Garrisons

The presence of more than 20,000 troops aimed to ensure tight imperial control over Xinjiang.[4] The court divided its armies into three military sectors to protect the most strategically vital areas of the colony (Fletcher 1978, 59-60). Under the command of the Ili military-governor, the northern division, with the largest number of troops, guarded the northern and western frontiers of Xinjiang. Five hundred kilometers to the east, in Urumchi, a military lieutenant-governor commanded a somewhat smaller number of troops in the eastern district. The southern circuit maintained only several hundred rotating troops from the northern and eastern sectors. The preponderant number of soldiers garrisoned in Zungharia reflects its greater vulnerability to outside intervention as well as the fact that it was the Zunghar homeland and thus perceived as potentially more dangerous. Southern Xinjiang, on the other hand, was judged more defensible because mountains formed protective barriers on all sides; in addition, the permanent garrisoning of large numbers of imperial troops, the court reasonably feared, might well provoke unrest among the Muslim population.

Manchu and Mongol bannermen constituted the greater part of the Xinjiang garrisons, although Han Chinese Green Standard soldiers also served on this frontier. Most of the Manchus came from Shaanxi and Gansu, while others were sent from Jehol (Wang 1987, 96). Two other Manchu peoples, the Xibo from southern Manchuria and the Solon from the Amur region, were resettled in Xinjiang where they served as border guards and herdsmen.[5] Several Mongol tribes were also organized into banners in Xinjiang: Zunghar survivors were resettled into the twenty-odd Oolod banners, the Chahar Mongols from Mongolia formed another two banners, and the Torguts who returned to China after a century in Russia were awarded pasturelands and supplies by the Qing authorities (Wang 1984, 81; Mish 1970).

From more than 250 strategic locations, rotating troops performed numerous responsibilities in Xinjiang (Ding [1944], 89; Wang 1987). Patrolling the borders from a series of watch towers (*kalun*), they denied passage to unauthorized individuals, monitored nomad migrations, and conducted government trade with the Kazakhs (XJSL 11; Lo 1983, 361-471). They also manned the post relay stations (*yizhan*), thereby maintaining communication networks within Xinjiang and between Xinjiang and Beijing. In peacetime, they participated in monthly sessions of military training; in crises, they suppressed internal rebellion or resisted foreign aggression. In addition to these military duties, the Xinjiang troops helped to develop the economy of the region. While Manchu bannermen bore primary responsibility for security, the Mongols played a central role in developing pasturelands, and the Green Standard soldiers assumed a leading part in agricultural production.

The Frontier Economy

The establishment of a large and permanent military force in Xinjiang necessitated the development of the frontier's economy. On the one hand, the court expected the new colony, like the rest of Inner Asia, to become self-supporting (*yibian yangbian*). More important, defense would be impossible without the ready availability of food and other supplies that were too cumbersome and exorbitant to transport from China proper. Qing authorities therefore developed a number of policy initiatives to promote the economy of Xinjiang. These included the establishment of state pasturelands, opening of mines, promotion of trade, and agricultural reclamation. The government actively fostered animal husbandry by opening up state pasturelands as it had done earlier in Mongolia (Xu 1987). Breeding stables and grazing lands produced horses, camels, sheep, and cattle for use by military and civilian colonists (Borei 1991). A special office under the Ili military-governor supervised these pasturelands, with Manchu and Mongol bannermen in charge of their daily operations (Ding [1944], 90). Another enterprise regulated by the government was mining. In northern Xinjiang, convict laborers and migrants from China proper extracted copper, lead, iron ore, gold, and coal for, among other uses, manufacturing coinage and weaponry (Sun 1967, 54-55; Ding [1944], 88-89; Fletcher 1978, 66). Jade, a government monopoly, was extracted by the Muslim inhabitants of Yarkand and Khotan and forwarded to Beijing as tribute (Fletcher 1978, 73, 80). The state also attempted to control foreign trade, especially in northern Xinjiang where the horse trade with the Kazakhs was regulated.[6] Licensed by the government, merchants migrated to northern Xinjiang with their families to provide necessities for the garrisons. In the south, private merchants conducted a flourishing trade between cities in Xinjiang and with China, India, the Central Asian states to the west. Chinese merchants, primarily from Gansu, Shaanxi, and Shanxi, journeyed to Xinjiang where they exchanged their tea, silk goods, porcelain, and rhubarb for jade, gold, and animal products (XJSL 8:23b; Fan 1987; Fletcher 1978, 49, 62-63, 66, 81-83).

Land Reclamation in Northern Xinjiang

Even more central to China's continued dominance over Xinjiang was land reclamation and the extension of agriculture, the major focus of this paper. From 1760 until 1820, the state concentrated its efforts on the development of agricultural resources in the northern steppelands, preferring not to disturb the Muslim settlements south of the Tianshan. Not until the 1830s, after the Jahangir rebellion had been crushed, did the Manchus attempt to develop agricultural colonies in the Tarim Basin. In contrast, northern Xinjiang, where the majority of the troops were quartered, became the focus of land reclamation after the conquest because its strategic importance and fertile (*feimei*) steppelands, watered by snows from the

Tianshan, appeared to provide both an essential and ideal site for cultivation. Two locations within northern Xinjiang were central to Qing efforts: the Ili Valley and Urumchi. The Ili region encompasses the fertile plain on both sides of the Ili River which flows westward to Lake Balkhash. The area is strategically vital because of its location just north of the Muzart Pass connecting the northern and southern circuits of Xinjiang and because it protected the Zungharian Gate to the northeast. Less arid than the rest of the Zungharian Basin because of its openness to moist westerly winds, the Ili Valley was particularly well suited for agricultural development (Zhao 1986, 178-79). Three hundred miles to the east of Ili was Urumchi, which commanded the northern end of the passage leading from southern Xinjiang into the Zungarian Basin. Although much of this basin is desert, there is a belt of fertile and well-watered land where agricultural settlements are feasible (Zhao 1986, 175-76). Assuming that its armies must guard Xinjiang in order to secure Mongolia and ultimately the capital itself, Beijing assigned different military and civilian groups to cultivate the Ili and Urumchi regions.

The military officials who set out to develop the agricultural potential of Zungharia faced several problems. Some of these were ecological: harsh climate, scant precipitation, shifting sands, and alkaline soil. Other problems resulted from human factors: scarcity of manpower, the inexperience and poor motivation of cultivators, the increasing number of troops in need of supplies, and frequent changes in military personnel and policies. What is remarkable, given the magnitude of these problems, is that the colonial government was as successful as it was in achieving its goals of defending and feeding the region. Without direct government intervention, it is unlikely that there would have been either sufficient manpower or productive resources to maintain a strong Qing presence on the frontier.

Labor Shortage and Colonization

An initial and long-standing obstacle to agricultural development in the northwest was the scarcity of labor in northern Xinjiang due to the region's physical geography, recent wartime destruction, and disease. Even under normal circumstances, desert and steppelands restricted dense concentrations of population. A century of warfare, with thousands of Mongol lives lost in battle and from disease, exacerbated the labor shortage.[7] In response to this demographic dilemma, the Qing state vigorously sponsored the migration of military and civilians into northern Xinjiang.[8] The Manchu bannermen, the elite of the Qing military establishment, functioned as the primary defense forces; even in the early nineteenth century, when the Ili military-governor completed the process of allocating lands to the Manchus, few actually tilled the soil, preferring to hire other laborers instead (XJSL 6:14). The Xibo and Solon, along with the Chahar and Oolod Mongols, were resettled in Banners in the Ili Valley where they grazed their herds and cultivated some land while pursuing their tasks as border guards.

Of all the military forces, the Han Chinese enrolled in the Green Standard army played the most important role in agricultural development, especially in Ili. They had first become important as food producers during the Kangxi and Yongzheng reigns when the army established its first military colonies (*bingtun*) in Hami and Turfan in order to supply Qing forces battling the Zunghars.[9] These early agricultural settlements, however, were not permanent; they were uprooted when Manchu forces retreated before the Zunghar armies. After the conquest, the Green Standard troops continued to perform military service when necessary and drilled on a regular basis, but most were organized into permanent military colonies and functioned as agriculturalists. The government helped establish the colonies by providing soldiers (and their families) with twenty *mu* (about one hectare) of land along with seeds, cattle, and tools produced in local shops (XJSL 6:10-b). In exchange, they paid an annual grain tax of twelve to eighteen *shi* (*piculs*) per *mu,* depending on the quality of the land. This grain, stored in official granaries, provided rations for the Manchu military officials and bannermen (XJSL 8:1). Divided into twenty-five colonies, they not only grew food for the Manchus, but also provided supplies and assistance to the civilian colonists who migrated to Xinjiang. The largest number of Green Standard farmer-soldiers were stationed in Ili, where the original one hundred in 1760 had grown to 2,500 by 1769 (XJSL 6:1-b).[10] By the late 1770s, approximately 80 percent of the Green Standard troops in Ili cultivated 50,000 *mu* (Wu 1987, 96). Another two thousand Green Standard soldiers farmed 31,000 *mu* in Urumchi and environs, a mere 17 percent of the acreage tilled by civilian settlers there (XJSL 2:40b-46).

In an effort to reduce the military's responsibility for food production, the Qing authorities also relied on criminal exiles to provide food for the Xinjiang garrisons.[11] One of the "five punishments" under the Manchus, exile to the northwest was the second heaviest penalty after death (Bodde and Morris 1973, 91). The government believed that, by exiling criminals to the distant frontier, they would be reformed through labor while simultaneously turning wasteland into a paradise.[12] In exile, these prisoners served as slaves to the troops, miners in the newly opened pits, and tillers of the soil. Organized into colonies (*fantun* or *qiantun*), these criminal exiles were provided with twelve *mu* of land, as well as seeds, draft animals, and tools in exchange for an annual grain tax of eight *sheng* (pints) of wheat per *mu*. The agricultural significance of exile colonies was limited because of the relatively small number of convicts involved. For example, court documents reveal that only about two thousand convicts served in both Ili and Urumchi in 1790 (Waley-Cohen 1987, 281). With an allotment of twelve *mu* per exile, that represents less than 24,000 *mu* in both sites. Although the state wanted to ensure rations for its troops, officials were even more concerned with the security of the frontier—a heavy concentration of dangerous prisoners in one area might well lead to serious disturbances. Once prisoners completed their sentences, the authorities registered them as civilians and allocated them twelve *mu* of land (Xu 1985, 91). Because criminal exiles, unlike political prisoners, usually remained in Xinjiang after serving their sentences, they brought their families with them and settled down, thereby providing a source of permanent labor on the frontier.

More important to the economic security of the Manchu troops in the Ili Valley were the agricultural colonies manned by the Muslim Uighurs from the Tarim Basin (*huitun*). First impressed into agricultural service by the Zunghars, the Muslims continued to be sent north after the Qing conquest.[13] Entire households packed up their farming equipment and trekked for a half a month over the Tianshan to the region south of the Ili River, where they had established nine colonies by 1773 (XJSL 6:24). From the original three hundred households in 1760, their numbers had increased to 6,383 within eight years (XJSL 6:1). In 1765 the single largest group, totalling 1,796 families, journeyed to northern Xinjiang (Wang 1990, 210). By the Jiaqing (1796-1820) period, more than 34,000 Muslims resided in the Ili Valley (Zeng [1936], 275). While the majority of Muslim households produced rations for the Manchu forces, others mined iron, labored in construction work, or grew wheat as payment to the *begs* brought north to rule them (XJSL 6:1b-2; 6:31-32). Each farming family was expected to produce sixteen *shi* of grain per *mu* for the army (Lin 1972a, 5, 8:11). The Muslim farmers, better known as Taranchis, were legally bound to the land and forced to work for the Manchus in exchange for rations. In Ili they cultivated 90,000 *mu* of land, nearly four times as much land as the exiles (Wu 1987, 96).

In addition to the agricultural colonies of the Green Standard troops, exiles, and Muslims, Han migrants came to Xinjiang from China proper to open up new lands (*hutun* or *mintun*). The decision to send non-military migrants to Xinjiang provoked a debate at the imperial court (Hua 1987). While some officials argued that the government had no business colonizing the border with civilians, others countered that the region would ultimately be easier to protect if it did so. The Qianlong Emperor supported those who favored civilian emigration, partly because of the lack of workers in Xinjiang, but also because of population growth in China proper. As early as 1760 the emperor declared:

> We are planning this matter and there are deep concerns [about it]. The nation's population is extremely large—from 1736 until today the number of people has so multiplied that it is impossible to count, yet we have only limited land and surplus profits are hard to come by. Moreover, the area beyond the Great Wall was known as a dangerous frontier by former generations who did not dare to go beyond it even a few feet or inches. The sons and grandsons as well as servants and slaves of our dynasty . . . have regarded [themselves] as one family. People on the border and those in China proper both engage in agriculture, establish homes, and raise children and [yet] their profits are extremely small. To prohibit them [from emigrating] will oppress the people. Today we know that the military colonies are flourishing in places like Urumchi and Pizhan, traders are continuously coming to carry on business, and houses [are being built] in various towns and villages. In the future, as roads increase and cultivation spreads, people from Gansu and other places who are without jobs or poor can come to conduct business or engage in agriculture . . . and so will have more to eat (DQSL: Gaocong 612:21; see also 604:16).

Concerned with both border security and the welfare of the common people, the emperor embarked on a program of government support for civilian colonies in northern Xinjiang (Hua 1987; Xu 1985).

In the Ili valley, these free settlers included a few small farmers, the relatives of Green Standard troops, and former exiles whose sentences had been completed. But the most wealthy were the merchants who had the resources to accumulate large landholdings. For example, Zhang Ziyi employed thirty-two households to cultivate 39,618 *mu* of wheat, while Zhang Shangyi hired two hundred families to grow rice and vegetables on his 10,668 *mu* (XJSL 6:5). Unlike other settlers, who paid a grain tax, merchants engaged in vegetable farming paid their taxes in silver. Ili agriculture, however, continued to be dominated by Green Standard and Muslim cultivators; fewer than 600 civilian households tilled 60,192 *mu* in the valley by 1820 (XJSL 6:5a-b; Fang 1989, 661).

In contrast, many more commoners from China proper migrated to the Urumchi region, where they had succeeded in opening up 181,866 *mu* by 1820 (XJSL 2:44b). The migrants travelled from Gansu and Shaanxi, through the Jiayuguan Pass in the Hexi Corridor, passed through Hami, and then settled in various sites in northern Xinjiang (Hua 1987, 126). In 1761 the earliest colonists were sent to Urumchi, where military units had recently been cut by two-thirds. The government permitted some of those released from military duty to settle in the area as farmers. These men were joined by civilian migrants from China proper in the same year. Because of the success of the Urumchi land reclamation efforts, similar civilian colonies were established in Barikol in 1763 and later in other sites west of Urumchi, including Ili. No civilians were permitted to migrate to southern Xinjiang until the 1830s, and then only after another heated court debate (Xu 1985, 89ff).

Civilian colonists in Urumchi included single men, some of whom later brought their families to the frontier, merchants who paid their own expenses in the hope of capitalizing on the rebuilding of the region, the children or relatives of Green Standard soldiers, and entire peasant households from China proper. Later, the male descendents of civilian colonists who had reached maturity could also establish their own households and receive government support (Xu 1985, 93). From 1761 to 1776, fewer than 1,000 families per year migrated to Zungharia. A devastating famine in Gansu during the years 1777 to 1778, however, caused the number of migrants to escalate sharply, with 5,648 households seeking refuge in northern Xinjiang. As conditions in Gansu improved, the total again dropped (Hua 1987, 121-23). The government continued to recruit and subsidize groups of Chinese migrants relocating in Xinjiang for twenty years, stopping only in 1782, after which the government simply relied on word of the prosperity of the new colony to attract new migrants. The plan appears to have worked because, although overall numbers declined, more people began to petition for government permission to homestead in the northwest. Between 1761 and 1790, approximately 49,000 individuals settled in northern Xinjiang with government backing (Hua 1987, 119, 121-22). A total of 52,250 people, it has been estimated, migrated during the entire Qianlong period (Hua 1987, 124). Eighty percent of this number came from Gansu while the other 20 percent migrated from Shaanxi (Hua 1990). Driven primarily by economic need, these settlers became a significant source of labor on the frontier, especially in the Urumchi and Barikol region, where they played a crucial role in agricultural development. Between 1772 and 1791 their labor enabled agricultural productivity in this area to increase by approximately 10 percent per year (Hua 1987, 130).

State Aid to Colonists

The strong commitment of the Qing state to these civilian migrations is especially evident in the direct financial and other support furnished to the migrants. First, the government covered all traveling costs to Xinjiang, just as it had for the bannermen. The Ministries of War and Works provided leather clothing needed for the cold weather migrants encountered on route, iron cooking pots, and rations according to the distance traveled and the age of the individual. It has been estimated that the court spent more than 281,700 *taels* of silver, or approximately ninety *taels* per household, on these costs between 1764 and 1770, when reductions were made in traveling allowances (Hua 1987, 126). The government continued to support the colonists once they arrived on the frontier by providing average allotments of thirty *mu* of land. Larger households could get more and smaller households less than the average thirty *mu*. Only exile families transferring to civilian population registers received a substantially lower amount of land (twelve *mu*). In addition to the land itself, the state provided loans amounting to eight *taels* with which to purchase seeds, draft animals, tools, a year's rations, and buildings. The military units worked closely with the new settlers, providing seeds and rations from their colonies as well as horses and oxen from the state pasturelands. Green Standard troops stationed nearby often aided in the contruction of homes, barns, and irrigation projects. The government expected migrants to repay these loans once their lands were reclaimed and entered on tax registers, a process (*shengke*) that took from three to, more commonly, six years (Xu 1985, 93; Hua 1990).

Labor Problems

The inability to provide a sufficiently large and skilled labor force able to meet the needs of an increasing Qing military presence continued to plague officials throughout the 1760-to-1820 period. When Jinchang became military-governor in 1812, he reported that banner lands, allocated to the Ili Manchus a decade earlier, still lay neglected because of insufficient manpower (XJSL 6:14b). According to Jinchang, even attempts to remedy the situation by renting these lands to Muslims or exiles had not improved this disturbing situation. Compounding this labor shortage was the lack of skill among many of the settlers. Several years later, another military-governor complained about the farming inexperience of both convict labor and Manchus (XJSL 6:b-12). Many of the new colonists, particularly the Banners, had no prior agricultural experience; many others—most notably the Muslims and convicts—were forced to farm against their will for the benefit of the Qing state. Even those with a farming background had to adapt to a physical environment that was entirely different from the rice-growing regions of China proper.

The problem of motivating workers loomed large in the minds of Xinjiang administrators. The military officials developed a variety of methods to induce greater productivity. One was to allow the families of colonists to accompany them to Xinjiang. From 1766 until 1799, for example, the families of convicts, even those not punished under the collective responsibility principle, were permitted to follow the exiles to Ili (Waley-Cohen 1987, 156-59). In 1778, Green Standard troops began to come with their families (XJSL 6:3b). The decision allowing the families of both convicts and troops to go to Xinjiang encouraged the men to work harder at the same time that it accelerated colonization, since many of these people became permanent residents. Officials also devised rewards and punishments to induce the colonists to increase food production. Quotas were established for exiles and Han soldiers; those who filled or exceeded them were rewarded with extra rations—grain for the criminals and salted vegetables for the soldiers—and silver (only for the troops). Both those who failed to meet the official quotas and their supervisors were punished (XJSL 6:3).

Manchu bannermen posed a special problem because their military duties traditionally kept them from engaging in productive activities. But as time wore on and their numbers expanded, the government found it increasingly costly to provide for them. As a result, the court decided to allocate lands for their support. After overcoming certain technical difficulties, Ili military officials divided 24,000 *mu* near Huiyuan and Huining among the banners in 1802, with each soldier allotted thirty *mu*. Another 40,000 *mu*, further out from Huiyuan and Huining, remained undivided and were to be collectively tilled for the welfare of all the banners. The government believed that these fields would provide employment for "unassigned" bannermen (*xiansan*), but in fact the bannermen hired others—Muslims or exiles—to cultivate the fields in their place. By 1812, when it became apparent that the collective lands were far less productive than those lands worked by individual bannermen, the Ili military-governor recommended parceling out most of the collective lands among the banners in order to improve their standard of living. In spite of resistance to this plan, the Grand Council finally approved of the distribution in order to promote better living conditions for the bannermen who, its members believed, would now have the incentive to work the fields themselves (XJSL 6:13b-15).

The above discussion illustrates the government's frustrations in trying to obtain a reliable labor supply, an issue which prompted the government to rely increasingly on civilian colonists for agricultural production. During the Kangxi, Yongzheng, and early Qianlong reigns, when Qing troops still battled with the Zunghars, military colonies had provided the major food supplies to the army. But the shifting or demobilization of units according to military demands inhibited the long-term stabilization of the frontier agrarian economy. Moreover, even after the conquest of Xinjiang, the primary focus of the military colonists remained defense, not food production. Once the Manchu armies had eliminated the Zunghar threat, the state shifted its focus to the establishment of civilian colonies which could produce food for the troops. The Qianlong court thus created a more stable labor force closely tied to the land and dependent upon increased productivity for an improved living standard (Hua 1987, 130). As a result, the ratio between soldiers and civilians in the Urumchi region shifted dramatically during the second half of the century. In 1766, the soldier-civilian ratio was 1:0.036; by 1795, the last year of the Qianlong reign, it was 1:11; and in 1805 there was only one soldier for every 15.1 civilians (Hua 1987, 131). This shift to civilian dominance in agriculture is also evident in the fact that the troops cultivated only 11 to 12 percent of the land tilled by the civilian colonists by the end of the eighteenth century (Hua 1987, 131).

Environmental Problems

In addition to the labor supply problem faced by the government, the colonists settling in Xinjiang encountered on-going environmental problems. Large portions of Zungharia, including the Gurbantunggut Desert, proved unfit for cultivation. Even arable soil contained little humus, decayed vegetable matter which provides nutrients for crops and helps retain water. The pebbles and shale underneath the topsoil not only made cultivation more arduous but also caused precipitation to run off quickly. A high water table and irrigation contributed to a concentration of soluble salts in the ground (Chang 1949, 60-61). Those allotted land of poor quality—either too sandy or too alkaline—found it difficult to sustain themselves. But the central dilemma for the settlers reclaiming vast expanses of steppeland was the availability of water. Although Ili and Urumchi, unlike southern Xinjiang, received sufficient annual precipitation (280 mm and 230 mm, respectively) to permit some dry agriculture, variable rainfall and low crop yields made irrigation necessary to support a large, concentrated population (Cressey 1955, 329-30).[14] Fortunately, the colonists did not have to dig the complex underground canals or *karez* (*ka'er* or *kanjing*) typical of oasis agriculture in the south.[15] Nevertheless, the primary texts clearly indicate the extent to which the establishment of dependable water resources in northern Xinjiang constantly preoccupied the authorities.[16] The major source of water for irrigation in Ili and Urumchi was snow from the tops of the Tianshan which, as the weather warmed in the spring and summer months, melted and flowed down to the basin in small streams, then fanned out over the flat steppe. These streams, and the rivers and tributaries they engendered, became the major source of irrigation for the new agricultural colonies.

The difficulty of providing sufficient irrigation for agricultural development was particularly evident in relation to the Manchu Banners. In 1802, when the Ili military-governor Songyun finally succeeded in settling some of the Manchu troops in agricultural colonies, he did so only after years of trial by earlier officials. Prior efforts had failed because of a lack of water. After assigning a special commissioner to investigate possible irrigation sites, Songyun ordered a major channel constructed on the north bank of the Ili River. Other channels were also built and eventually branch channels were dug and improved (XJSL 6:2,10).[17]

Nevertheless, the situation remained precarious. A decade later (1812) the 40,000 *mu* allotted to Banner use were still not being utilitized due to insufficient water and labor resources. These fields, located further from the mountains, were not as easily accessible to irrigation. A further difficulty in that particular year was the weather. Instead of the usual heavy winter snows and long cold springs typical of the region, the Ili Valley experienced a mild winter and a warm spring. The light snowfall quickly disappeared, and by midsummer, when the melted snow was most needed for the growing crops, water was scarce (XJSL 6:14b). Officials in Beijing and in Ili debated the proper response to this emergency, deciding finally to postpone cultivation until irrigation could be expanded in the future.

Other Difficulties

In addition to the irrigation problems involved in the reclamation of land, officials faced other difficulties. Seeds and methods of cultivation employed elsewhere in China were not suitable to the steppe and required considerable experimentation by the military authorities (Wu 1987, 98). In time, farmers in Zungharia were able to cultivate a variety of grains, including barley, millet, wheat, corn, oats, and rice (XJSL 8:1b-2; Lin 1972a, 5, 8:10). The relatively short growing season, however, limited production to one crop annually. Furthermore, the region's ecology did not allow annual cultivation of fields, which had to lie fallow for two or three years (XJSL 6:5,13; Lin 1972a:5, 9:7). These environmental factors contributed periodically to food shortages, a predicament that caused the government to construct and maintain official granaries to better regulate agricultural supplies. The Ili granaries, one for each of the Banners, stored the grain taxes collected from Green Standard troops and Muslims and later distributed these supplies as rations or welfare to the Manchus (XJSL 8:1-2). By 1795, the 330 granaries in Urumchi held more than 136,200 *shi* of grain, while the surrounding colonies maintained their own granaries (*Wulumuqi shiyi* 26b). In spite of these concerted efforts by the state, shortages could and did occur, as in 1803 when soldiers previously released from farm work had to be recalled and given the seeds and implements to recoup that year's losses (XJSL 6:4b). Even when harvests were plentiful, military-governors worried about rats eating the grain and spoilage due to mildew (*Da Qing huidian shili* 178:25b; XJSL 6:4).

A further problem, one rarely alluded to in contemporary documents, was the nature of the bureaucracy which administered Xinjiang. The officials who oversaw these agricultural projects were essentially military men, although they received assistance from officials exiled for political crimes. Frequently transferred, many found it difficult to accumulate the experience necessary for prudent decision-making or to implement long-range economic plans. Furthermore, their primary concern, as dictated by Beijing, was the military security of the frontier; economic development was secondary (XJSL 6:16; Lo 1983, 236). Yet officials recognized that defense could not be maintained without adequate resources. The court also expected Xinjiang to become self-supporting, not a drain on the state's resources (XJSL 6:9b, 11; SZJL 4:124). Thus, military-governors constantly had to counterbalance the two goals of military security and economic viability (XJSL 6:13b; SZJL 4:123-24).

Conclusion

During the late eighteenth and early nineteenth centuries, Qing military authorities in Xinjiang appear to have succeeded in meeting the goals of military and economic security. Despite occasional setbacks, peace on the frontier was preserved and colonists provided with basic necessities. The Qing state, believing that it must secure the northwestern frontier for its own survival, experimented with a variety of administrative methods to control the new territory. The contrast between Ili and Urumchi provides one example of this diversity. Because of its greater strategic value, the Ili Valley garrisoned the majority of the military forces in Xinjiang and was largely under the control of the military-governor. The center ruled the Mongols and Muslims sent there only indirectly, allowing them to retain their local leaders. Relatively fewer civilian migrants settled in Ili, although its physical geography was somewhat more favorable to agricultural development than Urumchi's. In part the government may have been reluctant to encourage a large number of civilians to migrate into what was essentially a military camp because of the difficulty of policing them. In contrast, Urumchi and neighboring settlements, closer to China proper, attracted the majority of the free settlers and quickly came under the civilian administration of the Shaan-Gan governor-general. This bureaucratic arrangement not only prevented one individual, namely the Ili military-governor, from accumulating too much power but also assured a tight rein over the Zungharian frontier. And the influx of large numbers of peasant settlers from China proper ensured that the troops keeping order would be fed.

In addition to these administrative maneuvers, the Qing state spent vast sums to assure that its policies in northern Xinjiang succeeded. Most of the new colonists came to Zungharia at the expense of the government, which continued to subsidize the colony until the end of the Qing (Borei 1991, 31). The state even loaned those not directly on its payroll the seeds, tools, and draft animals needed to get started in the new territory. Qing military authorities led the experimentation in seed varieties and cultivation techniques, saw to the construction and maintenance of water control projects, storehouses, and granaries, and oversaw the feeding and housing of thousands of new settlers. The magnitude of these projects, the distance between Beijing and northern Xinjiang where they were implemented, and the progress achieved all attest to the impressive organizational capacity of the Qing state.

Evaluating the success of Qing colonization and land reclamation efforts in quantitative terms is more problematic. Statistical data, even when they exist, are confusing and unreliable (Wiens 1966, 77). Population figures are scanty and recorded differently (by either household or individual) at various times. The statistics for cultivated acreage frequently reflect the entire region instead of a particular site such as Ili or Urumchi. Furthermore, figures for comparable sites or dates usually do not exist. Nonetheless, Chinese have attempted to verify the success of agricultural development in Xinjiang during the Qing with quantitative evidence. The

Xinjiang zhilue, the 1820 gazetteer, indicates that between 245,600 and 265,600 *mu* (depending on the amount of collective banner lands being tilled) were cultivated in Ili and another 181,866 *mu* in Urumchi. Writing several decades later, Wei Yuan justified Qianlong's conquest of Xinjiang by explaining that 100,000 colonists cultivated about 285,600 *mu* in both the northern and southern circuits by the 1830s ([1846] 4, 107). Recent PRC scholarship on Xinjiang also documents Qing success with agricultural development by detailing the number of *tuntian* opened, the total *mu* reclaimed, and the amount of grain harvested annually (Fang 1989; Wang 1990). Whatever the exact meaning of these figures, they are impressive, given the technical problems involved in land reclamation on the Zungharian steppe. It is clear that the Qing state triggered a process that ultimately altered the economy of northern Xinjiang over the course of the next two hundred years. Almost entirely pastoral at the time of the Manchu conquest, Zungharia gradually developed its agricultural potential so that by the 1940s the ratio between farmer to nomad was approximately 1:1.6 (Chang 1949, 63). The Qing state initiated this process in the mid-eighteenth century when it moved large numbers of people into the region for defense and food production.

The Qing state, rather than private individuals and groups, played the central role in the colonization and agricultural development of northern Xinjiang. The government had attempted, though with limited success, to prevent or at least control Han migration to other borders. For instance, a desire to protect the livelihood and cultural identity of the Manchus led to the banning of Chinese settlers from Manchuria, and legislation restricted the number of Han settlers who could migrate to Inner Mongolia (Lee 1970; Chia 1991). The court also prohibited emigration to Taiwan in an effort to placate its aboriginal tribes (Meskill 1979). The Manchu government even regulated the influx of outsiders into southern Xinjiang for fear that a large alien presence might lead to a repeat of earlier anti-Qing risings.

Security, of course, lay at the heart of all these decisions, as it did in the case of northern Xinjiang where, rather than prohibiting migration, the state vigorously sponsored settlement and land reclamation in order to defend the new colony. It is unlikely that much could have been accomplished in Zungharia without the inducement and intricate planning of the central government and local military authorities. This frontier was too isolated, its climate and topography sufficiently harsh, and its defense too uncertain to inspire large numbers of peasants to cross deserts and mountains in order to inhabit the remote valley. But by pursuing the policies of colonization and agricultural development, the Manchu state diversified the economy of northern Xinjiang and thereby pushed the northwestern border beyond the Great Wall.

Notes

1. Qing forces first conquered northern Xinjiang, where they discovered two brothers, sons of the *khoja*, or the alleged descendants of Mohammed who were religious and political leaders in the southern Muslim cities. After one was released and the other escaped, the brothers led a Muslim coalition against Qing rule. Following their deaths, descendants continued to harass the Chinese empire from Kokand (Fletcher 1968; Schwartz 1976).

2. The Zunghars (Zhunge'er), a branch of the Western Mongols, called themselves Oirats (Oolod). The Chinese referred to them as Zunghars before the Qing conquest and Eleuths (Elute) afterwards. Russian and Muslim records call them Kalmuks. Recent scholarship on the Zunghars includes Ma and Cai 1989; Ma and Ma 1984; Wang, H. 1984; and Zlatkin 1983.

3. Two of the Lifan yuan's six departments dealt with Xinjiang: the Outer Mongolian Bureau (Dianshusi) conducted affairs with the Zunghars; the Eastern Turkestan Bureau (Laiyuansi), established in 1761, conducted business with the Muslims in southern Xinjiang, including Hami and Turfan (Brunnert and Hagelstrom 1911, no. 495; Hucker 1985, nos. 3557 and 6648).

4. Troop estimates vary widely, in part because there were fluctuations in the totals over time. While Zeng records a range of 19,000 to 23,000 (1978, 266-68), Fang believes there were 38,701 troops in Xinjiang (1989, 547). My survey of the *Xiyu wenjian lu* reveals a total of approximately 26,000 troops in 1777. According to the *Shilu,* the Qianlong Emperor also sent troops to Xinjiang for reasons other than defense. He was concerned about improving the quality of those bannermen who had not experienced military discipline for some time; he also believed that frontier garrisons would be cheaper in the long run (Cited by Wang 1987, 96-97).

5. In 1764, approximately 3,000 Xibo journeyed for a year in small carts to serve for three years in Xinjiang. Despite efforts to return to their homeland, the Xibo stayed in Xinjiang where, organized into eight banners, they established walled villages along the Ili River. Today the Xibo celebrate their westward migration during the fourth lunar month by picnicking and holding martial arts contests (Bonavia 1988, 120-21; Benson and Svanberg 1988, 25; Wang, J. 1984, 81). The four Solon Banners originated in the Amur River region where they lived by hunting, fishing,

and breeding reindeer (Wang 1984, 81; Lee 1970, 14-16; ECCP 273). The term "Solon" disappeared after 1954 when the name was changed to "Daur" (Benson and Svanberg 1988, 24-25).

6. Trade between Xinjiang and the Russians did not become important until the mid-nineteenth century when treaties provided Russians access to duty-free trade in Ili and Tarbagatai.

7. Chinese sources, perhaps in exaggeration, record over a million deaths (Qishiyi 1777, 70). One Soviet historian estimates that more than half a million lives were lost (Zlatkin 1983, 303). Disease, especially smallpox, followed closely on the heels of the military carnage. For example, Amursana, a Khoit leader who turned first against the Zunghars and later against Qing authority, reportedly died of smallpox in 1757 (ECCP 11).

8. For a discussion of earlier government-planned migrations to populate the northern borders, including Xinjiang, see Lee 1978, 21-26.

9. *Tuntian* date back to the second century B.C. when soldiers and government-sponsored migrants were sent to the northern and northwestern frontiers to provision garrison units. For a discussion of Han *tuntian*, see Hsu 1980, 139-41. Qing military colonies appeared not only on the frontier but also in minority regions and "on land assigned to grain transport detachments" (Kuhn 1970, 22).

10. In 1778, there were 2,500 Green Standard troops divided into twenty-five colonies. Five hundred men performed military duties while the remaining two thousand cultivated the soil (XJSL 6:3b).

11. The Manchus exiled both officials guilty of political offenses and ordinary criminals to Xinjiang. The former served as administrators or clerical personnel while the latter worked as laborers. For a detailed study of Xinjiang exiles, see Waley-Cohen 1987.

12. DQSL 744:4b. Criminal exiles were sent to sites further east, such as Anxi, Hami, and Barikol as early as 1761. (Chou 1976). Not until 1764 were they sent to Ili where at first they freed soldiers from such tasks as cooking, cutting wood, and cultivating the land. The decision to allocate land to the exiles and their families came three years later (Wu 1987, 96). For a detailed study of the legal aspects of exile in Xinjiang, see Waley-Cohen 1987. Convicts were also employed in the mines and boatyards, as clerks in government offices and as slaves to the *begs* in southern Xinjiang (Waley-Cohen 1987, 270-91).

13. For a fuller discussion of the Muslim cultivators under the Zunghars and the Manchus, see Saguchi Toru 1964.

14. Although these figures are for the twentieth century, the fact that there is no indication of major climatological changes suggests that these figures can be used for the late eighteenth and early nineteenth centuries.

15. For a fuller description of the *karez* or *kariz*, see Cressey 1955, 331. The XJSL does not mention the construction of any of these canals in the Ili Valley.

16. The first local gazetteer of Xinjiang, presented to the emperor in 1821, describes water conservancy (*shuili*) efforts in the Ili region in the chapter on agricultural matters (*tuntian*) (XJSL 6:6b-8b, 20b-23b, 26-27).

17. The XJSL lists ten irrigation projects for the Manchu banners in the area around Huiyuan and another five around Huining (XJSL 6:20b-22b).

References

Barfield, Thomas J. 1989. *The Perilous Frontier. Nomadic Empires and China.* Cambridge, Mass.: Basil Blackwell.

Bonavia, Judy. 1988. *An Illustrated Guide to the Silk Road.* London: William Collins.

Benson, Linda and Ingvar Svanberg, eds. 1988. *The Kazaks of China: Essays on an Ethnic Minority.* Uppsala: Studia Multiethnica Upsaliensia.

Bodde, Derk and Clarence Morris. 1973. *Law in Imperial China: Exemplified by 190 Ch'ing Dynasty Cases Translated from the Hsing-an huilan.* Philadelphia: University of Pennsylvania.

Borei, Dorothy V. 1987. Images of the Northwest Frontier: A Study of the *Hsi-yu Wen Chien Lu. The American Asian Review* 5, 2:26-46 (Summer).

_____. 1991. Economic Implications of Empire-Building: The Case of Xinjiang. *Central and Inner Asian Studies* 5:22-37.

Brunnert, H. S. and Hagelstrom, V. V. 1911. *Present Day Political Organization of China.* Shanghai.

Cai, Jiayi. 1986. Xinjiang Chahe'er ying, Elute ying gaishu (A summary of the Chahar and Eleuth troops of Xinjiang). *Menggu shi yanjiu* (Study of Mongol history). N.p.: Inner Mongolian People's Press.

Chang, Chih-yi. 1949. Land Utilization and Settlement Possibilities in Sinkiang. *The Geographical Review* 39:57-75.

Chia, Ning. 1991. The Li-fan Yuan and its Economic Policy in Ch'ing Mongolia. Conference paper, Southeast Region, Association for Asian Studies, Rock Hill, S.C.

Chou, Nailene. 1976. Frontier Studies and Changing Frontier Administration in Late Ch'ing China. Ph.D. diss., University of Washington.

Cressey, George B. 1955. *Land of the 500 Million*. New York: McGraw-Hill.

Da Qing huidian shili (Collected statutes and sub-statutes of the Qing). 1909. Shanghai: Commercial Press.

DQSL. *Da Qing lichao shilu* (Veritable records of successive reigns of the Qing dynasty). 1937-38. Tokyo.

Ding, Shicun. [1944] 1981. "Ili jiangjun shezhi zhi qiyin yu qi zhiquan" (The origin of the establishment of the Ili military-governor and his duties). In *Zhunge'er shilun wenji* (Collected essays on Zunghar history) 1:85-90. Reprint. N.p.

Drew, W. J. 1968. Sinjiang: The Land and the People. *Central Asian Review* 16, 3:205-216.

Dreyer, June Teufel. 1976. *China's Forty Millions*. Cambridge, Mass.: Harvard University Press.

ECCP. Hummel, Arthur W., ed. [1943] 1970. *Eminent Chinese of the Ch'ing Period*. Reprint. Taibei: Chengwen.

Fan, Jinmin. 1987. *Qingdai Jiangnan yu Xinjiang diqu de sichou maoyi* (Silk trade between Jiangnan and Xinjiang in the Qing dynasty). Nanjing: Nanjing daxue lishi yanjiuso.

Fang, Yingkai. 1989. *Xinjiang tunken shi* (A history of land reclamation in Xinjiang). Urumchi: Xinjiang Qingshaonian. Vol. 2.

Fletcher, Joseph F. 1968. "China and Central Asia, 1368-1884." In *The Chinese World Order*, ed. John K. Fairbank. Cambridge, Mass.: Harvard University Press.

————. 1978. "Ch'ing Inner Asia c. 1800." In *The Cambridge History of China, Vol. 10: Late Ch'ing: 1800-1911*, Part I, ed. John K. Fairbank. Cambridge: Cambridge University Press.

Hambly, Gavin, ed. 1969. *Central Asia*. New York: Delacourt Press.

Hsu, Cho-yun. 1980. *Han Agriculture*. Seattle: University of Washington Press.

Hua, Li. 1987. Qianlong nianjian yimin chuguan yu Qing qianqi Tianshan beilu nongye de fazhan (Emigration beyond the Great Wall in the Qianlong reign and the development of agriculture north of the Tianshan in the early Qing). *Xibei shidi* (History and geography of the northwest) 4:119-131.

————. 1990. Interview by author. Beijing.

Hucker, Charles O. 1985. *A Dictionary of Official Titles in Imperial China*. Stanford: Stanford University Press.

Kuhn, Philip A. 1970. *Rebellion and Its Enemies in Late Imperial China. Militarization and Social Structure, 1796-1864.* Cambridge, Mass.: Harvard University Press.

Lee, James. 1978. "Migration and Expansion in Chinese History." In *Human Migration: Patterns and Policies*, ed. William H. McNeill and Ruth S. Adams. Bloomington: Indiana University Press.

Lee, Robert. 1970. *The Manchurian Frontier in Ch'ing History.* Cambridge, Mass.: Harvard University Press.

_____. 1979. "Frontier Politics in the Southwestern Sino-Tibetan Borderlands during the Ch'ing Dynasty." In *Perspectives in a Changing China*, ed. Joshua A. Fogel and William T. Rowe. Boulder: Westview Press.

Lin, Enxian. 1972a. *Qingdai Xinjiang kenwu yanjiu* (Study of land reclamation in Xinjiang during the Qing dynasty). Taibei: Zhonghua wenhua.

_____. 1972b. Qingdai Xinjiang zhouxian zhidu zhi yanjiu (Study of the system of *zhou* and *xian* in Xinjiang during the Qing). *Renwen xuebao* 2:185.

Liu, Zhixiao. 1985. *Weiwu'er zu lishi* (History of the Uighur people). Beijing: Minzu. Vol. 1.

Lo, Yunzhi. 1983. *Qing Gaocong tongzhi Xinjiang zhengce de tantao* (Inquiry into Qing Gaocong's administrative policies in Xinjiang). Taibei: Liren.

Ma, Ruheng, and Ma Dazheng. 1984. *Elute Menggu shi lunji* (Essays on Eleuth Mongol history). Xining: Qinghai Renmin.

Ma, Dazheng, and Cai Jiayi. 1989. *Weilate Menggu shi rumen* (The Basics of Eleuth Mongol history). Xining: Qinghai Renmin.

Meskill, Johanna Menzel. 1979. *A Chinese Pioneer Family: The Lins of Wu-feng Taiwan, 1729-1895.* Princeton: Princeton University Press.

Mish, John L. 1970. The Return of the Turgut. *Journal of Asian History* 4, 1:80-82.

Naquin, Susan, and Evelyn S. Rawski. 1987. *Chinese Society in the Eighteenth Century.* New Haven: Yale University Press.

Qishiyi. 1777. *Xiyu wenjian lu* (Record of experiences in the Western regions). N.p.

Rossabi, Morris. 1975. *China and Inner Asia from 1368 to the Present Day.* London: Thames and Hudson.

Saguchi, Toru. 1964. Taranchi nin no shakai. *Shigaku zasshi* (History journal) 73,11:1-52.

Schwartz, Henry G. 1976. The Khwajas of Eastern Turkestan. *Central Asiatic Journal* 20, 4:266-296.

Sun, E-tu Zen. 1967. "Mining Labor in the Ch'ing Period." *Approaches to Modern Chinese History,* ed. Albert Feuerwerker, Rhoads Murphey, Mary Wright. Berkeley: University of California.

SZJL. Hening. [1805] 1968. *Sanzhou jilue* (Summary of the three regions). Reprint. Taibei: Chengwen.

Treager, T. R. 1970. *An Economic Geography of China.* New York: American Elsevier.

Waley-Cohen, Joanna. 1987. The Stranger Paths of Banishment: Exile to the Xinjiang Frontier in Mid-Qing China. Ph.D. diss., Yale University.

_____. 1991. *Exile in Mid-Qing China: Banishment to Xinjiang, 1758-1820.* New Haven: Yale University Press.

Wang, Hongjun. 1984. *Junge'er de lishi yu wenwu* (History and cultural relics of the Zunghars). Xining: Qinghai Renmin.

Wang, Jianmin. 1984. Qing QianJia shiqi Xinjiang tuntian fenbu (Preliminary survey of the distribution of troops garrisoned for the purpose of defense and farming in the Qianlong and Jiaqing reigns of the Qing dynasty). *Xibei shidi* (History and geography of the northwest) 1:76-84.

Wang, Xilong. 1987. Qingdai Xinjiang de zhufang baqi yu 'qitun' (Eight banners garrisoned in Qing Xinjiang and their agricultural colonies). *Xinjiang shehui kexue* (Xinjiang social sciences) 6:96-104.

_____. 1990. *Qingdai xibei tuntian yanjiu* (Study of military colonies in the northwest during the Qing period). Lanzhou: Lanzhou University.

Wei, Yuan. [1846] 1962. *Shengwuji* (Chronicle of imperial military campaigns). Reprint. Beijing: Zhonghua.

Wiens, Herold J. 1966. Cultivation Development and Expansion in China's Colonial Realm in Central Asia. *Journal of Asian Studies* 26, 1:67-88.

Wulumuqi shiyi (Conditions in Urumchi). 1795. N.p.

Wu, Yuanfeng. 1987. Qing Qianlong nianjian Ili tuntian shulue (Summary of Ili military colonies in the Qianlong period during the Qing). *Minzu yanjiu* (Research on nationalities) 5:92-99.

XJSL. Songyun, comp. 1820. *Xinjiang shilue* (A summary of Xinjiang). N.p.

Xu, Bofu. 1985. Qingdai qianqi Xinjiang diqu de mintun (Civilian colonies in Xinjiang during the early Qing dynasty). *Zhongguo shih yanjiu* (Research on Chinese history) 2:85-95.

_____. 1987. 18-19 shiji Xinjiang diqu de guanying xushouye (Government-run animal husbandry in Xinjiang during the eighteenth and nineteenth centuries). *Xinjiang shehui kexue* (Xinjiang social sciences) 5:101-112.

Zeng, Wenwu. [1936] 1978. *Zhongguo jingying xiyu shi* (History of China's management of the western regions). Taibei: Wenhai.

Zhao, Songqiao. 1986. *Physical Geography of China.* New York: John Wiley.

Zlatkin, I Ia. 1983. *Istoriia Dzhungarskogo khanstva* (History of the Zunghar khanate). Moscow.

4

The State's Resources and the People's Livelihood (*Guoji minsheng*): The Daoguang Emperor's Dilemmas about Grand Canal Restoration, 1825

Jane Kate Leonard

Introduction

In late 1824, major floods destroyed the Grand Canal in northern Jiangsu and crippled the grain transport system. During the early months of 1825 as regional officials sought in vain to ship the 1825 grain tax quotas through the Huaiyang section of the canal, it became clear that the Grand Canal was no longer functional. If the state intended to continue canal shipments of tribute grain in the dangerously unstable period ahead as the Yellow River lay poised for its northward shift of course, it would have to mount a massive program of canal restoration to open up the lower course of the Yellow River and rebuild the lake dikes west of the Huaiyang Canal (Map 2).

The tasks were herculean in scope and the costs staggering. Yet from the newly enthroned Daoguang Emperor's point of view, canal restoration was essential to guarantee the shipment of strategic grain reserves to the capital—grain that was "the imperial granaries' main source of supply" (P5.8.9). Because this issue went to the very heart of Qing strategic views of empire and the intimate connections between economic and strategic power, the emperor launched a critical review of current approaches to

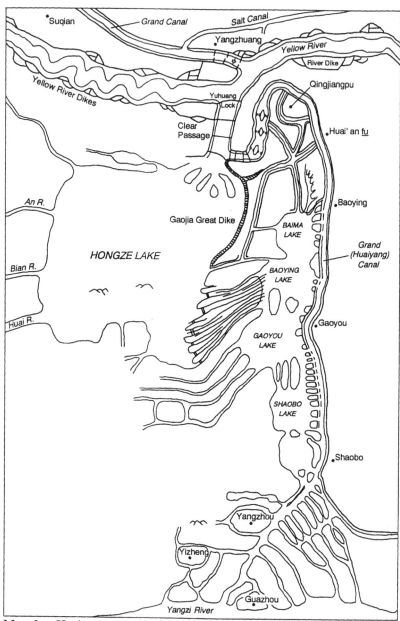

Map 2. Huaiyang Canal and Grand Canal-Yellow River Junction, ca. 1820.

regional management of the canal–grain transport system. He forced regional officials to put aside their repertoire of time-worn strategies for operating the canal because it had proved incapable of coping with canal conditions in the wake of the flood disaster of late 1824 (Leonard 1991, 244-69). He insisted that they prepare, instead, to implement a bold new plan for canal restoration. The centerpiece of the plan was an elaborate scheme for commuting the 1826 grain tax to silver in order to finance system-wide repairs of the Grand Canal–riverine network in northern Jiangsu, especially the dredging and diversion of the lower course of the Yellow River. The initial intention was to close down the canal completely for a year to concentrate human and material resources on reconstruction tasks while shipping a limited amount of grain to Beijing by sea to maintain minimum granary reserves in the capital.

The debate over commutation took place in mid-1825 during the darkest hours of the canal crisis when canal blockages, the shortage of small craft called lighters (*bochuan*), and siltation of the canal–Yellow River junction seemed to threaten the completion of the 1825 grain shipments. To the emperor and his central advisers, commutation seemed to provide an effective way to raise money for canal restoration. In the end, the commutation plan was abandoned, and with it any hope of ameliorating geophysical barriers that threatened continued canal operations. Yet, the debate on this issue and the companion issues of transfer-shipping (*panba jieyun*) and sea transport for 1826 raised fundamental questions about the Qing state's ability to control fiscal-administrative processes at the district level of government and to guarantee the state's fiscal resources and the people's livelihood (*guoji minsheng*). These questions, in turn, cast doubt on the imperium's ability to maintain the Grand Canal system and the vast logistical network that sustained the empire.

The purpose of this paper is to examine the major issues raised in the debate on commutation and to interpret their significance for defining the Qing leadership's view of the strategic significance of economic stability and the state's responsibility for assuring the people's livelihood at the subdistrict level.

The Tradition of Qing Stewardship of the Economy

Throughout the Qing dynasty, imperial leadership vigorously upheld the economic interests of the peasant, trader, and craftsman and acted to stop the "mean and corrupt" (private interests and officials) from bankrupting the state and "harming the people." Their reasons for doing so were closely tied to the Qing view of empire and their definition of strategic imperatives associated with the vast expansion of the empire into the borderlands and the special problems of pacifying China proper. Two major assumptions shaped their imperial adventure. First, the logistical network that sustained the empire depended on the wealth generated in the grain-producing regions of China. Second, the uninterrupted flow of revenue and food grains to the capital depended on peace and security in the grain-producing heartland, especially the eight-province canal zone that linked the heartland to the capital (Leonard 1987). These two assumptions shaped the Qing dynasts' view of the strategic-logistical significance of economic issues to the long-term security of the empire, and they account for Qing administrative activism in fiscal-economic matters. An understanding of the strategic significance of economic ordering was not unknown in earlier periods. Indeed, it expressed the Confucian view that economic stability provided the conditions necessary for moral-political ordering. Qing imperial leadership was, however, unique for its careful scrutiny of economic conditions, facilitated by the use of the secret communications system, and for its flexibility and responsiveness to changing economic realities.

Even though the state's power to control the economy was relatively limited, the Qing monarchs used their power to encourage prosperity and growth in the various regional economies of China. Because their strategic view of empire linked the survival of the dynasty directly to the people's livelihood, the Qing emperors showed a great willingness to intervene in the economy to restore and promote prosperity and assure fiscal-economic justice in ways that accorded with the ''limited'' prerogatives of the state at the subdistrict level (Bao 1982; Metzger 1970; Ng 1983, 184-212; Perdue 1987, 1-24, 164-96; Shang 1981, 111-20). These efforts created an environment throughout the Qing period where economic enterprise expanded, developed, and diversified in both the agricultural and commercial sectors; and even when the state's ability to control the disruptive effects of economic change was limited by the weakness of local government in the nineteenth century, the desire to do so remained undiminshed as did their sense of responsibility for the ''state's fiscal well-being and the people's livelihood.''

The term, *guoji minsheng*, expressed the Qing leadership's view of the integral linkage between the state's strategic-fiscal needs and prosperity in the people's sphere, or private economy. It suggests an identity of interests between the people and the imperial state, in which no clear distinctions were made between economic and strategic necessity, only between economic and strategic function. The former, economic function, was the people's sphere, where resources were used to create a stable livelihood. Strategic function was the state's sphere. To maintain that sphere, the leadership had the prerogative to extract only that portion of the people's wealth that was necessary to accomplish its political-moral mission. The people and the state, therefore, shared a common interest in economic prosperity and order that linked their separate and independent functions. Policies that served one, served the other as well. This notion guided the Qing leadership's administration of fiscal-economic issues and sparked imperial involvement in a wide range of economic matters that were perceived as crucial to economic ordering.

The character of that involvement varied over time and space. One finds direct management, regulation, and funding of enterprises and infrastructure projects in the early reigns, but more mediation and selective involvement in the eighteenth century (Bao 1982; King 1965; Metzger 1962; Ng 1983; Perdue 1987; Quan and Kraus 1975; Rowe 1983; Schoppa 1989; Shang 1981; Vogel 1983; Wang 1973; Will 1985; Will and Wong 1991). These initiatives were paralleled by imperial moves to eliminate economic exploitation and abuse that might prompt rebellion and disorder, such as curbing local magisterial prerogatives over budget and tax collection, the elimination of gentry privilege, the expansion of *baojia* networks, and the extension of state control over specialized bureaucratic functions at subprefectural level (Ch'u 1962; Dodgen 1989; Hsiao 1960; Watt 1972; Will 1985; Zelin 1984). In general, the imperial posture was one of restraint and circumspection, expressing the preference for "storing wealth among the people" (Rowe 1991, 22-28; Wang 1973, 110-33).

Even in enterprises where state management and funding were constant and on-going due to scale of enterprise or strategic significance, efforts were made to serve the economic interests of the community as well as the state. The Grand Canal-grain transport system was the largest enterprise of this kind. It was designed to guarantee imperial strategic control over the disposition of vital grain surpluses, and, especially, to maintain the grain self-sufficiency of the capital at Beijing—a Manchu island in a sea of Chinese (Hinton 1970; Quan and Kraus 1975). Yearly grain shipments on the canal totalled nearly 3.5 million *shi*. The safe, orderly shipment of these grain reserves depended on government reconstruction and yearly maintenance of the canal's complex hydraulic engineering works. It also depended on peace and security in the agricultural communities that straddled the canal. The Kangxi Emperor understood the necessity of both when he undertook the reconstruction of the Huaiyang section of the canal. Besides rebuilding and expanding the large water control facilities connected to the canal, he also undertook the improvement of local, small-scale drainage and flood control networks in the adjacent Xiahe region to protect the area from floods, enhance its prosperity, and thus guarantee its security and the security of grain shipments (Map 3). Later, in the eighteenth century, the drainage outlets on the Yangzi were expanded for the same reasons (Bao 1982; Liu 1961; Liu 1981; Gandar [1894]; Zhu 1962). Both of these undertakings show the Qing regime's desire to avoid economic turmoil stemming from flood disasters in the strategically sensitive canal zone, and they express the leadership's broadened view of the intimate relationship between economic well-being and imperial security.

As the dynasty progressed, one also sees a readiness to step beyond the confines of government agencies and administrative law to work with sectors of the private economy to cope with changing conditions affecting

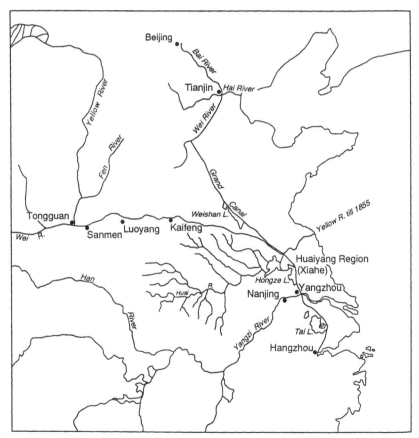

Map 3. Confluence of Grand Canal, Huai, and Yellow Rivers (1288-1852).

canal-transport operations. As the rolls of government transport workers declined, the government adjusted, albeit reluctantly, to the use of private wage labor to man the government grain junks (Kelley 1986). In the early nineteenth century when siltation of the canal required the use of smaller craft, or lighters, for grain transport, hundreds of private canal shippers were routinely hired to supplement the fleets of regular grain junks. When the canal was severely damaged in 1825, the government recruited (*zhaolai*) private coastal shippers from Shanghai to undertake the sea transport of grain tribute from Jiangnan in 1826. All of these examples show the Qing state's willingness to use private economic groups to pursue non-bureaucratic solutions to achieve the state's strategic-fiscal goals. Joint ventures of this kind were also used in other strategic-fiscal areas, such as the provisioning of military campaigns, famine relief, inter-provincial grain transfers, and copper mining to assure adequate supplies of monetary copper (Perdue 1989; 1991; Quan and Kraus 1975; Shulman 1989; Sun 1968; Vogel 1983; Will 1980; 1990).

In summary, throughout the dynasty, the Qing leadership pursued what can only be called a very activist and creative approach to the economy. Its purpose was to promote prosperity and growth in the private economy to safeguard the logistical network joining China and the borderlands. Its intention was, of course, to generate reliable tax revenues, but it did so in ways that strengthened and enhanced economic stability in the agricultural heartland. As impending crises loomed over the Grand Canal–grain transport network in the late eighteenth and early nineteenth centuries, the standard against which plans for canal restoration were measured was their ability to benefit the state without disrupting the people's livelihood.

Canal Restoration and the Debate on Grain Tax Commutation

The debate on commutation took place in mid-1825 after emergency plans to repair the canal system and manuever the grain fleets through the canal–Yellow River junction collapsed. It was clear to the emperor and regional official alike that the canal in northern Jiangsu was no longer operational. The use of Yellow River backspills at the junction earlier in the spring, the resort to lighterage on the Huaiyang Canal, and then the scheme for transfer-shipping across the junction embankments had all broken down. The emperor entreated regional officials to face the need for canal restoration if strategic grain shipments were to continue (Leonard 1991, 150-240).

Two basic approaches to canal reconstruction were discussed. The first, favored by regional officials, proposed limited repairs to those specific water control facilities that had been damaged by the floods in late 1824. The second option, pushed by the emperor and his allies (both central advisers like Yinghe and highly trusted regional officials transferred in to key positions in northern Jiangsu, such as Qishan and Tao Zhu), sought to reverse long-term deterioration of the canal system as well as to complete emergency reconstruction. Both called for rebuilding the lake dikes west of the Huaiyang Canal and for a system-wide program of silt removal to dredge open the lower course of the Yellow River.

Each of the plans had its merits and drawbacks. Neither boasted a permanent solution to the fundamental problem which was the Yellow River and its destructive pattern of siltation and meandering that anticipated the river's impending northward shift. Yet the actual design of the programs and the reasons for their acceptance or rejection bear close analysis. They were shaped primarily by the long-standing principle that imperial decisions should serve both the state's strategic needs and the economic needs of the people and should protect both from economic exploitation and abuse. During the crisis, with its complexity of fiscal, logistical, and economic problems, the only options that did both were plans that avoided any participation or involvement of district-level government. In other words, the acceptance or rejection of alternative courses of action depended on the extent to which these plans required the participation of department and district officials and whether the so-called "mother and father of the people" could be trusted to carry out crucial organizational and fiscal functions. In a number of important instances concerning transfer-shipment from grain junks to lighters, sea transport, and, of course, the conversion of grain tribute to currency to pay for canal reconstruction, key decisions were determined by the extent to which district-level officials played a role in the planning and execution of these strategies. If their role was large, the plans were often scrapped. If minimal, plans went forward. Similarly, those plans for grain transport that received the greatest support were those organized by top regional officials to bypass district-level government and rely instead on the organizational resources of private interests on the canal and on the coast.

The crux of the imperial plan for canal restoration was the commutation of grain tax to currency (*zhecao*) to pay for reconstruction. Without massive funding in this period of escalating costs, the state could never hope to undertake the scale of work required to rebuild the canal system in northern Jiangsu. The vision of the plan was very broad and unorthodox in that it called for the closure of the canal and a ban on canal shipments of grain for one entire year so that labor, material, and bureaucratic resources, normally used to perform regular cyclical repair and transport tasks, could be diverted wholeheartedly to reconstruction on a scale unknown since the early Qing period. The Daoguang Emperor first raised the commutation issue in early lunar four (S/TJ5.4.10a); then in late lunar five, he distributed a more detailed version of the plan in which some of its concrete provisions were sketched out (S/TJ5.5.22a). A month later (5.6.28), the emperor forged decisively ahead and ordered all southern canal-zone officials to study the plan and assess its applicability to conditions in each of their respective jurisdictions (TJ5.6.28c).

The conversion of grain tribute to silver was neither new nor impossibly difficult, in principle, to implement. Since the early Qing period, part of the grain quota had been paid in silver in the more distant southern provinces of Jiangxi, Hunan, and Hubei although never in Jiangsu and Zhejiang, primary suppliers of premium grade polished rice destined for imperial use. This category of commuted grain was called "permanently commuted tribute" (*benseyin, yongzhe, zhese;* CAT 512; Hinton 1970, 9). Although a great deal of variety existed in the manner of grain tax collection at the local level, permanently commuted tribute was generally paid in cash by the peasant, which meant that he undertook the conversion of grain to currency. His currency payment was determined by the market price of a *shi* of grain at the time of conversion (CAT 734; Hinton 1970, 8-9; Wang 1973, 60-61).

The second type of conversion was temporary commuting (*zhese, zhecao*) and was allowed when the actual grain could not be collected in kind. Temporary commuting occurred when crops failed, the shipment process broke down locally or on the Grand Canal, or when provincial officials deemed it necessary to sell the grain locally to stabilize grain prices. In the first two cases, the taxpayer undertook the conversion transaction, while in the last, the magistrate did so. The local sale of grain tribute to achieve stable grain prices was a common practice; and even if it was done in a number of districts, it did not threaten metropolitan granary supplies because extra reserves were kept for just such contingencies. The whole shipment of 3.5 million *shi* could be held back for one year, or 2 million *shi* for three consecutive years without depleting the capital granaries (CAT 785; Hinton 1970, 7-8; Quan and Kraus 1975, 28-39).

Grain tribute quotas were never widely commuted until the post-1850 period, when the shift of the Yellow River, the Taiping occupation of the lower Yangzi valley, and the availability of steamship transport dramatically altered the grain transport system. Yet, a variety of local practices did develop after 1750 that involved currency transactions in the collection and delivery of grain tax (Hinton 1970, 8-9; Hsiao 1960, 122-24, 139-43; Rowe 1983, 33-86; Wang 1973, 52-66). In these cases, the grain tax was increasingly paid in copper cash rather than silver. Peasants who lived in areas remote from the district seat or official granaries often paid their tax in currency as did peasants who produced cash crops in highly commercialized districts like Jiangnan. The latter paid their grain tax in currency, either directly to district government or indirectly to groups or individuals who acted as tax brokers and arranged for the purchase and delivery of grain to the district authorities. These brokers included *li* headmen, gentry *baolan* organizations, and *yamen* clerks and their cronies. As the population increased in the late eighteenth century and the district magistrate found it increasingly difficult to perform many of the basic functions of office, these tax brokers played an ever larger role in the grain tax collection process (Zhou 1982, 89-93). Although these practices were generally fairly well established and widely used by the 1820s, rarely had commutation been carried out on such a large scale as proposed in the emperor's plan and never associated with the complete closure of the Grand Canal—a highly symbolic and strategically important government operation in the late imperial period.

The emperor asked regional officials to consider three approaches to handling the 1826 grain tax (TJ5.6.28c). The first was peasant commutation of grain tax obligations. In this case, theoretically at least, the peasant undertook the market sale of his grain and the delivery of the proceeds from the sale to the district magistrate. The second was magisterial sale of tribute grain. In this case, the local magistrate collected the grain tax in kind as usual from peasants, arranged for its sale on the open market for silver, and then forwarded the proceeds to its designated use, in this instance, canal authorities in northern Jiangsu. Third, if there were locales where neither peasant nor magisterial commutation was appropriate and canal shipping was temporarily stopped, officials were asked to plan for the storage of 1826 grain quotas until 1827 when the canal presumably would be functioning normally again.

From early lunar six to lunar eight, regional officials considered these three options in light of local conditions and practices in each of their respective provinces. In general, they were uniformly and adamantly opposed to peasant commutation. They argued that it would be far too "difficult" to carry out, both for the taxpayer and the tax collector (TJ5.6.22; S5.7.3a/b). Additionally, it would unleash uncontrollable official corruption that would "harm the people." Tao Zhu argued that in Jiangsu, which had a large grain tax quota, the sale of huge quantities of tribute would flood the market and drive down prices, reducing the income from its sale and destabilizing the market (TJ5.6.29a; TJ5.7.17).

Taking a slightly different line, the governors of Jiangxi and Anhui both proposed complicated plans for peasant commuting in which peasants paid half their grain tax in unhusked rather than the normal form of husked rice and the other half in currency (S5.7.21; TJ5.8.10). The reason for suggesting the collection of unhusked rice was the fear that if the grain had to be stored for a year in the hot humid south, there would be less risk of spoilage with unhusked than with husked rice. The Anhui governor, furthermore, urged that part of the grain and currency collected in 1826 be used locally to replenish local granary supplies, especially relief granaries, with the remainder forwarded to canal authorities. This, the emperor rejected out of hand, asserting that the "original purpose of the plan was to pay for canal-river reconstruction," not local administration (S5.7.21).

The Jiangxi governor's proposal hinted that official corruption (manipulating the rates of collection) could be controlled if the peasants undertook the commutation plan, and he pointed out that just such a plan had been discussed earlier in the Yongzheng reign. The emperor was intrigued by the idea of minimizing official corruption, but he also worried that such a plan might be too burdensome for the peasants. He ordered the governor to publicize his plan throughout Jiangxi and test the people's (*xiangmin*) reaction to it and simultaneously warned local officials not to hide the response of the people just to please the governor. He also showed caution and not a little skepticism about the reference to similar proposals in the Yongzheng reign, saying that the governor had not explained whether or not the plan had actually been implemented at the time nor whether it had been successful. Even if it had, past plans don't necessarily work for the present!

> In the Yongzheng reign although they discussed this issue, did they actually carry it out? In the memorial, it does not state this clearly. The situation now and in the past are not the same. Was the plan absolutely free of obstructions? (S5.7.6).

While regional officials generally opposed peasant commutation, they were more receptive to official commutation, where district officials undertook the market sale of grain and/or copper cash for silver. The greater support for official sale can be explained in several ways. First, throughout the Qing period, local officials had been responsible for and experienced in a wide-range of fiscal-marketing functions connected to interprovincial grain transfers, the provision of relief grains, and price stabilization measures; and regional officials probably thought that official commutation of tribute would be a fairly easy and routine task to perform, easier than changing the procedures for grain tax collection. Even so, they must have been reluctant to add another task to the already overburdened magistrates who were scarcely able to perform the minimal responsibilities of their office.

Financial need must have provided the second reason for regional official support of official commutation. District-level officials and their provincial superiors depended on the manipulation of fiscal-market transactions to fund the basic operations of provincial government. The opportunity to manipulate the ratios between husked and unhusked grain prices, between grain and silver, and between copper cash and silver, would have provided a golden opportunity for raising money during a period when they were all strapped for funds and constrained by an inelastic budget.

Yet other officials recoiled from official commutation precisely because they felt local officials would go too far in raising the rate of collection for the taxpaying peasant, as well as extorting money from merchants by arbitrarily manipulating the market price of grain, silver, and copper cash. In the latter case, they feared that local officials would demand an arbitrarily high price for grain and thereby destabilize market conditions. This was a legitimate fear in the 1820s, a period that was already experiencing deflation of rice prices, an oversupply of copper, and shortages and inflation of silver (King 1965; Lin 1989; Quan and Kraus 1975; Wang 1973, 115; 1979).

Earlier in the debate, Qishan had warned against these evils, asserting that "corrupt officials might deliberately increase the price of grain and harm the people" (S5.6.28c). Tao Zhu feared that dumping grain tribute on the market would depress rice prices in Jiangsu. Li Hongbin, governor-general of Huguang, asserted that although magisterial sale of grain was more practicable than peasant commutation, he had deep misgivings about the former:

> I fear it will cause *zhouxian* officials to coerce and exploit the
> merchants and the people. The officials in charge of buying
> silver can make a false price and carry out all the corrupt
> practices of increasing the amount of silver (S5.7.3b).

This fear was echoed by the Hunan governor who asserted that *zhouxian* sale of grain would inevitably lead officials and their clerks to demand that merchants buy grain at artificially high prices (TJ5.7.17).

These discussions highlighted the multitude of ways that local officials could manipulate the local tax collection process and fiscal-market functions associated with their administrative responsibilities. In light of these abuses, the two proposals for collecting unhusked grain and currency from the peasants in Jiangxi and Anhui take on new significance. While peasant commutation to unhusked grain and copper cash appeared on the surface to reduce the risk of official corruption, it, in fact, provided local officials with a double opportunity to make money. They could manipulate the rate of collection of unhusked to husked rice and husked rice to copper cash when collecting from the peasant, then turn around and sell both at artificially high prices on the market for silver.

The response of top regional officials to the commutation scheme is significant because it reveals what they perceived as the greatest obstacles to its implementation, or to the implementation of any major imperial undertaking that relied on the administrative actions and fiscal integrity of local government. Their comments are less condemnatory than expressive of an awareness of a malaise, or paralysis, in local government that seemed to preclude the assignment of additional tasks to this beleaguered sector of provincial government.

In retrospect, it is clear that local government struggled unsuccessfully to cope with the effects of economic change and demographic crisis because it used fiscal-administrative tools crafted in and intended for a seventeenth-century reality. Times had changed. Institutions had not. The district magistrate was as much the victim of early nineteenthcentury conditions as the villain. His resources were inadequate to the tasks he faced, and he was viewed, with varying degrees of hostility or sympathy, as either ineffective or corrupt, or both. In light of these problems at the district level, top regional officials were marginally willing to support official sale of grain tribute in 1826 even though they were reluctant to add more responsibilities to local government. However, they made clear the daunting obstacles to its implementation—obstacles that they knew would dampen the Daoguang Emperor's enthusiasm for the plan, given the long-standing Qing suspicion of magisterial tampering with the fiscal process.

Although official discourse on commutation centered on the difficulties of district-level administration and fears of corruption, another unspoken issue, equally important, motivated officials to reject the plan and argue for the retention of the usual pattern of grain collection and shipment. The normal pattern was intimately linked to networks of private organizations on which the dynasty depended for the successful yearly transport of grain tribute. These organizations included labor, marketing, and shipping interests that undertook a range of functions, including ship-building and repair, private lighterage, canal engineering, reconstruction and dredging, and the tracking and haulage of grain cargoes (Hoshi 1960; 1971; Kelley 1986). All were deeply enmeshed in the yearly canal-transport cycle and formed a complex network of government-private interests. To disrupt these networks was to disrupt economic conditions along the canal and invite hardship and perhaps rebellion. A censor clearly expressed this fear when commutation was first raised. If the canal was closed down for a year, he felt certain that the hired crews on the government grain junks connected to the Luo Sect would cause trouble when thrown out of work (TJ5.6.6b).

The reliance on these organizations arose from complex structural changes in the Chinese economy since the mid-eighteenth century, including the commercialization of the economy in the lower Yangzi valley, the specialization of labor functions along the Grand Canal, and the Qing practice of cultivating non-bureaucratic organizations to perform essential aspects of grain shipping (lighterage) and marketing. Lighterage, for example, in silt blocked sections of the canal in northern Jiangsu was now a routine part of the shipment process. Any changes in government grain shipping, therefore, were bound to affect the canal zone very profoundly, particularly if those changes were made rapidly, as was proposed in 1825, giving shippers little time to adjust to the economic consequences. Rhetorical arguments about "*zhouxian* corruption" and "maintaining the old regulations in canal transport" at least partially masked the issues of government-private networks, the political-economic power they represented, and the fear of economic turmoil that would result from sweeping changes in 1826.

Some of these same officials also wanted to maintain the status quo in grain transport because they had serious misgivings about the wisdom of investing huge sums in canal reconstruction. They doubted that much could be done to reverse the deterioration of the canal system and the centuries of siltation that had caused it. Muddling through until the shift of the Yellow River seemed to be the wisest course. To spend on reconstruction at this stage seemed to be throwing good money after bad. In sum, three issues—district-level corruption, economic disorder from the disruption of offical-private networks connected with grain shipping, and the impossibility of achieving significant improvements in the canal system—caused regional officials to reject the plan for commutation of grain tribute! All three reflect the leadership's fear of the strategic consequences of fiscal-economic instability.

When the emperor initially launched the debate on grain tax commutation, he had been hopeful of its potential for raising money for canal restoration. He appears, at first, to have favored peasant commutation, apparently because he thought it was the less vulnerable to official extortion than official sale. When regional officials rejected this plan out of hand because it was unworkable and would surely encourage official manipulation of the tax collection process, he quickly realized that an undertaking like commutation could never be implemented successfully because it relied so heavily on *zhouxian*-level administration.

The emperor was generally more hostile to plans for official sale of grain on the open market because of its effect on merchants and market conditions. The exploitation of merchants seemed, at the outset, to pose a more serious problem of corruption to him than did official manipulation of the rates of collection that adversely affected the peasant. The reason for this may have been that there were fewer legal restraints on official manipulation of merchants and market transactions, compared to the regulations on tax collection and surcharges. His fear of market instability must also have shaped his view. Because regional officials routinely reported on market conditions, he would have been aware of growing instability in the grain, copper, and silver markets. He must also have feared the economic consequences of flooding the market with tribute grain after Tao Zhu raised this issue. In any case, by late lunar seven, he was convinced that both commutation plans were seriously flawed because they would lead to widespread official extortion and exploitation of both the peasant and merchant and would adversely affect regional economic conditions. The arguments of regional officials had made a deep impression on the Daoguang Emperor, as they were obviously intended to do, because of the significance that the Qing dynasts had always attached to the integrity of the tax collection process and their direct personal responsibility for maintaining fiscal equity and economic stability. Both were seen as pivotal in protecting the livelihood and security of the people as well as that of the state.

From the beginning, the emperor asserted that if a commutation scheme was adopted for 1826, it must work to benefit both the state's revenues and the people's livelihood (*guoji minsheng*; TJ5.6.29a). "The most important thing to keep in mind when considering this plan," he stated, "is that both the officials' and the peoples' interests must be served" (S5.6.28c). He argued against official commutation precisely because it gave officials free rein to jack up the price of grain and increase unfairly the amount of silver they made from market transactions (S5.7.3a/b). When he considered the Jiangxi plan for peasant commutation to unhusked rice and cash, he was reluctant to proceed with the plan until he was sure "the people" were in favor of it. It was important "that this entire matter contribute to the government's fiscal security and the people's livelihood. I still fear we can't avoid myriad troubles. Placing responsibility on *zhouxian* officials to collect and convert unhusked grain will unleash the evil practices of deceit and extortion'' (S5.7.6).

By the time the Anhui proposal arrived later in lunar seven, the emperor stated that the plan of collecting the tribute in unhusked rice and copper currency was too complicated and too vulnerable to official corruption. ''How can peasant families decide how much to deliver in grain and how much in currency? Originally, the plan for commuting grain was a temporary expedient (*quanqie*) to pay for canal-river reconstruction.'' It was best, he ordered, that Anhui officials collect the grain in the usual way and if the canal was closed in 1826, simply store the grain until the following year. Commutation ''will only benefit the state if it does not cause trouble for the people nor excite corrupt practices by *yamen* clerks'' (S5.7.21). The latter robbed both the people and the state.

In early lunar eight, the emperor scuttled the plan completely. In a public edict summarizing official response to the commutation plan, he explained that regional officials had insisted that peasant commutation would give rise to uncontrollable corruption. To undertake commutation on a large scale would also disrupt the collection, shipment, and marketing of grain. Therefore, he decided to abandon the plan and adhere to the normal process of grain collection:

> Grain tribute is the dynasty's main supply. Levying and collecting grain tribute in kind has been the established way of doing things for a long time. Now, changing the system and receiving commuted silver will give rise to corrupt practices. Therefore, I have sent down an edict to terminate all discussion of this matter in Jiangsu, Anhui, Zhejiang, and Huguang (P5.8.9a).

The autumn harvests had begun, he explained, and officials were busy preparing for grain collection. He ordered all officials to collect the grain tax in the normal way so that ''unfilial (*buxiao*) officials will not have any excuses for using commutation to extort money and injure the people'' (P5.8.9a). The barrage of official arguments against commutation had, indeed, convinced the emperor to abandon the plan.

The abandonment of grain tax commutation, the fiscal underpinnings of canal restoration, requires some explanation. Why, in the face of the overwhelming fiscal need in canal-grain transport administration, particularly for canal restoration, was the commutation plan jettisoned so easily? Can we take at face value the imperial and official arguments about magisterial corruption at the department and district levels? Can we accept the views and assumptions of the emperor, his officials, and modern scholars alike who identify *zhouxian* corruption as the major problem limiting the Qing state's ability to cope with herculean problems in the early nineteenth century, such as Grand Canal restoration?

The answer to this problem is complex and scholarship has lagged on this subject because many aspects of the fiscal collection system were informal and non-statutory, and therefore, are extremely difficult to ferret out. It is much easier to cry "corruption" at the *zhouxian* level, just as the Qing emperors did, than to find the answers (Hsiao 1960, 95-105, 122-24, 139-43; Morse 1913, 76-113; Zelin 1984, 167-219). As noted above, throughout the Qing period, local magistrates undertook a wide range of fiscal-market functions connected to the performance of routine tasks of office (Ch'u 1962, 140-44; Hsiao 1960, 105-20; Huang [1694], 31-37, 203-207; Watt 1972, 197-209). These tasks included the buying and selling of grain, copper cash, silver, and other commodities. The procedures and usages were long established, including those connected to the retention of grain tax for local uses. In view of this, why was there such fear of local-official corruption and market instability in the mid-1820s?

There are two aspects of this question: first, the structural nature of official corruption and second, its relationship, in the minds of the emperor and regional officials, to the disruption of the economy and internal security in the canal-zone. Because the Qing regime regarded the private, non-statutory charges of the fiscal system with abhorrence, they acted early in the dynasty to deprive local officials of the initiative to levy these charges; they fixed and legalized some of the surcharges and prohibited all the others, condemning them as illegal and immoral, a device, they argued, that corrupt local officials used for their own private enrichment.

Many of these measures were unworkable and patently unfair. They locked the magistrate into a hopeless situation with ever-increasing local administrative responsibilities, especially as population mushroomed, but with a fixed revenue and budget to perform them. In addition, he had to provide contributions to his superiors, hire his own staff, and rely on local *yamen* personnel to perform the basic functions of his office (Ch'u 1962; Littrup 1981; Liu 1968). The costs, of course, multiplied as population and prices increased (Deng 1958, 102-103, 844; Huang [1694], 31-37; Zhou 1982, 85-103). Both the state and the local community recognized the magistrate's legitimate need for funds, and even though non-statutory surcharges were illegal, they were generally condoned. They were customary and, it would appear, they were determined consensually by the magistrate and the local community power brokers.

The most balanced and convincing analysis of this problem is that of Wang Yeh-chien, who argues that, for the most part, the collection of taxes in the last 150 years of the Qing was orderly and stable. Both statutory and non-statutory surcharges increased, but not capriciously. Non-statutory surcharges, he asserts, rose primarily due to the effects of population increase and changes in the value of money. They should be seen as a flexible response to changing times that were accepted as customary and necessary (Wang 1973, 49-83; Watt 1972, 197-209; Zhou 1982, 92-93).

If local government was not wholly the problem, who or what was? The answer seems to lie in the special fiscal and monetary problems of the Daoguang reign and their relationship to funding both central and local government operations. These problems posed a threat to the long-established Qing principle of fostering the people's livelihood (*minsheng*). Serious shortages of imperial revenue appeared in the Jiaqing and Daoguang reigns (1796-1850) that were caused by tax arrears and remissions and by the military expenses associated with the suppression of internal rebellion and unrest in southwest Turkestan. To offset these shortages, imperial government embarked on a vigorous effort to collect tax arrears and to expand the sale of office (*juanna*), the latter providing 36 percent of central government income in the Daoguang reign (Wang 1973, 12-19). These mounting shortages must have heightened imperial and central government awareness of fiscal problems at both the central and local levels.

Even more important in the early nineteenth century was the growing instability of the monetary system which exacerbated fiscal problems at both the central and local levels of government, and unsettled market conditions in the private economy. From 1750 to 1850, the monetary system was disrupted by a general rise in the price of silver in relation to copper cash. This trend was apparently driven first by copper shortages and then, in the Daoguang reign, by an oversupply of copper cash (King 1965, 140-43; Vogel 1983, 377-96; Wang 1973, 60-61, Zhou 1982, 61-105). At the same time, there appears to have been a simultaneous, market-generated scarcity of silver which may also have been somewhat influenced by the expansion of the illegal smuggling trade in opium in the 1820s, at least in the major cities and markets on the coast and the lower Yangzi valley (Chang 1964, 39-40; King 1965, 121-63; Lin 1989; Wang 1979).

In spite of this instability, however, the economic picture was generally positive from 1750 to 1910. Wang Yeh-chien shows that during this period, agricultural acreage increased by one-half, land yields increased by 20 percent, and prices tripled which suggests that the tax burden in 1910 was one-third that of the mid-eighteenth century. However, within this relatively positive picture, the period from 1820 to 1850 (the entire Daoguang reign) experienced considerable turmoil. From 1815 to 1850, grain prices fell by one-half which meant a 100 percent appreciation in the value of silver relative to grain. This placed an enormous burden on the taxpayer when paying his land tax in silver. The general deflationary forces at work also decreased the taxpayer's income from cash crops and off-season employment (Lin 1989: Wang 1973, 110-15; 1986; Zhou 1982, 61-105).

Technically, the fall in grain prices should not have affected the commutation of grain tax because the amount of *shi* determined the tax liability. Yet the rising price of silver and the ups-and-downs in the monetary and market systems, placed a burden on the magistrate who had to send on the commuted portions of the grain tax in silver. To meet his needs, the magistrate generally raised the rate of collection for both the land and the grain tax. That is, he increased the add-on surcharges to keep pace with the rising price of silver. Because of these key price movements, taxes in the early Daoguang reign were rising, and at the end of the reign, taxes were twice as heavy as in the 1820s and three times as heavy as those in the Qianlong and Jiaqing reigns (Wang 1973, 102-103; 110-28). The net effect of the declining price of cash, the inflation of silver, the drop in grain prices, plus the increased rate of collection placed a burden on the taxpayer and the tax collector alike. It became impossible for the magistrate to fund the spiralling costs of local administration with a budget structure designed for an earlier age and a population of one-half or one-third the size.

The turmoil in the fiscal, monetary, and market systems in the 1820s, with its accompanying symptoms of unrest, litigation, tax revolt, local government paralysis, and general market instability, must have evoked a picture of economic and fiscal crisis at the local level—a picture which could readily be interpreted as exploitive of the peasant and merchant, and the result of district-level mismanagement or corruption, or both. The emperor and his Grand Council advisers would, of course, have been aware of the growing turmoil in the fiscal, monetary and market systems because of their close supervision of these issues. Yet the causes and the effects of these phenomena were not clear at the time (nor are they altogether clear today). Instead of responding equally to the hardships created for both the magistrate and the taxpayer, the emperor and the upper levels of bureaucracy seem to have identified the source of the problem as district-level corruption and mismanagement, giving us yet another historical case of blaming the victim!

The debate on grain tax commutation and alternative methods of grain transport in 1825, I would suggest, reflected the mood of uncertainty about the economy and fears about the impact of economic instability on the imperial fiscal system and on internal security in the canal zone. Although these economic conditions have yet to be researched and fully explained, the perception of those conditions during the Grand Canal crisis seems clear. They were viewed primarily as strategic security issues. Even though regional officials must have had a clearer and more sympathetic picture of the fiscal crisis that gripped local administration, they rejected commutation out of hand because of fears that magisterial abuse of fiscal power might well trigger economic instability and rebellion. The emperor did not need much persuasion to go along with this view. He saw magisterial mis-management and corruption as dangerous and subversive forces, capable of undermining the imperial alliance with the people, his commitment to their livelihood and his, and the very foundations of the state. These strategic-economic assumptions mandated the rejection of grain conversion, the only plan that promised effective, if temporary, reconstruction of the canal system. And it predisposed the emperor and his advisers to turn to the private economy to solve the problems of grain transport.

What remained were two plans for grain transport: transfer-shipping and sea transport. Both avoided local government involvement and promised to help the imperial state overcome persistent and recurring canal blockages for the immediate future while the Yellow River hovered precipitously on the brink of its massive northward course change. Both plans were essentially joint, or cooperative, ventures, directed and organized from the top levels of central and regional government but reliant on and responsive to the organizational and technical resources of private shippers. The emperor directed the investigation and organization of these ventures, while top-level regional officials worked out the details directly with the shippers. These officials investigated, assessed, and reported the feasibility of the plans. The emperor then questioned, revised, and finally authorized their implementation, giving regional officials great latitude to work out details to benefit both the state and the people (Leonard 1991, 208-240, 335-42). Emperor and regional official alike recognized the state's need for and dependence on private shippers. They had no other viable alternatives.

The sea transport plan was designed purely as a temporary expedient for 1826 while the canal was under repair (He Changling 1826). Transfer-shipping, in contrast, provided a slightly longer-term solution to the problems of canal shipping in this risk-prone period. Regional officials in northern Jiangsu were familiar with various forms of lighterage, haulage, and transfer-shipping, all of which had been used with increasing frequency since the late eighteenth century to overcome barriers to navigation on the canal. The complexity of water conservancy tasks designed to overcome these barriers is readily apparent in the 1815 compilation of the *Regulations of the Board of Works* (*Gongbu celi* 1815:55-62). By the 1820s, the procedures for organizing these various shipping methods were well established and caused little comment. This is demonstrated by the speed and efficiency with which private craft from Henan, Shandong, and Jiangsu were mobilized in 1825 (Leonard 1991, 208-240). It is clear that imperial planners saw transfer-shipping on the canal as the most practical way to cope with shipping problems for the immediate future. Sea transport, on a large scale, was impractical for the decade ahead because of a shortage of ocean-going craft available for government hire from the lower Yangzi to the northeastern ports. Yet, both forms of shipping were taken seriously enough that regulations and procedures were included in the revised Hubu regulations in the 1830s and 1840s, a fact that demonstrates the Qing leadership's belief that the days of the regular grain transport system were numbered (*Hubu caoyun quanshu* 1845:89-92; *Hubu celi* 1831:19-24; 1865:19-24).

Conclusions

The two plans for grain transport are significant for what they tell us about the operation of the Qing state in this select area of administration. During the crisis from late 1824 to 1826, the Daoguang Emperor undertook the disciplined supervision of canal-transport affairs and the direction of the decision-making process during the heat of crisis; he pursued a flexible approach to its management that was determined by changing realities in northern Jiangsu, rather than a mindless adherence to the regulations and traditions of the imperial ancestors. Regional management of the crisis also proceeded remarkably well because of close imperial supervision and because of impressive regional leadership. What both shared in common was a certain flexibility and willingness to address problems realistically and deal with them as practically and efficiently as conditions permitted. In the case of the canal-transport system, there were only a few short-term options available for muddling through a prolonged Yellow River crisis—one that could only get worse.

The problems they faced were twofold. The first was obvious and insurmountable—the Yellow River and its course shift. The second was administrative paralysis at the lower levels of provincial administration.

Whatever ameliorative solutions they worked out for the canal and grain shipping, these plans would have to be done without burdening district-level government and further exacerbating its problems. So, with remarkable ease, they turned to private canal and ocean shippers whose resources and institutional outlines had grown, developed, and matured during the Qing period in response to the commercialization of the lower Yangzi valley and the growth of north-south trade on the canal and the China coast (Liu 1987; Ng 1983). Their ability to tap private resources grew out of long-standing patterns of interaction with the private economy that were shaped by the belief that the state and private economy shared common needs and goals, that the security of both were served by economic prosperity and growth, and that private organizations could perform certain tasks more effectively than the state's bureaucratic apparatus.

These patterns had emerged, grown, and changed over the years, but as they did so, they helped define the Qing approach to the economy. This approach was characterized by a practical-minded sense of fairness, restraint, and reciprocity, born of the need to protect its sources of revenue. When the canal–grain transport enterprise began to falter and the lowest levels of administration seemed incapable of meeting the challenge, the state turned again with surprising speed to those private economic organizations that had been allowed to grow and develop under benevolent Qing rule. These organizations were recruited (*zhaolai*) to undertake what was considered to be one of the most strategic and sensitive operations of the imperial state—the shipment of strategic grain supplies. This demonstrates the resilience and organizational capacity of the Qing state at the top levels of central and provincial government in its efforts to protect its strategic fiscal interests in a period of economic uncertainty. It also reveals the leadership's preference for non-bureaucratic solutions to pressing political-administrative problems, rather than reforming or extending bureaucratic government at the local level. Finally, it presents an impressive example of practical institutional change and readjustment designed to protect the *guoji minsheng*—the resources and the security of the state and the people.

References

The following abbreviations appear in the text notes. Citations of Qing inperial edicts start with an abbreviation that indicates whether it is a public (P) edict or a secret edict (S or TJ). The abbreviation is followed by a three-number sequence that indicates reign year, lunar month and day, e.g., P5.2.11a (the first of several public edicts of Daoguang five, second month, day eleven). This system is used to indicate the category of the edict, its archival location, as well as to facilitate reference in the *Ta Qing Shilu*.

CAT Sun, E-tu Zen. *Ch'ing Administrative Terms*.

P Public edict (*mingfa shangyu*). Shangyu dang: fangben (Record book of ordinary Grand Council affairs). National Palace Museum, Taibei.

PM Palace memorial. Gongzhong dang (Palace memorial archive). National Palace Museum, Taibei.

S Secret edict. Shangyu dang: fangben (Record book of ordinary Grand Council affairs). National Palace Museum, Taibei.

TJ Court letter drafts (*tingji*). Jiaobu tingji dang (Record book of court letter drafts). National Palace Museum, Taibei.

Bao, Hongzhang. 1982. Kangxi yu zhihe (The Kangxi Emperor and river management). *Beifang luncong* (Harbin) 5:29-32.

Chang, Hsin-pao. 1964. *Commissioner Lin and the Opium War*. Cambridge, Mass.: Harvard University Press.

Ch'u, T'ung-tsu. 1962. *Local Government in China under the Ch'ing*. Cambridge, Mass.: Harvard University Press.

Cressey, G. B. 1934. *China's Geographic Foundations*. New York: Mc-Graw-Hill.

Deng, Yunte. 1958. Zhongguo jiuhuang shi (The history of natural disaster in China). Beijing: Sanlian.

Dodgen, Randall. 1989. Controlling the Dragon: Confucian Engineers and the Yellow River in the Late Daoguang Reign (1835-1850). Ph.D. diss., Yale University.

Elvin, Mark. 1975. On Water Control and Management during the Ming and Ch'ing Periods: A Review Article. *Ch'ing-shih wen-t'i* 3, 3:82-103.

Gandar, Domin. [1894] 1903. *Le canal impérial: étude historique et descriptive*. Variétés sinologiques, no. 4. Shanghai: The Catholic Mission.

[Qinding] Gongbu celi (Regulations of the Board of Works). 1815. 142 *juan*. 20 *ce* in 2 cases. n.p. Jiaqing 20.

He, Changling. 1826. *Jiangsu Daoguang liunian fen haiyun quan'an* (Complete record of Jiangsu sea transport in Daoguang six). 12 *juan*. Microfilm.

Hinton, Harold C. 1970. *The Grain Tribute System of China (1845-1911)*. Cambridge, Mass.: East Asian Research Center, Harvard University.

Hoshi Ayao. 1960. Shinmatsu koun yori kaiun eno tenkai (Late Qing change from canal to sea transport of tribute grain). In *Tōyoshi ronso*. Tokyo: Kodansha.

_____. 1971. *Tai unga: Chūgoku no sōun*. (The Grand Canal and Chinese grain transport). Tokyo: Kondo.

Hsiao, Kung-chuan. 1960. *Rural China. Imperial Control in the Nineteenth Century*. Seattle: University of Washington Press.

[Qinding] Hubu caoyun quanshu (Imperially endorsed Board of Revenue complete book on grain transport). 1845. Pan Shi'en, comp. 92 *juan*. 45 *ce* in 4 boxes.

[Qinding] Hubu caoyun quanshu (Board of Revenue complete book on grain transport). 1875 completed. 1876 printed. Cai-ling, comp. 96 *juan*. 48 *ce* in 4 boxes.

Hubu celi (Regulations of the Board of Revenue). 1831. 99 *juan*. 72 *ce* in 6 boxes.

[Qingding] Hubu celi (Regulations of the Board of Revenue). 1865. 100 *juan*. 48 ce in 4 boxes.

Huang, Liu-hung. [1694]1984. *A Complete Book Concerning Happiness and Benevolence. "Fu-hui ch'uan-shu."* Trans. and ed. Djang Chu. Tuscon, Arizona: University of Arizona Press.

Kelley, David E. 1986. Sect and Society: The Evolution of the Luo Sect among Qing Dynasty Grain Tribute Boatmen, 1700-1850. Ph.D. diss., Harvard University.

King, F. H. H. 1965. *Money and Monetary Policy in China*. Cambridge, Mass.: Harvard University Press.

Leonard, Jane Kate. 1987. Qing Perceptions of Geopolitical Reality in the 1820s. *The American Asian Review* 5, 2:63-97.

_____. 1988. "Controlling from Afar": Open Communications and the Tao-Kuang Emperor's Control of Grand Canal-Grain Transport Management. *Modern Asian Studies* 22, 4:665-99.

_____. 1991. "Controlling From Afar." The Daoguang Emperor's Management of the Grand Canal Crisis 1824-1826. Unpublished manuscript.

Lin, Man-houng. 1989. Currency and Society: The Monetary Crisis and Political-Economic Ideology of Early Nineteenth-Century China. Ph.D. diss. Harvard University.

Lin, Renchuan. 1987. *Mingmo Qingchu siren haishang maoyi* (Private sea trade in late Ming and early Qing). Shanghai.

Littrup, Leif. 1981. *Subbureaucratic Government in China in Ming Times. A Study of Shantung Province in the Sixteenth Century.* Oslo: Universitetsforlaget, Institute for sommenligneude kulturforskning.

Liu, Danian. 1961. On the Kangxi Emperor. *Lishi yanjiu* 3:5-21 (June).

Liu, Deren. 1981. Lun Kangxi de zhihe gongji (On the Kangxi Emperor's achievements in river management). *Fuyin baokan ziliao* (Beijing) K2, 14:115-20.

Liu, Kwang-ching. 1968. "Nineteenth-Century China: The Disintegration of the Old Order and the Impact of the West." In *China in Crisis*, eds. Ho Ping-ti and Tsou Tang. Chicago: University of Chicago Press.

Metzger, Thomas A. 1962. T'ao Chu's Reform of the Huaipei Salt Monopoly. *Harvard University Papers on China* (East Asian Research Center) 16:1-38.

_____. 1970. The State and Commerce in Imperial China. *Asian and African Studies* 6:23-46.

_____. 1972. "The Organizational Capabilities of the Ch'ing state in the Field of Commerce: the Liang-Huai Salt Monopoly 1740-1840." In *Economic Organization in Chinese Society*, ed. W. E. Willmott. Stanford: Stanford University Press.

Morse, Hosea B. 1913. *The Trade and Administration of China.* Rev. ed. London: Longmans, Green.

Needham, Joseph. 1971. *Science and Civilization in China.* Vol. 4, pt. 3, *Physics and Physical Technology. Civil Engineering and Nautics.* Cambridge: Cambridge University Press.

Ng, Chin-keong. 1983. *Trade and Society. The Amoy Network on the China Coast 1683-1735.* Singapore: Singapore University Press.

Perdue, Peter. 1987. *Exhausting the Earth. State and Peasant in Hunan, 1500-1850.* Cambridge, Mass.: Council on East Asian Studies, Harvard University.

_____. 1989. The West Route Army and the Silk Road: Grain supply and Qianlong's Military Campaigns in Northwest China (1755-1760). Massachusetts Institute of Technology. Photocopy.

_____. 1991. Three Qing Emperors and the Northwest. Conference paper, annual meeting, Association for Asian Studies, 13 April, New Orleans, Louisiana.

Quan, Hansheng and Richard A. Kraus. 1975. *Mid-Ch'ing Rice Markets and Trade: An Essay in Price History.* Cambridge, Mass.: East Asian Research Center, Harvard University.

Rowe, William T. 1983. Hu Lin-i's Reform of the Grain Tribute System in Hupeh, 1855-1858. *Ch'ing-shih wen-ti* 4, 10:33-86.

_____. 1991. State and Market in mid-Qing Economic Thought: The Career of Chen Hongmou (1696-1771). Conference paper, Symposium on the Qing State and the Economy, 22-23 February, University of Akron.

Schoppa, R. Keith. 1989. *Xiang Lake—Nine Centuries of Chinese Life.* New Haven: Yale University Press.

Shang, Hongkui. 1981. Kangxi nanxun yu zhili Huanghe (The Kangxi Emperor's southern tours and harnessing the Yellow River). *Fuyin baokan yuankan* (Beijing), K2, 16:111-120.

Shulman, Anna See Ping Leon. 1989. Copper, Copper Cash, and Government Controls in Ch'ing China (1644-1795). Ph.D. diss., University of Maryland.

Sun, E-tu Zen. 1961. *Ch'ing Administrative Terms. A Translation of the Terminology of the Six Boards with Explanatory Notes.* Cambridge, Mass.: Harvard University Press.

_____. 1968. Ch'ing Government and the Mineral Industries before 1800. *Journal of Asian Studies* 27,4: 835-45.

Treager, Thomas R. 1965. *A Geography of China.* Chicago: Aldine Press.

_____. 1980. *China. A Geographical Survey.* New York: Halsted.

Vogel, Hans Ulrich. 1983. Chinese Central Monetary Policy and Yunnan Copper Mining in the Early Qing (1644-1800). Ph.D. diss., University of Zurich.

Wang, Yeh-chien. 1973. *Land Taxation in Imperial China, 1750-1911.* Cambridge, Mass.: Harvard University Press.

_____. 1979. "Evolution of the Chinese Monetary System, 1644-1850." In *Modern Chinese economic history.* ed. Chi-ming Hou and Tzong-shian Yu. Taibei: Institute of Economics, Academia Sinica.

Watt, John R. 1972. *The District Magistrate in Late Imperial China.* New York: Columbia University Press.

Will, Pierre-Étienne. 1980. Un cycle hydraulique en Chine: La province du Hubei du XVIe, au XIXe siècles. *Bulletin de l'École française d'extreme-orient* 68:261-87.

_____. 1990. *Bureaucracy and Famine in Eighteenth-Century China.* Trans. Elborg Forster. Rev. ed. Stanford: Stanford University Press.

_____. 1985. "State Intervention in the Administration of a Hydraulic Infrastructure: The Example of Hubei Province in Premodern Times." In *The Scope of State power in China,* ed. Stuart Schram. New York: St. Martin's Press.

Will, Pierre-Étienne, and R. Bin Wong. 1991. *Nourish the People. The State Civilian Granary System in China, 1650-1850.* Ann Arbor: Center for Chinese Studies, University of Michigan.

Zelin, Madeleine. 1984. *The Magistrate's Tael. Rationalizing Fiscal Reform in Eighteenth-Century Ch'ing China.* Berkeley: University of California Press.

Zhang, Zhelang. 1942. *Qingdai de caoyun* (Grain tribute in the Qing dynasty). Taibei.

Zheng, Zhaojing. 1986. *Zhongguo shuili shi* (The history of water conservancy in China). Taibei.

Zhou, Yuanhe. 1982. A study of China's population during the Qing Dynasty. *Social Sciences in China* 3, 3:61-105 (September).

Zhu, Xie. 1962. *Zhongguo yunhe shiliao xuanji* (Compliation of historical materials on the Grand Canal of China). Beijing.

5

Household Handicrafts and State Policy in Qing Times[1]

Susan Mann

Comparing the peasant economy of the Yangzi delta and the North China plain, Philip Huang commented that the "most important" feature of the delta's rural labor market was that "a substantial part of the productive labor force—especially women—remained outside of it." The primary factors restricting the market for women's labor, he suggested, were "cultural constraints against women venturing outside the home, plus the logistical difficulties of managing female labor that came with those constraints" (Huang 1990, 111). How and why did these constraints develop?

This paper examines one source of the cultural constraints on women's labor: an ideology propagated by the Qing state that helped to shape the strivings of families in local communities in late imperial times. Through the assiduous campaigning of Qing magistrates, prodded by the central government and also fired by their own Confucian zeal, househeads and community leaders were reminded constantly that economic welfare and social status were linked to the productivity of women in the household economy. Qing policies promoting a strict division of labor in the home ("men plow, women weave") simultaneously made women's place an emblem of status for individual families, and even for entire communities and local systems, so that "native place" pride was conflated with norms that bound women to their looms and spindles. "Going out" to work, by contrast, was a stigma reserved for lowborn women from peripheral areas.[2]

75

The Qing ideology confining respectable women's roles to home work was thus an integral part of its larger program to promote handicraft skills and technologies in peasant households. Unlike the early Ming government, which sought to constrain commercial commodity production through taxation (Huang 1974, 226-37) and by registering artisans as a hereditary class (Xu and Wu 1985, 112ff.), early Qing rulers believed that household self-sufficiency would supply the crucial brake on rapid commercialization in the agrarian economy. Commercialization was welcome, but markets that grew too fast threatened to draw labor off the land, which could reduce income from the land tax. Qing administrators were also concerned about a growing population in the towns that might turn to riots if food supplies or jobs ran short.

The account that follows focuses on household spinning and weaving. It begins by outlining briefly the transition to a "free" artisanal labor market in the late Ming–early Qing period, sketching the ideological and practical priorities of the Qing state as it guided the changing economy. Next it shows how women's work in the home, a central theme in Qing policy towards handicrafts, assumed moral as well as economic and political significance. Finally, contrasting evidence from Tokugawa Japan, where similar attempts to restrict labor markets failed utterly, suggests that Chinese local officials and househeads embraced Qing policies for reasons of their own.

The Ming-Qing Transition

The classic survey of China's proto-industry in Ming and Qing times documents the decline of state-sponsored handicraft industries under the Ming, the result of competition from small-scale commercial production in the rural economy. The early Ming state-sponsored system (*guan shougongye*) was based on a model of a stable agrarian economy in which each peasant household would meet its own needs for food and clothing, specialized artisans being required only to supply the official elite. These craftsmen, who produced a range of items, such as ceremonial garments, ritual vessels, army uniforms, weapons, pottery and utensils, and ships and transport vehicles, were registered as a hereditary class in a special section of the population records. In 1393, registered artisans and their dependent workers comprised an estimated 3 percent of the population (Xu and Wu 1985, 112-15).

As the Ming consumer economy expanded, several processes combined to erode the state-sponsored hereditary artisan system. The system was eroded from within by flight: registered artisans simply absconded, despite severe penalties imposed on those who were caught (Xu and Wu 1985, 116-18). The system also was permeated from without, as artisans outside the hereditary registers attached themselves to registered artisans as adopted sons or sons-in-law, opening shops under their in-laws' or adopted parents' name (Xu and Wu 1985, 313). More devastating still to the registered artisan system was the rapidly increasing population in the sixteenth century and the resulting specialization and commercialization of the peasant economy. The major centers of silk-weaving production and marketing during the late imperial period sprang up during this century, not only in the lower Yangzi region (Shengze, Zhenze, Huangqi, Puyuan, Wangjiangjing, Shuanglin), but also in Shanxi, Sichuan, and Fujian. Cotton weaving centers appeared in Songjiang, Jiading, and Changshu (Xu and Wu 1985, 124, 127-28).

During this time, the peasant household emerged as the primary production unit for the commercial spinning and weaving of cotton and silk. Increased commercial production drew prices down, bringing silk and cotton textiles within the means of ordinary consumers. Between the Song and the Ming periods, the real price of silk in Jiangnan fell by nearly 60 percent (Xu and Wu 1985, 124-25). By the fall of the Ming dynasty, the moribund registered artisan system had been entirely displaced by the new commercial economy.

Qing rulers released all registered artisans from the official rolls in 1645 (Peng [1964], 391), then set to work formulating policy for the commercial handicraft production system. They had before them several classical models. The first was a model of imperial patronage for household-level sericulture found in descriptions of Zhou society. The second was a long history of state encouragement for peasant sericulture as a source of tax revenue, with important precedents in Song administrative practice. The third was a more recent model, inherited from the Ming period, which promoted home cotton production as the linchpin in a plan for peasant household self-sufficiency. As we shall see, each of these models played an important role in the policies toward peasant proto-industry crafted under the leadership of the Kangxi, Yongzheng, and Qianlong Emperors. Women's work was at the center.

Qing Policy

Having released registered artisans, the Qing state sought a means to ensure that a new artisan class would not grow up to take its place.

Doubtless Qing rulers feared labor unrest, a scourge of late Ming rule. But other considerations also appear to have been important in their calculations. The first was a notion about the commercial economy set forth in a Yongzheng edict dated 22 June 1727:

> Among the four classes of people, next to the scholars, farmers are the most valuable. All artisans and merchants rely for their food on farming, which is why farming is the basic pursuit (*benwu*) throughout our realm, while crafts and trade are merely secondary (*mo*). With the rising demand today for ever more elaborate and finely crafted implements, clothing, and amusements, we are surely going to be needing more artisans. One more artisan in the market place, however, means one less farmer in the fields. Moreover, when the simple people see how much more artisans make than farmers do, they are sure to stampede to learn a trade. A sudden increase in the number of artisans will mean a glut of manufactured goods on the market, which will make it harder to sell things, as blockages develop and prices fall. Thus not only will an increase in people who pursue secondary occupations harm agriculture . . . , it will also have a harmful effect on the artisans themselves! (Cited in Peng [1964], 419; see DQSZSL, 57:2b-3)

The implication of the Yongzheng Emperor's strategy was the following: it might not be possible to get artisans to return to farming, but surely the state could prevent farmers from turning to the trades.

This program took the form of a campaign to promote household self-sufficiency that deployed two slogans: "enough to eat" (*zushi*) and "stable income" (*hengchan*). Every peasant family was exhorted to produce all of its own food and clothing instead of relying on the market. Though the Yongzheng Emperor's concern in the document above was for the artisans, clearly the government was more fearful of a collapsing farm economy, in which insufficient labor on the land would lead to a fall in government tax revenues. The concern about flight from the land is understandable, since contemporary documents indicate that artisan wages ranged as high as an incredible 3,000 cash a month in the 1770s (Peng [1964], 411). The Yongzheng Emperor was well aware of the *mentalité* that had faced Chinese rulers since Han times, summed up in this ancient rhyme that describes the lure of commercial towns for both men and women:

For the poor to seek riches
Farming is not as satisfactory as crafts;
Crafts are not as good as trading.
To prick embroidery does not pay
As much as leaning upon a market-door.[3]

Most mid-Qing officials were resigned to the fact that, as one statecraft writer put it, "the common people think only of profit" (*xiaomin wei li shi tu* ; JSWB 37:6). Farm policy thus required a constant struggle to keep peasants from leaving the land and becoming wholly dependent on the market for survival. Qing policy-makers advocated a plan to promote peasant household self-sufficiency, and to anchor men firmly to stable farm households, so that individual families could weather periodic shortfalls, and their land would remain as insurance against impoverishment (not only of their own households, but of the government's coffers as well).

The man who contemplated moving into town was reminded that he should plan ahead. A family would need more than two or three thousand *jin* a year to make it:

> It's not like the countryside, where you can oversee the tilling of several *mu* and earn rents in excess of your expenses that will feed eight mouths; where you're raising chickens and pigs in a pen, where you're growing vegetables in your garden and raising fish and shrimps in your pond, where you can gather fuel on the hillsides, so that for month after month, you never need any cash at all. Besides, when you live in the country, then your relatives can take care of you if you need help or fall on hard times, . . . and if the women in your family work hard, they can learn spinning and make your clothes for you (JSWB 36:46b).

Zhou Models: The Lei Zu Cult of Imperial Patronage

To keep people down on the farm, Qing policy depended on the full mobilization of all members of the peasant household for labor, and especially, as the remarks above suggest, on a strict gender division of labor. For this they invoked the ancient ideal of the woman worker valorized in the Guliang commentary on the *Spring and Autumn Annals*:

> The Emperor himself plows in order to supply millet for the
> sacrificial vessels; the Empress herself tends the silkworms,
> in order to supply the robes for the sacrificial rites. A realm
> cannot be without good farmers and working women. In
> sacrificing to the ancestors, in order to achieve the fullest
> expression of the human spirit, nothing can match what you
> yourself have produced (*Guliang zhuan* 4:7b; Duke Huan,
> 14th year, 8th month).

The ancient female counterpart of the emperor's plowing of the fields
was revived in late imperial times, and never more extravagantly than under
Qing rule (Williams 1935). Following the prescriptions of ancient texts,
every year Qing empresses worshipped Lei Zu, patron goddess of
sericulture, at a shrine complex located a kilometer north and slightly west
of the rear gate of the Forbidden City. This ritual, the only public function
at which women presided as imperial officials, was observed in the most
elaborate detail. The shrine itself, especially constructed by the Qianlong
Emperor in 1742, included dressing rooms, an altar, a terrace from which
the audience could observe the gathering of mulberry leaves, and an
enclosed courtyard with a large pool and rooms for the hatching of the silk
worms and for weaving silk. Sluices carried water from a stream for
washing the silk; a sanctuary housed the tablet of the deity herself.

The Lei Zu rites commenced each year on a propitious spring day
selected by court astronomers. The empress herself presided. Preparations
for the ritual began with two days of fasting, to purify sacrificers and their
attendants. They then presented cooked food and wine to delight the spirit
of the goddess, and made additional offerings of incense, candles, and silk.
On the day following the sacrifice, the Empress led two imperial con-
cubines, along with princesses and other noble ladies, in the ceremony of
gathering mulberry leaves. Ideally this was done on a day when the
silkworms at the shrine complex had hatched; the leaves gathered by Her
Majesty were then scattered over the frames for the worms to feed on.
Another delay followed while the worms matured and spun their cocoons,
after which an auspicious day was again selected and the empress returned
to Lei Zu's altar to offer silk personally reeled for the goddess with the
empress's own hands. The empress was required to supply three basins of
silk in all, dyed vermilion, green, and deep yellow, to be set aside for use
in embroidering garments for ritual sacrifice. The scale of this great rite
may be gauged by the 117 persons who participated in the first sacrifice,
including 56 women and 34 eunuchs. Those who took part in the initial

sacrifice were then admitted to the rites of gathering mulberry, feeding the worms, and reeling silk that followed.

The Lei Zu ritual was part of a complex of symbols and stories celebrating the supervision of women's work by mythical founders and elite patronesses. Drawings depicting scenes from the daily lives of the Qing empresses frequently portrayed them inspecting the silkworms raised by their court ladies (Headland 1914, 103-5). Beyond court circles, a tradition well predating the Qing, called on elite women to emulate the empress and work alongside their servants while supervising them. For example, in Changshu, Jiangsu, at the end of the fourteenth century, a concubine left in charge of the estate of her late wealthy husband won fame because she "braved the cold, heat, dew and frost to *personally supervise the family servants working in the fields* . . . ."[4] In the early fifteenth century, the widow of an estate-holder managed the deployment of field labor on her late husband's lands and "personally led all the female bondservants in weaving and spinning. Every evening they divided and needled the cocoons, never missing a day's work."[5] Ladies of distinction were honored for their ability to work like servants. A Ming period epitaph for the mistress of an upper-class household employing large numbers of bondservants in a home industry recorded the following:

> The Lady nee Yang was ennobled with a fourth-class honor. She was the wife of governor-general Zhang Xuye. The Yang family came from Wujili. . . . After the governor-general retired and returned home, he spent his days at leisure, writing poetry and drinking, studying, and teaching the Confucian classics to the children. He never inquired about family affairs. His lady, in contrast, worked diligently, leading the bondservant women in spinning. Even though she was of high rank, she wore the same *jingbu* cloth garments as the commoners. She educated her family in the ways of frugality.[6]

Such accounts show that marriageable women from elite families had long been trained for manual labor for two reasons: first, to meet the exigencies of widowhood or poverty; second, to set an example of industry in the home for the servants. But in Qing times, the ideal of women as supervisors of other women's labor on large estates was shifting towards a model of women as partners in a household economy where they worked at handicrafts alongside their farmer husbands.

Qing policy presented the working "goodwife," referred to in the four-character phrase "men plow, women weave" (*nangeng nüzhi*), as the key to both household self-sufficiency and family honor. Early Confucian texts invoked by Qing policy makers stressed the moral values embedded in the ideal gender division of labor. Thus the first Confucian moral tracts on womanly conduct which set forth "the wifely way" (*fudao*), emphasized that "womanly work" (*nügong*) was one of the "four virtues" that every young girl must cultivate. Women's work (work, or *gong*, often written with a silk radical, evoking images of thread and fine embroidery) was glossed in Han sources as a reference to "hemp and silk." In other words, work with the needle, spindle, and loom. When it came to womanly work, upper-class and commoner women were held to the same moral standard. Confucian "gentlemen" (*junzi*) were supposed to eschew manual labor, but Confucian gentle*women* were expected to work with their hands alongside their servants and tenants. The ability to do womanly work was a sign that a woman possessed the three attributes most essential to her family's future success: thrift, frugality, diligence. Among poor families, these womanly qualities were the key to survival. For women of the upper classes, the same attributes were essential to the proper discipline and management of domestic help—the mistress set the standards for her servants' work by her own example. For a woman, in other words, manual labor suited to her station was never demeaning.[7]

Lei Zu's cult, so extravagantly patronized by the court in the Qianlong period, was therefore part of a larger statecraft agenda focused on the moral education of the populace. Moral education had several common themes. It exalted the farm community, exhorted the population to frugality, and deplored both decadence and idleness. Qing moral education campaigns make it clear that both work and proper ritual practice were central to all these issues (JSWB 54:20). Writers in the mid-Qing statecraft compendium, *Collected Essays on Statecraft* spoke eagerly of extending the rites into commoner households (lit. "into the neighborhoods"; JSWB 54:24). In that sense, the lavish imperial ritual devoted to Lei Zu, honoring silk workers, was the symbolic pinnacle of a program aimed at spreading sericulture throughout the farm economy.

Song Models: Sericulture Bureaus

Qing rulers also embraced Song precedents for promoting household sericulture through county-level agricultural extension bureaus (Xu and Wu 1985, 123). Handbooks designed to illustrate the proper techniques of sericulture in model households were published for the edification of local officials and farm families. The *Imperially Commissioned Illustrations of Farming and Weaving* (*Yuzhi gengzhi tu*), printed in 1696, provided careful illustrations depicting the gender division of labor in sericulture households: men and young boys plucked the leaves, women tended and fed the worms, sorted the cocoons, and reeled the silk. Women then wove the silk thread into cloth (Sun 1972, 82; Li 1981, Figures 1-4; Sung 1966, 36-59).

Silk was, in fact, the favored form of weaving, as evidenced by the Qing preference for another phrase representing the normative division of labor: *nongsang* (farming and mulberry). The *Collected Essays on Statecraft* includes numerous essays naming sericulture a fundamental underpinning of state agricultural policy.[8]   For example, Huang Liuhong's "Four Policies To Nurture the People" (Yangmin sizheng) lists in order: irrigation and water conservancy, expansion of the arable into undeveloped lands, fruit orchards, and mulberry trees (JSWB 28:16-18). A lengthy report on conditions in Shaanxi province by Chen Hongmou recommended six remedial measures, of which the first was "broad promulgation of sericulture" (JSWB 28:12-15).

The model for statecraft writers was an essay by Gu Yanwu titled "The Profitability of Weaving" (Fangzhi zhi li). Gu's essay, which later writers cited frequently, proposed that the state promote silk weaving in households in border areas by bringing in master weavers from the outside to teach them. The purpose was practical, in keeping with statecraft thought: silk weaving would bring down the cost of living by making households more self-sufficient. And, Gu suggested, it would thereby free up resources for the state's tax coffers: "household budgets steadily shrink; government tax arrears steadily mount" (JSWB 37:1).

Tang Zhen, in an essay titled "Teaching sericulture," makes the point still more bluntly. In sericulture areas, even poor people pay their taxes.

> Wu silk clothes the world. It is collected in Shuanglin, and people flock there from the lower Yangzi and the southeast coast, even from the islands in the sea. In the fifth month they all come to the market carrying their silver; they stack up like potsherds. So all the rural areas in Wu and southward (the lower Yangzi) make over 10,000,000 [*taels*] in profits every year. That is why, although the tax burden is heavy in that area, even poor people are not driven to destitution. Indeed, their ordinary dwellings and vessels surpass those of other places. Such is the wealth to be gained from sericulture! (JSWB 37:3-4)

Tang likewise proposed that local officials import master weavers from sericulture areas to instruct women living in regions where silk was not produced. He predicted that with the right official leadership ("reward those who produce a lot, warn those who produce little, punish those who don't produce any"), sericulture would spread to every part of China within ten years (JSWB 37:3b, 8-13).

Ming Models: Promoting Household Cotton Industries

Cotton, a latecomer to China's household production systems, was assimilated into the model for sericulture in Qing official policy, which followed late Ming precedents in encouraging the cotton home handicraft industry (Xu 1981, 34ff.). In 1808, the Jiaqing Emperor endorsed a special reprint of the *Imperially Endorsed Edition of Wide-ranging Instructions on the Provisioning of Clothing (Qinding shouyi guangxun)* that contained an annotated collection of illustrations entitled "An Illustrated Guide to Cotton" (Mianhua tu) by Fang Guancheng. This text, presented to the throne with an accompanying memorial in the spring of 1765 and inscribed in the emperor's own hand three months later, was embellished with poems written by the Kangxi and Qianlong Emperors. It presents idealized drawings of large happy families engaged in cotton cultivation and manufacturing, beginning with the sowing of the seeds and ending with the final bolts of cloth. (See Dietrich 1972 for reproductions of some of the illustrations.)

The illustrations also show clearly the gender division of labor in cotton cultivation and manufacturing. The initial preparation of the soil (hoeing, irrigating), the sowing and weeding, all were done by men (including hired laborers, young boys, and servants). Women then took charge of the cotton plants: pinching back the shoots (zhejian) and plucking the cotton. Fluffing the cotton for market was servants' work, mainly men's. Male brokers bagged the cotton and sold it to other households where men and women began the manufacturing process by ginning it to remove the seeds. Spinning and weaving were women's work; dyeing was done by men. The preface to the guide declares emphatically that the ordinary clothing produced by the people for their daily use should be honored alongside farming and sericulture as a "basic occupation" (benye; SYGX 1808, fanli, 1b).

At the same time, Qing statecraft policies tried to curb, rather than promote, the cotton industry in areas where specialization was so far advanced that it threatened household self-sufficiency in grain. Thus in the lower Yangzi, cotton's very success was viewed as a threat to the *zushi* campaign, and in this case, the Qing government attempted to restrict local handicraft operations. Guo Qiyuan, for example, tried to argue that cotton weaving was too unprofitable and too demanding to serve as a worthy complement to ploughing. His essay "Cotton and silk: shrinking profits" (Bu bai ying shu), claims that women had to work too hard for too little when they wove cotton:

> The value of one length of cotton cloth is less than one-tenth that of a comparable roll of silk. The labor is great, the profit small—not enough to feed even one individual. A young girl [trying to support herself by weaving cotton] would find it difficult to avoid starvation. Only the profits from sericulture are a worthy complement to farming (JSWB 37:5).

In a different vein, Gao Jin, writing in 1776 as Liangjiang governor-general, advocated state programs to return to rice cultivation 30 percent of the 70 percent of paddy land planted to cotton (JSWB 37:6-7). He opposed cotton cultivation because it threatened the grain supply, stressing that of food and clothing, the two most important concerns of peasant households, food was the more vital. Why, then, he complained, did peasants living in the Jiangnan regions near the sea prefer planting cotton to rice? By his estimate, no more than 20 to 30 percent of Jiangnan peasants planted paddy; the rest raised cotton. When he polled some peasants on this question, they explained that cotton was cheaper to plant and more profitable to sell than rice; rice, they said, was expensive to plant because of high labor costs, and brought low profits (JSWB 37:6). So this official advocated programs to induce peasants to restore half of their landholdings to paddy, perhaps with state subsidies for irrigation to reduce the labor costs of planting rice (JSWB 37:7-b). In contrast, in areas where home handicrafts were underdeveloped, we find a prefect like Li Ba in Fuzhou trying to encourage cotton cultivation and complaining about the fact that peasants in his area purchase cotton textiles from Jiangsu and Zhejiang instead of growing their own and teaching the women how to weave it into cloth (JSWB 37:17).

Li Ba's disdainful comparison of the women in Fuzhou with women weavers in the lower Yangzi region suggests that Qing statecraft programs promoting women's household handicrafts simultaneously asserted a hierarchy of local systems. Within the lower Yangzi macroregion, fine cotton weaving in the Jiangnan area was held up as a model for the poor areas of Subei, in the Huai region (Peng [1964], 223-24), and great pains were taken to stress the exquisite fineness of this cotton. In Jiading, the local product had a softness "like the nap on the wool blanket the emperor uses for ancestor worship" (Xu 1981, 14). Jiangnan women weavers put other women workers to shame. In Yenan, proclaimed an entry in the *Gujin tushu jicheng*, women barely were able to weave enough cloth to cover their own bodies (Xu 1981, 17). Jiangnan cotton culture was the pace-setter even for the Fujianese (as in Li Ba's writing); Shandong sericulture became the inspiration for Guizhou's new proto-industry. Compilers of a local gazetteer in Anhui derided local people for their refusal to learn sericulture, "so that the women here don't know how to spin or weave" (Xu 1981, 22).

Plainly, in the minds of Qing statecraft writers, those regions in China where "women wove" were culturally and even morally superior to areas where women had no specialized home handicrafts. Like Li Ba and Song Rulin, who carried home handicraft models to the southeast coast from the lower Yangzi, and from the North China plain to the upper Yangzi, Chen Hongmou and Bi Yuan used their knowledge of sericulture from areas where they had lived or served to promote it in areas where they held office (JSWB 37:26-32, 37:10, 36:48, 36:2).

In every case, officials introducing handicraft industries into new areas remarked on their utility as an antidote for indolence and a tonic for morality:

> The customs of Xinghua favor indolence (*tou'an*). . . . Poor women here do not do their work diligently, but let their hands and feet rest idle, as a result of which their whole manner appears loose and profligate. . . . Our county *yamen* has been extremely concerned to remedy this situation, and we have already contributed a modest sum to establish a Weaving Bureau (*fangju*). Any young woman from a poor commoner family between the ages of 11 and 13 *sui* can come here to learn (Peng [1964], 224).

One even finds sericulture explicitly touted as a means of controlling female sexuality, in an essay by Zhou Kai, written while he was holding office in Xiangyang, Hubei. Zhou's essay begins with a classical injunction quoted in official statements about agricultural policy in Qing times: "If one man does not plough, then the people will starve; if one woman does not weave, then the people will freeze" (JSWB 37:19-22). Zhou goes on to discuss the value of silk as a commodity. He cites Mencius and the *Shiji* on mulberry and notes that though field crops are vulnerable to flood and drought, silkworms can be tended by women in the home regardless of the weather. Additionally, the trees were completely profitable: the leaves fed silkworms, the fruits could be made into liquor, the wood used for kindling and the bark for paper. At the end of a tree's ten-year lifespan, every physical aspect was put to practical use. For the subsistence farm economy, sericulture was a good thing.

But Zhou's larger concern was the connection between a sharp gender division of labor in peasant households and sexuality, between women's work and wifely fidelity (JSWB 37:21-22):

> I especially pity the women of Xiang. They have no way to develop specialized work of their own and thereby affirm their commitment as faithful wives. The woman who has no work of her own should take up sericulture. Whether she comes from a gentry or a commoner household, a wife can personally tend silkworms in order to clothe her husband. When she sees that her own strength is sufficient to provide for her family's subsistence, her heart will be pure.
>
> Once when I was walking out in the country, I saw some poor women. They were at work breaking up clods of earth with a hoe, and they were even ploughing in pairs (*za gengyu*). This shocked me deeply, for when the *Odes* refer to women in the fields, they speak only of women who bring food to their husbands while their husbands do the ploughing ["The husband ploughs, the wife brings him food"; *fu geng, fu yan*]. I was certain it would not be long before these same wives would be suing their husbands, and husbands their wives. To be sure, there are those women in Xiang who "warn their husbands about the crowing of the cock" [i.e., are goodwives (*qiaijiming*)] and who "swear to be a cedar vessel" [vow to preserve their chastity (*shibozhou*)]. But most women do not stop at even one remarriage, and they simply take their cue from everyone around them: families seeking a bride see nothing wrong with a twice-married woman, and families marrying off a daughter do not think it shameful if she marries more than once.
>
> All human beings have "feelings of shame and dislike" (*xiuwu zhi xin*); can it be that these women's hearts are inhuman (*shuren*)? Truly the cause of their behavior is that they have no specialized work of their own to do, and they have no commitment to wifely fidelity. As a result, their

labor is not sufficient to provide for themselves. All of this
is due to the fact that they grow no mulberry"[9]

A less emotional statement about the linkage between stable farm
families and women's work appears in the essay "Treatise on Farming"
(Nong shu) by Zhang Lüxiang, a magistrate of Tongxiang county, Zhejiang
province:

> In the western districts [of my county], women's work may
> consist of weaving silk or twisting hemp and straw. In the
> eastern districts, women's work may be a mixture of farming
> and sericulture, or it may be spinning. As for my own
> district, here women's work is mainly cotton spinning and
> weaving, or rearing silkworms for floss. Although this is a
> rural area, each woman earns income to help support her
> husband. Where a woman works diligently, her family will
> surely rise; where a woman is lazy, her family is certain to
> fall. What a woman works at may be nothing more than
> hemp and silk, but whether she is industrious or lazy has
> profound implications for her family. Thus, if she is hard-
> working, all the family's undertakings will prosper; if she is
> lazy, everything the family tries will fail. Thus it is said:
> "The family that is poor longs for a good wife; the country
> that is in chaos longs for a good minister." The family's
> circumstances will be reflected in the measure of support a
> woman gives it. Take an ordinary married couple. The man
> can till perhaps ten *mu* of land. The woman can rear perhaps
> ten baskets of silkworms, and weave two rolls of cloth a day,
> or spin eight *liang* of thread. Would they need to worry about
> hunger and cold? (JSWB 36:27b)

In Yunnan in 1737, a magistrate struggling to promote *zushi* policies
listed ten guidelines for selecting worthy peasants capable of instructing
others in improved farming techniques. The first requirement was that the
person be "muscular and hardworking" (*jinli qinjian*); the second, that in
his household, the women and children share in the work (*fuzi xieli*) (JSWB
36:17b).

Magistrates were thus continually promoting programs to keep women
busy. They abhorred the silence in households where looms were not
clacking away; they worried about places where families were constantly on
relief; they associated women's idle hands with dependency and sloth (Peng

[1964], 224). The specter of social disorder that haunted these local officials drove them to spend money from their near-empty treasuries to teach *nügong*—women's handwork—in the districts under their control.

Conclusion

Qing state policy toward home handicraft industries interwove three themes. The first was a paradigm for the gender division of labor: most ideally, farming and mulberry (*nongsang*), or more broadly, men ploughing, women weaving (*nan geng, nü zhi*). The second theme constructed a hierarchy of value in which certain modes of production were set forth as models for the realm, reaffirming and reconstituting hierarchies of culture and localism through the production of commodities. The third was a strategy for sustaining and reproducing the kinship system through a stable, self-sufficient farm household economy that kept women safely in the home, out of the traffic in women associated with poverty and unemployment. By extension, women busy in the home were seen as the anchors of stable farm families, supporters of their menfolk in the off-season, and producers of the goods that could carry the family through the dearth between planting and the harvest—and pay the taxes.

The Qing state worked on other fronts as well to maintain the household as the center of spinning and weaving. For example, during the seventeenth and eighteenth centuries, as commercialization and proto-industrial development reached their peak, the Chinese government, unlike the governments of some European states, never adopted protectionist measures designed to help guilds compete with cheap female labor in the home. The Prussian notion that "the right to work was conditional—a concession granted, modified, or refused by the sovereign 'according to times and customs' " (Quataert 1985, 1123) would have met with stares of disbelief from Qing dynasty statesmen. In Chinese political theory, hard work was part of moral conduct. Even the gentleman worked diligently, at his studies; and keeping home industry alive in the peasant population was one of the state's obligations to the body politic. Moreover, as Qing policy-makers show us, keeping home industry alive required the skills and energies of women.

How successful were these policies? Though earlier evidence is lacking, anecdotes from the early part of this century show that disdain for women who "went out" was widespread even in poor households (Pruitt 1967, 26, 175). Women who could be seen on the streets or in the fields, working or not, were of questionable reputation or at least a lower class. To what extent footbinding abetted the cloistering of women in late imperial times is a matter of some debate among scholars.[10]   In any case, it appears that in most parts of China, even poor peasant women rarely worked in the fields outside the small plots owned by their own households, where they might regularly weed and water. Public opinion held that only at the peak of the harvest season was it permissible for women to participate in regular field labor, as John Lossing Buck discovered during his surveys of Chinese villages in the late 1920s:

> When both the millet and the wheat are yellow ripe,
> Even the spinning girls have to come out to help.
> When it's busy on the farm
> Girls may leave their rooms to help (Buck 1956, 240, 307).

These strict norms keeping Chinese women at home, even in rural areas, contrast sharply with the norms in Japanese peasant villages during the Tokugawa era. Although the shogunate too attempted to keep farmers on the land (Smith 1955, 29), village custom sent young women as well as men off the farm to work, frequently outside their home villages, for a year or two before marriage (Hanley and Yamamura 1977, 254-55). It is unclear if the common practice of working outside the home or even the community made it easier for early Meiji companies to recruit women workers from "good" families.[11]   In any case, Thomas C. Smith has found suggestive demographic evidence that the expansion of secondary and tertiary sectors in rural areas lowered the rate of female infanticide during the Tokugawa period, indicating that farm families made good use of their daughters' earning power outside the home (Smith 1977, 152-56; Smith 1988, 85, 93).

Comparison with the Japanese case also dramatizes the close connections between Confucian moral values and women's work in Qing policy, and the particular characteristics of the Chinese family system. In the grand family ideal, to which commoners in increasing numbers aspired in Qing times, all sons were to take brides and remain at home, where their wives became servants of the larger family economy, under the direction of the mother-in-law. This ideal contrasts sharply with its counterpart in Tokugawa farm families, where only the heir was expected to marry and remain at home.

The obligation of every Chinese bride to serve her husband's parents was compatible with the priorities of the Qing state aimed at anchoring male and female labor in the countryside. As a result, the senior couple in every Chinese farm family remained a staunch ally of Qing home industry policies, long after the growth of proto-industry and the development of a flourishing system of trade and craft guilds in the late empire. Qing policymakers and heads of peasant households shared an interest in programs promoting female productivity in the home. At the same time, these shared interests produced "cultural constraints" and "logistic difficulties" that reduced the numbers of women available to work in China's factories on the eve of industrialization.

Notes

1. The author gratefully acknowledges generous bibliographic assistance from Chi-kong Lai and critical readings by Jane Kate Leonard, K.C. Liu, G. William Skinner, and E-tu Zen Sun, and is especially indebted to John Watt for provocative comments that helped to shape the present essay.

2. Thus high-status native places (Ningbo, for example) drew female wage laborers from low-status places ("hill country"). Women factory workers in Shanghai were hierarchically stratified by native place, with the cream of the jobs as "Number Ones" and highly paid skilled weavers reserved for workers from the Jiangnan core, leaving the dregs of the spinning mill work to women who hailed from peripheral Subei (Honig 1986, 62-70). In North China, where local custom strictly forbade women to work outside the home in farming or handicrafts, women were noticeably absent from the factory work force until after 1930, even in the cotton mills (Hershatter 1986, 54-56). And when the Huguang governor-general Zhang Zhidong established China's second spinning mill in Wuchang shortly after 1890, he refused to hire women workers because it would be a violation of Confucian morality and a threat to China's "national essence" (Ono 1989, 24).

3. This saying from the Early Han period (perhaps two centuries BCE) is quoted in the oft-reprinted Ming dynasty agricultural handbook, *Nongzheng quanshu*. See Xu [1639/40], *juan* 7:40. The translation here is from Yang 1952, 101.

4. Oyama Masaaki, Large landownership in the Jiangnan delta region during the late Ming-early Qing period, *Shigaku zasshi* 66 (1957), cited in Grove and Daniels 1984, 107.

5. Grove and Daniels 1984, 108.

6. See Nishijima Sadao, The Formation of the Early Chinese Cotton Industry, *Chûgoku keizaishi kenkyû* (1966), cited in Grove and Daniels 1984, 62.

7. Embroidery was the elite female handwork, something more akin to art practiced and cultivated in all families whose women could manage the time (Feng Hefa 1933, I:300-301). Work in the fields was considered

demeaning for women in many parts of China, not simply because it was coarse, heavy work, but because it took respectable women outside the home. For examples of upper-class women working with their hands, see Ho 1959, 210-11; Oyama in Grove and Daniels 1984,107-8, 110.

8. See the three chapters on "Agricultural Policy" (Nong zheng) in JSWB *juan* 36-38. More than half of the forty-nine essays in these chapters refer to home weaving, and one entire chapter containing nineteen essays (*juan* 37) focuses exclusively on cotton and silk home handicraft industries.

9. The essayist here alludes to poems in the *Book of Odes* both of which invoke images of the faithful wife. In the first, which is the title poem in the collection of odes from the state of Qi, the good wife admonishes her husband to rise early and attend to his duties (rather than languishing in connubial indulgence). See Legge 8,1:150. The second allusion to cedar vessels is likewise the title poem in the collection of odes from the state of Bei. The metaphor is that of a boat "floating uselessly about with the current," in Legge's words (Legge 3,1:38-39). Like the official without a lord, the widow without her husband is a cedar vessel. The allusion invokes both sorrow and rootlessness. In the case of women, it specifically alludes to the young widow who resists pressures to remarry.

10. Adele Fielde noticed during her ten-year sojourn in Swatow, Guangdong (1877-87) that only the rich could afford really to incapacitate their women, binding their feet starting at the age of six or eight; poor families did not begin binding until thirteen or fourteen years. Still, she observed, "even middle-class bound-foot women sometimes had to walk four or five miles daily." (Quoted in Levy 1966, 274; c.f. 213, 224, 226, 230). Especially in North China, bound feet appear to have presented no barrier to working in the fields. On the other hand, in the south, bound feet appear to have been more closely associated with indoor work. See Justus Doolittle's observations on Fuzhou, in Doolittle 1867 1:61; 2:202.

11. Of the 371 women employed in the Tomioka silk filature, 40 percent were said to come from aristocratic (*shizoku*) households (Hane 1982, 174-75). Hirschmeier (1964, 302, n.13) observes that Yonezawa silk cloth, woven at home by samurai women, achieved "national fame" in Tokugawa times.

References

Buck, John Lossing. [1937] 1956. *Land Utilization in China.* Reprint. New York.

Cole, James H., trans. 1989. Why the Sprouts of Capitalism Were Delayed in China, by Fang Xing (excerpt from Xu and Wu 1985). *Late Imperial China* 10, 2:106-38.

Dietrich, Craig. 1972. "Cotton Culture and Manufacture in Early Ch'ing China." In *Economic Organization in Chinese Society*, ed. W. E. Willmott. Stanford: Stanford University Press.

Doolittle, Rev. Justus. 1967. *Social Life of the Chinese.* 2 vols. New York: Harper and Brothers.

DQSZSL. *Da Qing Shizong Xianhuangdi shilu* (The Veritable Records of the Yongzheng reign). 1964. Vol. 6, pt. 2. Facsimile reprint of 1937 edition. Taipei: Huawen shuju.

Elvin, Mark. 1984. Female Virtue and the State in China. *Past and Present* 104:111-52.

Fang, Guancheng. [Edition of 1808, presented to the throne in 1765]. 1957. *Shouyi guangxun.* Facsimile edition, Shanghai: Guji chubanshe.

Fei, Hsiao T'ung. 1939. *Peasant Life in China.* London: Routledge and Kegan Paul.

Feng, Hefa, ed. 1933. *Zhongguo nongcun jingji ziliao.* 2 vols. Shanghai: Liming shuju.

Fu, Yiling. 1956. *Ming Qing shidai shangren ji shangye ziben* (Merchants and commercial capital during the Ming and Qing dynasties). Beijing.

Grove, Linda, and Christian Daniels, eds. 1984. *State and Society in China: Japanese Perspectives on Ming-Qing Social and Economic History.* Tokyo: University of Tokyo Press.

Guliang zhuan (The Guliang commentary on the Spring and Autumn Annals). [1927-36] 1965. Sibu beiyao, ed. Facsimile reprint. Taibei: Zhonghua shuju.

Hane, Mikiso. 1982. *Peasants, Rebels, and Outcastes: The Underside of Modern Japan.* New York: Pantheon Books.

Hanley, Susan B., and Kozo Yamamura. 1977. *Economic and Demographic Change in Preindustrial Japan, 1600-1868.* Princeton: Princeton University Press.

Headland, Isaac Taylor. 1914. *Home Life in China.* London: Methuen and Company.

Hershatter, Gail. 1986. *The Workers of Tianjin, 1900-1949.* Stanford: Stanford University Press.

Hirschmeier, Johannes. 1964. *The Origins of Entrepreneurship in Meiji Japan.* Cambridge, Mass.: Harvard University Press.

Ho, Ping-ti. 1959. *Studies on the Population of China.* Cambridge, Mass.: Harvard University Press.

Honig, Emily. 1986. *Sisters and Strangers: Women in the Shanghai Cotton Mills, 1919-1949.* Stanford: Stanford University Press.

Huang, Philip C. C. 1990. *The Peasant Family and Rural Development in the Yangzi Delta, 1350-1988.* Stanford: Stanford University Press.

Huang, Ray. 1974. *Taxation and Governmental Finance in Sixteenth-Century Ming China.* New York: Cambridge University Press.

JSWB. *Huangchao jingshi wenbian* (Collected essays on statecraft of our August Dynasty). [1826] 1963. Comp. Wei Yuan. Preface dated 1826. Reprint. Taibei.

Legge, James, trans. [N.d] 1966. *The Chinese Classics, vol. IV, The She King.* Reprint of the last editions by Oxford University Press. Taibei: Wenxing shudian.

Levy, Howard S. 1966. *Chinese Footbinding: The History of a Curious Erotic Custom.* New York: Walton Rawls.

Li, Lillian M. 1981. *China's Silk Trade: Traditional Industry in the Modern World, 1842-1937.* Cambridge, Mass.: Harvard University Press.

Luo, Qiong. 1935. Zhongguo nongcunzhong de laodong funü (Women workers in China's villages). *Funü shenghuo* 1, 4.

Mann, Susan. 1987. Widows in the Kinship, Class, and Community Structures of Qing Dynasty China. *Journal of Asian Studies* 46,1:37-56.

Ono Kazuko. 1989. *Chinese Women in a Century of Revolution, 1850-1950,* ed. Joshua A. Fogel. Stanford: Stanford University Press.

Peng, Zeyi. [1964] 1984. Zhongguo jindai shougongyeshi ziliao (Materials on the history of China's modern handicraft industries). Reprint. Beijing: Zhonghua shuju. Vol. 1.

Pruitt, Ida. [1945] 1967. *A Daughter of Han: The Autobiography of a Chinese Working Woman.* Reprint. Stanford: Stanford University Press.

Quataert, Jean H. 1985. The Shaping of Women's Work in Manufacturing: Guilds, Households, and the State in Central Europe, 1648-1870. *American Historical Review* 90, 5:1122-1148.

Smith, Thomas C. 1955. *Political Change and Industrial Development in Japan: Government Enterprise, 1868-1880.* Stanford: Stanford University Press.

_____. 1977. *Nakahara: Family Farming and Population in a Japanese Village, 1717-1830.* Stanford: Stanford University Press.

_____. 1988. *Native Sources of Japanese Industrialization, 1750-1920.* Berkeley, University of California Press.

Sun, E-tu Zen. 1972. "Sericulture and Silk Textile Production in Ch'ing China." In *Economic Organization in Chinese Society*, ed. W. E. Willmott. Stanford: Stanford University Press.

Sung, Ying-hsing. [1637] 1966. *T'ien-kung K'ai-wu: Chinese Technology in the Seventeenth Century*. Trans. E-tu Zen Sun and Shiou-chuan Sun. University Park: The Pennsylvania State University Press.

SYGX. *Qinding shouyi guangxun* (Imperially authorized edition of the Wide-ranging Instructions Concerning the Provision of Clothing). [1808] 1988. Reprint. *Zhongguo gudai banhua congkan* (Collected classics in the original woodblock editions). Shanghai: Guji chubanshe.

Williams, Edward T. 1935. The Worship of Lei Tsu, Patron Saint of Silk Workers. *Journal of the North China Branch, Royal Asiatic Society*, new series 66:1-14.

Xiangyan congshu (Collection of feminine fragrance). Preface dated 1909/10. N.p.

Xu, Dixin and Wu Chengming, eds. 1985. *Zhongguo ziben zhuyi de mengya* (The sprouts of capitalism in China). Beijing: Renmin chubanshe.

Xu, Guangqi. [1639-1640] 1900-1901. *Nongzheng quanshu* (The complete book of agricultural policy). Reprint. Shanghai.

Xu, Xinwu. 1981. *Yapian zhanzhengqian Zhongguo mianfangzhi shougongye de shangpin shengchan yu ziben zhuyi mengya wenti* (Commercial production in China's cotton spinning and weaving protoindustry before the Opium War and the problem of the sprouts of capitalism). Yangzhou: Jiangsu renmin chubanshe.

Yang, Lien-sheng. 1952. *Money and Credit in China: A Short History*. Cambridge, Mass.: Harvard University Press.

6

Qing Administration of the Tea Trade: Four Facets over Three Centuries

Robert Gardella

"Immobilism" and "rigidity" are labels that historians in the West persist in applying to Qing administration, yet the more we learn about the almost three centuries of Qing rule, the less accurate such epithets appear to be. Mid-Qing policy regarding coastal security and maritime trade did become inflexible and rigid, yet Qing policy towards Inner Asian trade repeatedly exhibited considerable pragmatism and adaptability. These differences are seen in Qing administration of the tea trade. They reflect a changed outlook on the relationship between commerce and imperial security, and they flowed inevitably from the enormous expansion of the domestic tea market that resulted from the conquest and incorporation of the Inner Asian borderlands into the empire and from China's gradual absorption into larger global patterns of commerce. A review of Qing tea policy, in contrast to that of Song and Ming, and an analysis of four regional cases of the tea trade serve to document and explain the nature and significance of these changes in Qing administration of this trade.

The four regional vignettes point up the disjunction between trade within the Qing imperium versus China's own incorporation into a global trading system over the full span of Qing rule. The first case (trade with Mongolia) illustrates the pragmatic adaptability of early Qing trade policy in an age of expanding continental empire, while the second (the Fujian-Canton trade) stresses the hyper-cautious, restrictive mid-Qing approach to maritime commerce. The third case (the Mongolian-Russian trade) follows from the demise of the restrictive approach, leading to dislocation of indigenous caravan trading patterns. The final case shows the endurance of Sino-Tibetan commercial linkages beyond the Himalayas and serves as a counterpoint to its predecessor.

Revenue, Security, and Qing Tea Policy

Among the most enduring tenets of Chinese imperial administration was the regulation and taxation of domestic and external commerce. The influence of regulatory and fiscal measures over time played a key role in defining the scale and scope of major commodity trades, not the least of which was the tea trade.[1] From the Song to the Qing, tea was a valued article of commerce, one of few staples able to stand the cost of long-distance transport within and beyond shifting imperial frontiers. It did not

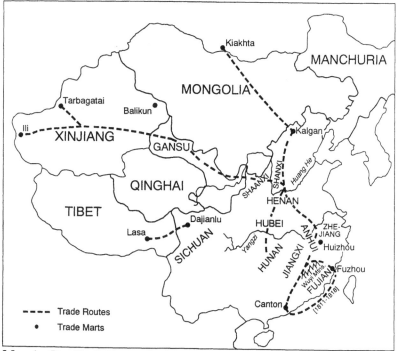

Map 4. Tea Trade Routes in the Qing Period.

lend itself to official oversight in the manner of a dietary necessity like salt, or a scarce medicament like Manchurian ginseng. In the words of one authority, "The tea trade was not a uniform whole." There was a world of difference between the sources of supply and demand, the routes followed, the agents involved, and goods exported in the mid-Qing overland trade between Sichuan and Tibet and the Canton trade to England, to cite one example (Adshead 1988, 288-90). This non-standardized commodity, with its fragmented, highly dispersed mode of production and complex array of markets, recurrently tested imperial regulatory and fiscal capacities.

Qing policy towards the tea trade is more intelligible in the light of Song and Ming precedents (Yuan tea policy is a special, lesser case that will be ignored here). The Song comprehensively sought to administer both tea production and trade. According to Saeki Tomi, Song tea policy had three objectives: financial enrichment of the state, facilitation of logistical support for northern frontier garrisons, and control of the terms of border trade with Inner Asians (1962, 163-65). Tea monopoly regulations under the Song thus incorporated both revenue and security goals; they were so complex and mutable as to defy brief summation (Smith 1983). Song officials' implication in managing tea growing and processing required special bureaucratic posts, collecting agencies, and credit systems to facilitate these operations. Tea distribution also was controlled by a system of official certification of merchants, the so-called *yin* licenses.

Ming tea policy was far less ambitious and interventionist than that of the Song because the Ming were preoccupied with distribution rather than production. The same description, of course, would apply to most aspects of the Ming political economy (Huang 1974, 316-17). The main elements of continuity from Song to Ming were the *yin* licensing system and a strategic preoccupation with Inner Asian trade. As Jack Wills affirms, "defensiveness" was the leitmotif of the Ming era on all frontiers, maritime and continental (1988, 227; Martynov 1981). It stands to reason that security rather than revenue emerged as the dominant focus of Ming tea administration, and security came to be linked to what Arthur Waldron terms "the fundamental issue in Ming security policy . . . the approach to the Mongols" (1990, 84).

Two overlapping expressions of this theme were the *kaizhong* policy and the border tea-horse trade with Tibetans and other nomadic peoples. *Kaizhong* refers to the state's co-optation of groups of merchants to provision the northern frontiers, granting them in return licenses to pursue the lucrative salt and tea trades (Rossabi 1970, 152; Waldron 1990, 83). The Ming tea-horse trade resuscitated a Song monopoly system of annually bartering tea for the Inner Asian horses required by imperial armies.

Officials staffed a network of tea-horse trading offices (*chamasi*) along the northwest frontier to enforce the monopoly and curb smuggling. Controlling the trade was thought to give China "life or death" leverage over nomadic "barbarians" whose greasy diets required tea. In reality, of course, Ming officials were usually in greater need of horses than the Inner Asians were desperate for tea (Rossabi 1970, 136-63; Martynov 1981, 186-87).

The Qing carried over virtually intact the provisions of the Ming tea code (*chafa*), including draconian penal laws mandating capital sentences for forging tea *yin*.[2]   Yet, Qing tea policy was no mere statutory legacy. Codified, presumably universal norms only mattered in the context of "routinized procedures forming regionally unified patterns of action" (Whitbeck 1965, 18-20). In contrast to both the Song and Ming, these routines were seldom carried out by functionally discrete officials, but by provincial and local magistrates acting under the central oversight of the Board of Revenue (Whitbeck 1965, 20-21; Sun 1962-63; Ch'u 1969, 147).

In operational terms the system can be described without prejudice as a patchwork, doubtless reflecting the sheer size and baroque complexity of the late imperial economy itself. Provincial exemptions and idiosyncratic local variations affected *yin* license quotas, "miscellaneous taxes" (*zafu*), and regional patronage networks. To cite one example from a mid-nineteenth-century survey, while Zhejiang topped all provinces annually with 210,000 *yin*, other major tea producing provinces would have no *yin* quota (Fujian) or only token quotas (Hubei's 248 and Hunan's 240 *yin*). Each tea *yin* commonly authorized the marketing of a hundred *jin*. Some 508,000 were issued for the entire country in the mid-1800s, covering perhaps 32,000,000 kg of tea (Whitbeck 1965, 23-24, 51). Comparing this figure with Wu Chengming's estimate of China's total tea output in 1840 (158,000,000 kg), however, indicates that 80 percent of the empire's annual tea production simply would have been excluded from licensing regulations (Wu 1983, 99).

Above and apart from the *yin* system, the miscellaneous taxes on tea included duties (*ke*) and tariffs (*shui;* Sun 1962-1963, 206). In the early Qing, these assessments were somehow classified among the empire's primary revenues (*zhengxiang*; Zelin 1984, 27). While such taxes might have been elastic local sources of income (Mann 1987, 41), they accounted for only 70,000 *taels*, or a mere 0.14 percent, of annual central government revenues in the mid-Qianlong era (Wu Hui 1990, 43; Whitbeck 1965, 28-29).

In Qing tea policy, revenue and security concerns intermingled, especially regarding trade along the empire's vulnerable land and sea frontiers. In comparison to all previous dynasties save the Yuan, the Qing realm itself represented an enormous expansion of China's own domestic market into Inner Asia and Manchuria. The new empire afforded a greatly expanded scope of operations for Chinese merchants and suppliers in the late seventeenth and eighteenth centuries, who penetrated vast dominions initially established by *force majeuré* (Rossabi 1975, 163). In the nineteenth century, Qing policy fell from grace, as the empire struggled to adapt to and contain expansive Western political and commercial interests. Still, as late as the 1911 Revolution, native traders backed by imperial regulations could more than hold their own in domestic commercial competition with foreigners in Inner Asia.

Mongolia and the Superannuation of the Tea-Horse Trade, 1644-1735

Under the Northern Song, the tea-horse trade both commenced and reached a height of logistical efficiency. Each year, up to five million *jin* of tea was bartered for steeds on the northwest frontier. Official control of this strategic trade became far weaker during the Ming, with only one million *jin* exported per annum. By the sixteenth century, over half of the border tea-horse exchanges were, in fact, being contracted out to groups of private merchants. The *kaizhong* system, by which merchants supplying grain to Shaanxi received permits to trade in official tea, gave way to virtually unimpeded free trade in the commodity. By the late Ming, authorities commonly were procuring only three to six thousand horses per year (Huang 1974, 257-61; Martynov 1981, 195-97; Rossabi 1970; 1975, 78-82; Smith 1983, 586-87; Wu Juenong 1990, 10-16).

During the troubled course of the late sixteenth and early seventeenth centuries, trade on the northwest frontier was constantly disrupted. The vestiges of the Ming tea-horse system rapidly unraveled, exacerbating the general economic and political insecurity in Shaanxi and the borderlands in the early 1600s (Rossabi 1979, 184-89). The consequent inability to obtain mounts crippled hard-pressed Ming frontier defenses (Rossabi 1975, 82-83). As the *Ming shi* tersely notes in retrospect, "the tea laws, the horse administration, and the border defenses were all ruined" (cited in Rossabi 1970, 162).

While they were major beneficiaries of this debacle, the Manchus too needed horses to facilitate their conquests. Over the period 1644 to 1668, the Qing tried to revive the tea-horse trade in Shaanxi and Gansu on the basis of Ming institutional precedents, especially the tea-horse trading offices and the tea-horse censors (*chama yushi*). Despite reinvigorated controls, not many more than 3,000 horses per year were procured in barter for 310,000 *jin* of tea (Wu Juenong 1990, 1; Lin 1982, 102-109). In the 1670s, in fact, most of the tea officially obtained for barter actually was diverted to pay Qing troops serving on the northwest border, who then resold it to obtain provisions (Rossabi 1979, 191). The new regime had done little better with a ramshackle system than the old.

A longer-term solution was to render the tea-horse trade expendable, as the Qing dynasty forged a vastly expanded imperium across Inner Asian frontiers (Leonard 1987, 67-76; Waldron 1990, 167-68). The *raison d'être* of the trade evaporated during the period 1669-1735, as state horse-raising and private tea-marketing penetrated the borderlands. Between Kangxi's 1669 *coup d'état* and the end of Yongzheng's reign in 1735, the Qing pacified Inner Asia and gained direct control over its equine pasturelands. Thirteen large-scale breeding stations were created in Gansu and Xinjiang in the late eighteenth and early nineteenth centuries. These enterprises provided many times the number of mounts supplied in the palmiest days of the tea-horse exchanges, and at a time when military demand was diminishing. In 1805, for instance, just one such operation at Balikun (Barkol) in Xinjiang stocked 31,359 horses (Lin 1982, 109-16; Kano 1963).

The Kangxi and Yongzheng reigns also witnessed an aggressive commercial penetration of Mongolia by Chinese merchants, often from Shanxi, who became the indispensable *bête noire* of Mongol daily life. Along with the encouragement of Lamaist Buddhism and the sedentarization of nomadic society, Han commercial exploitation has been taken to indicate a studied Qing policy of emasculating and weakening Mongol society. The phenomenon also might be described as a less artful symbiosis emerging over time between Qing garrison officials and vigorous, very well-organized Han commercial interests (Jagchid and Symons 1989, 20-21; Leonard 1987, 69-71).

No longer was trade a matter of Mongol-initiated border bartering. It now entailed the ubiquitous presence of several private trading firms amongst a people whose innocence of commercial practice was as proverbial as their dislike of deceptive middlemen (Bawden 1968, 94-100; Jagchid and Hyer 1979, 304; Lattimore 1975, 178). One such Han firm was the Dashengkuai, the largest trader in Inner Mongolia. Founded sometime between the late 1600s and early 1700s and active down to the early twentieth century, this Shanxi company had six to seven thousand employees and numerous branches in China proper. Its provisioning of Qing garrisons and Mongol nobles and commoners with tea and other goods was soon overshadowed by its extensive banking and credit operations. The Dashengkuai and at least one other firm were commonly known amongst the

Mongol banners as guarantors, or paymasters (*tongshi*; NMZ, 1-10; Pozdneyev 1892, 179, 208-11).

Introduced along with Yellow Sect Lamaism from Tibet only in the last quarter of the sixteenth century, tea rapidly became the import in greatest

Fig. 1. Coolies Carying Brick Tea. From T.T. Cooper. *Travels of a Pioneer of Commerce.* London: 1871.

demand in the grasslands (Jagchid and Symons 1989, 46). Estimates of annual tea consumption per Mongol family range from as few as twelve to as many as fifty-four bricks per year. Bricks of tea also were commonly valued as a commodity money because they were highly portable, quite durable, and came in several denominations or sizes. Contemporary reports describe frequent manipulations of exchange rates between tea bricks and livestock, as well as usurious credit terms calculated in brick tea. Perhaps it does not overstate the case to suggest that, by dominating the tea trade, sojourning Han merchant-bankers also gained ascendancy over a sizable portion of Mongolia's incipient money supply (Sanjdorj 1980, 48-49, 89-91).

Curtailing Coastal Commerce: The Broken Link between Fujian and Canton, 1816-1818

Chinese seaborne commerce flourished during the early to mid-Qing, and particularly along the southeast littoral, where Ng Chin-keong's research confirms the vigorous activity of Amoyese and other Fujianese merchant-shippers (Ng 1983; 1990). While Qing authorities in general favored this trade, they appear to have balanced it uneasily against a strategic imperative—the security of the southeastern coastline. The confinement of a growing Sino-Western maritime tea trade to Canton after 1759 certainly accords with a strategic outlook depicting southeast China as the first line of defense for the imperial lifeline, the Grand Canal (Leonard 1984, 65-75; 1988, 232-34).

Between 1760 and the Opium War, the teas of South Anhui and the Wuyi Mountains followed a tortuous overland route through Jiangxi on their way to Canton. The trek involved up to seven inconvenient transshipments *en route* from Anhui. Seven internal customs barriers intercepted the riverboats and portage traffic from the Wuyi range to the Pearl River delta. Samuel Ball, the East India Company's resident tea expert in early nineteenth-century Canton, once estimated the cost of shipping a *picul* (60 kg) of *congou* tea from north Fujian downriver to Fuzhou at a mere 11 percent of the cost of overland transit (0.42 *taels* versus 3.92; Ch'en 1989, 2-3; Ball 1848, 356). As John Crawfurd put the issue in 1820:

> The natural and obvious channels by which the teas of China would be exported to foreign countries are wholly different from that to which the Chinese force it. . . .

[Why], while there exists an extensive coasting trade between the provinces of Fokien and Quantong, [are] teas not invariably conveyed by sea? (Crawfurd 1820, 3:527-29)

A straight-forward answer suggests itself. The court wanted to confine this commerce to "natural and obvious channels" where it could be conveniently controlled and regularly taxed. The fact is, however, that teas actually were "conveyed by sea" on several occasions. Ch'en Kuo-tung's use of India Office records reveals that sea shipments intermittently took place during the Qianlong era (1736-95). They were interdicted not by Qing statutes, but by the massive eruption of piracy on the Guangdong coast between 1795 and 1810, demonstrating anew the vulnerability of the southern littoral (Ch'en 1989, 3; Murray 1987).

Beginning in 1811-1812, East India Company officials evidently began arranging with Fujian merchants to convey tea again by sea to Canton. After a down-river haul to Fuzhou, cargoes of three to four thousand chests per junk arrived at Canton within two weeks instead of the customary forty to sixty days by interior routes. By 1816, almost four million kilos of tea arrived by sea, or about one-fourth of Canton's annual tea exports. Since this reduced the incidence of both transport fees and transit taxes, the company's court of directors formally sanctioned the new route in 1817 as a cost-saving option (Ball 1848, 167-69; Ch'en 1989, 3).

That very same year, Liangguang Governor-general Jiang Youxian memorialized the throne to prohibit coastal shipments of tea destined for Canton. His rationale stressed coastal security. It was easier to supervise overland commerce than control a coasting trade that might carry contraband goods as well as teas. Similarly, he minimized the impact that the seaborne trade was having on imperial revenues. The argument was plausible, yet Jiang also may have been concerned that Guangdong's inland customs proceeds, thus the Hubu's fixed annual revenue quota, were now being jeopardized (Liang [1838], 3:1267-69; Ch'en 1989, 4). The Jiaqing Emperor concurred with this proposal. An edict of 1818 prohibited use of the seaborne route and ordered the governors of Fujian and Anhui, who apparently had been loose constructionists regarding the matter, to enforce strictly the old landbound transit route. In the future, those Chinese merchants resorting to the coastal route to Canton were to be punished as smugglers and their tea confiscated (Liang [1838], 3:1267-70). In this early nineteenth-century instance, forceful regional interests supporting a well-established commercial and fiscal network were validated by the court's strategic anxieties. The procedural inflexibility evident in the Canton system, irreconcilable with a rapidly expanding Sino-Western commerce, was again confirmed (Leonard 1984, 75).

Shifting Networks of Merchant Clientage: The Overland Trade to Inner Asia and Russia from Mid- to Late Qing

In the seventeenth century, Shanxi and Shaanxi merchant guilds (*bang*), along with the Huizhou traders of south Anhui, were numbered among the great commercial capitalist networks of China. The profits of the two northern groups had long been associated with the Ming *kaizhong* system (Wu 1985, 241-46). Shanxi and Shaanxi merchants were resourceful enough to survive the demise of the Ming, of *kaizhong*, and the tea-horse trade. When an overland tea trade to Russia and Inner Asia grew during the early to mid-Qing era, it virtually became their preserve. By the late nineteenth century, however, shifting political winds that once fostered their rise, hastened their fall, as alien competitors and domestic rivals with new sources of patronage appeared.

From the Wuyi Mountains of Fujian to the villages of southern Hubei and northern Hunan, expatriate Shanxi merchants fanned out across the countryside buying tea for the Kiakhta and Mongolian markets. Called "Western guests" (*Xike*) or the "Western group" (*Xibang*), these amply funded traders—capitalizations of 200,000 to 1,000,000 *taels* per firm are reported—came to dominate the long-distance caravan trade to the north (Gardella 1990, 332-33; Li 1987, 50-51, 55; Shigeta 1962, 49-52). Notwithstanding the arduous 2,300-kilometer final leg of the journey from Kalgan (Zhangjiakou) to Kiakhta, the trade grew in the early nineteenth century. In 1817 a total of 2,500 camels and 1,420 oxcarts comprised its logistical support. A dozen years later, the mustering of 9,670 camels and 2,705 carts denoted the rapid growth of Sino-Russian tea traffic (Li 1987, 50-51, 55; Cai 1982, 120-21).

Trade to Kiakhta was designated as the "Northern route" (Beilu), while trade to what would later become known as Xinjiang was called the "Western route" (Xilu). Even though the brick tea trade continued in the hands of Gansu licensees, unlicensed Shanxi traders were allowed to export leaf tea to the growing Qing colonies in Xinjiang after the region's conquest in 1760 (Fletcher 1978, 82). The 1851 Sino-Russian Kulja Treaty additionally gave Shanxi merchants full access to the border trade at Ili and Tarbagatai. Buying tea in southern Anhui, they then would convey it to Xinjiang and Russian Central Asia via Henan and Shanxi (Cai 1982, 125).

For Shanxi-Shaanxi caravan traders, the longer-term consequences of the treaty system and the disruption of new and old trading patterns, caused by the mid-nineteenth-century rebellions, proved disastrous. Russian tea firms from 1862 onward gained and quickly utilized the right to buy, process, and ship tea directly from the middle Yangzi and Fujian without utilizing Chinese middlemen. In 1880, only three out of twenty-eight Chinese firms were still active on the Northern route, the Kalgan to Kiakhta trade, while Russian merchants began to sell instead of buy tea in Xinjiang (Cai 1982, 130-33; Cheng, Wang and Xu, 1984).

The *coup de grâce* for Western route caravans ironically was delivered not by Russians but by domestic competitors. It is traceable to Governor-general Zuo Zongtang's establishment of a rival group of licensed Hunanese tea merchants, the so-called "Nanzhu," during his military campaigns in Xinjiang from 1874 onward. Some three thousand *yin* permits were issued to authorize their trade. Zuo's patronage of his fellow provincials underscored and further contributed to the decline of the northern merchant groups already hampered by the empire's prolonged civil strife. The growing wealth and regional influence of the Nanzhu merchants epitomized the dramatic expansion of Hunan's export tea trade after 1842, and its increased control by home-grown traders rather than by northern sojourners (Cai 1982, 125-27; Chu 1936, 104; Wu Juenong 1990, 485).

Maintaining a Monopolized Market: The Sichuan-Tibet Trade at the Turn of the Nineteenth Century

"Dogs and thunder must have voice. Men and horses must have class. Tea and beer must have strength" (Duncan 1964, 47). The colorful maxim encapsulates the central role of Chinese tea in the Tibetan popular diet in the nineteenth and twentieth centuries, the end result of a staple trade dating from the Song era (Smith 1983, 167-68). Only at the very end of the Qing was Sichuan's dominance of this commerce in compressed or brick tea challenged by newly established British plantation interests in Assam (Cooper 1871, 409-10; Cammann 1951, 100, 147).

Unlike the situation prevailing on the northern frontier, the Ming-Qing interregnum marked a decisive end to the tea-horse trade system on the Sichuan-Tibetan border. Eager to rehabilitate the ravaged province and expand commerce with Inner Asia, the new dynasty attached some importance to facilitating the controlled development of Sichuan tea exports. The Qing tea code was instrumental in this process (Gu and Chen 1988, 166-76; Wu Juenong 1990, 579-80).

Provincial authorities quickly opened the trade to those merchants purchasing official *yin* licenses and paying some additional local taxes (tariffs and duties totalling 45,942 and 13,128 *taels,* respectively, in the early Qing). Judging by the number of *yin* in circulation, the tea trade flourished under the new conditions. During the Shunzhi era (1644-1661), 106,127 *yin* were issued, and by the end of the Jiaqing era (1796-1820), 146,713. Estimated Sichuan tea production rose two-and-a-half times (to

Fig. 2.   Tea Porters on the Road to Dajianlu. From W.W. Rockhill. *Land of the Lamas.* N.Y.: 1891.

250,000 *piculs*, or 15,000,000 kilograms) over the same period. The trade was carried on mainly at the frontier commercial center of Dajianlu, which had been designated officially for this role in 1696, and also at the lesser border towns of Litang, Batang and Songpan (De Rosthorn 1895, 14-15; Gu and Chen 1988, 197-99; Huang 1972, 40; Wu Juenong 1990, 706-709).

Regulating the annual volume of trade, *yin* permits were central to an elaborate system administered by a special tea intendant (*yancha daotai*), resident at Chengdu, a post rarely found in the Qing administrative system. Each *yin* issued by the Board of Revenue covered a hundred *jin* of tea, which in practice amounted to five packages (*bao*). The licensing procedure involved three categories of permits specifically designated either for export to Tibet (*bianyin*), trade along the Sino-Tibetan frontier (*tuyin*), or trade within the province (*fuyin*). Export licenses were by far the most important, accounting for two-thirds of the tea in transit and as much as or more than the yearly revenue. To further complicate matters, Sichuan officials in need of additional revenue also issued a variety of special permits (*piao*) to increase the volume of trade (De Rosthorn 1895, 15, 17-21; Huang 1972, 42-43; Peng 1986, 79).

Taking the year 1815 as an example, a grand total of 139,354 *yin* were issued, 92,327 of which were export permits for the Tibetan trade. The total annual revenue realized was 111,693 *taels*, and 72 percent of this stemmed from the export trade (De Rosthorn 1895, 15-17). Local insecurity and weak administration brought setbacks to the trade in the troubled mid- to late nineteenth century (Gu and Chen 1988, 206-17). Nonetheless, in the 1890s, some 133,840 *taels* per annum in revenue were still being collected on exports of 6,000,000 to 6,500,000 kilograms, or enough to satisfy the yearly consumption of about two million Tibetans (De Rosthorn 1895, 18-19; Rockhill 1891, 280-81).

Chinese licensees arranged for the processing, collection, and transport of the several brands of tea for the Tibetan market, ranging in price and quality from bricks of first-class leaf to fifth-class crude woody stems. Transported to Dajianlu on the overburdened backs of Sichuan porters, who could heft loads of over a hundred kilograms for a twenty-day trip of 220 kilometers, the cargoes were consigned to Tibetan traders who conveyed them home by pack trains (Rockhill 1891, 278-80; De Rosthorn 1895, 31-33). With a total resident population of upwards of three hundred thousand monks, the great Tibetan monasteries were dependable markets for the commodity. Monasteries also profiteered by serving as distribution centers to the general populace (Goldstein 1989, 21; Wiley 1986, 10). This is clear enough in the following unfriendly observation:

The Lamas, keeping in their hands the retail, as the Chinese monopolize the wholesale trade, by this means reduce the people to absolute dependence upon them, exacting in return for the precious article, labour and produce. Grain, yaks, sheep, horses, and even children, are given to the rapacious priesthood in return for tea (Cooper 1871, 409).

As the value of tea shipments would rise twenty-fold *en route* from Dajianlu to Lhasa, the trade was even more lucrative from the vantage point of Chinese merchants (Huang 1972, 47). The annual profit from the licensed trade in the 1890s was a healthy 437,536 *taels*. Available *yin* were snapped up quickly, as "the privilege to participate in the trade is a valuable one, and one not easily obtained" (De Rosthorn 1895, 36-37).

In order to acquire a permit, one had to be on the lists of applicants annually supplied by two department (*zhou*) and three district (*xian*) magistrates to the sub-prefect of Dajianlu. Those so favored were required to have financial guarantors among the local merchant and gentry elite. Some licensees even turned a profit by renting out their permits to other parties with more capital to conduct the business (De Rosthorn 1895, 17, 32). More information on just how closely and by whom *yin* privileges were held would be interesting. The Ba district archive near Chengdu evidently contains numerous records indicating that a closed corporate group (*chaguan*) of fifty-three families restricted entry into Sichuan's tea business, which must have encompassed the Tibetan trade (Ran 1986).

Since the early days of the company *raj*, exaggerated prospects of commerce with Tibet had spurred interest and avarice in British India (Cammann 1951). Turn-of-the-century English observers' accounts of Sino-Tibetan trade frequently and boldly proclaimed their own commercial agenda, as in this 1895 pamphlet:

The hope of being able yet to supersede China in her commercial supremacy in Tibet, which rests entirely on the tea trade, and perhaps the knowledge also, that the commercial dependence of that country is a political lever of no small importance, have no doubt made the opening of Tibet on the Indian side to appear to Englishmen highly desirable, while to the Chinese they have furnished an excellent pretext, if not a powerful motive, for refusing their assent to any proposal in that direction (De Rosthorn 1895, 6).

The same sources just as often expressed doubt about the prospects of a trans-Himalayan tea trade, both because of indigenous consumer demand and effective Chinese competition. Tibetans' traditional preference for the various grades of Chinese tea, and well-organized efforts of Sichuan merchants to supply their wants handicapped Indian tea exports, which had otherwise bested Chinese tea on the world market (De Rosthorn 1895, 37-39; Hutchison 1906, 54). Sir Charles Bell noted that by the late 1920s, Tibetans of all social classes could still select among five "brands" of Chinese tea, and they also

> found the Chinese tea more nutritious, more wholesome, and more pleasant to the taste. Consequently, they rated the Indian varieties only slightly above the lowest grade of Tibetan tea. There is unlikely to be any real market for Indian tea in Tibet, until it is made like the Chinese in appearance and flavour (1928, 121-22).

Qing policy also played a strong and even innovative role in support of the Sichuan tea industry. A Sino-British agreement of 1890 halted importation of Indian tea until 1904, when the Younghusband expedition forcibly opened Tibet to British trade (Gu and Chen 1988, 242-44). Curzon's obsession with India's security undoubtedly figured more in this *démarché* than any machinations of Assam tea planters, which, in any case, were soon frustrated (Cammann 1951, 147; Snellgrove and Richardson 1986, 235). Zhao Erfeng, the governor whose subsequent behavior fueled the 1911 Revolution in Sichuan, established a *guandu shangban* (official supervision and merchant management) corporation to modernize the tea trade and insure China's continued monopoly. Titled the Border Tea Limited Liability Company (Biancha Gufen Youxian Gongsi), this organization made some headway during the last three years of the empire in rationalizing production and marketing conditions (Gu and Chen 1988, 248-62; Grunfeld 1987, 50-51).

After the 1911 Revolution, commercial relations between an increasingly autonomous Tibet and warlord-ridden Sichuan suffered frequent breakdowns because of chronic border hostilities. Yet Tibetans failed to accustom themselves to mechanically processed Indian tea "tasting of machine oil." The greatest competition Sichuan tea faced in the early twentieth century came not from Assam, but from Yunnan teas laboriously transshipped across Burma and India. In one form or another, China's control of the tea markets of the Roof of the World appeared as durable as the region's lofty summits (Chen and Chen 1988; 53; Hill 1989, 325-27).

Conclusions

Joseph Esherick and Mary Rankin remark in a recent study that "the Chinese [empire] in effect reversed the European evaluations of domestic and foreign trade" by officially encouraging the former, and restricting or at least disparaging the latter (1990, 332). This is, of course, true. By comparison with all previous dynasties save the Yuan, the Qing realm represented an enormous expansion of China's own domestic market into Inner Asia and Manchuria. The new empire afforded a greatly expanded scope of operations for Chinese merchants and suppliers in the late seventeenth and eighteenth centuries, who penetrated vast dominions initially established by *force majeuré* (Rossabi 1975, 163). At the same time, restrictiveness toward the maritime trade reflected the Qing imperium's response to changing conditions in maritime Asia in the nineteenth century, as the empire struggled to adapt to and contain expansive Western political and commercial interests.

The four episodes considered above reveal these changed conditions in domestic and foreign trade. The greatest dichotomies occur between domestic and foreign trade and between continental and coastal regions engaging in one or the other. Simply put, Qing imperial expansion, in varying degree, domesticated vast areas of Inner Asia that lay beyond Ming frontiers. The domination of Han commerce throughout Mongolia, its penetration of Xinjiang, and the resilience of Sino-Tibetan trade played no small part in this complex process. Private and semi-official trade flourished under the new regime's more liberalized administration, serving to enhance both state security and popular welfare.

But overseas trade in coastal regions could not be viewed in the same light nor administered with quite the same confidence. Early Qing realism and pragmatism regarding the regional economic necessity of maritime commerce gave way to mid-Qing defensiveness and restrictions. The ocean was one frontier that could never be domesticated, and the suspect activities of private and semi-official maritime traders were far less amenable to control. By the mid-Qing, expansion of foreign trade along the seacoast increasingly appeared to diminish imperial security and even endanger popular welfare. The scenario was thus in place for a tragic denouement, and the compulsory reordering of Qing political and economic relations with the wider mid-nineteenth century world.

Notes

1. The writer is most grateful to John Watt, E-tu Zen Sun, Andrea McElderry, Jane Leonard, and Nailene Chou Wiest for their generous critiques of earlier versions of this paper. He is indebted also to Kwan Man-bun for providing a copy of an important *neibu* study of the Dasheng-kuai, and to Lai Chi-kong for sharing his edition of a recent comprehensive history of the Sichuan tea industry.

2. A translation of a tea *yin* certificate appeared in the *Canton Register* of 17 March 1835 (Klaproth 1835, 43-44) and is reproduced verbatim as follows:

> Tea Permit, Issued by the Minister of Finance: The Minister of Finance having received a report from the administration of teas in the district of _____, I have carefully examined it, and find that it is in perfect conformity to the imperial decree concerning the teas, and with all local regulations &c. The minister, therefore, has caused this tea permit to be made, containing the following heads, and which is given to merchants to prove that they are authorized to sell tea.
>
> 1. The merchant receives one of these permits for each box or basket of tea, of whatever quality, weighing one *pecul*[*sic*]. Upon one of these permits is marked the weight; the other, carrying half of the impression of the seal, authorizes the sale of the tea. These tickets are a sufficient guarantee for the merchants, if they have paid the price into the treasury.
>
> 2. The merchant who sells tea should possess the necessary tickets (for the purposes of trade). If he omits taking this precaution, his tea will come under the class of prohibited goods, and the proprietor incur[*sic*] the same punishment as those who sell contraband salt (The goods are confiscated, and the offenders bambooed).
>
> 3. When a parcel of tea arrives at a customhouse, the officer should carefully examine the tickets which accompany it. If he finds them according to rule, he will cut one corner; the tea can then pass, if there are not other undeclared goods packed with it. If anyone secrets tea in a house, and conceals it with an old permit, the master of the house is as a receiver of stolen goods, liable to the same punishment as the defrauder.
>
> 4. If tea is carried into a city, the mayor[*sic*] should examine the billets; if he finds them good, he will cut one corner, and permit the sale of the merchandise.

5. He who forges false tea permits, shall lose his head, and all his property be forfeited to the state. The informer shall be rewarded with twenty ounces of silver.

6. If the proprietor of a tea plantation sells to a merchant unprovided with the necessary permits, he shall receive sixty blows with the great bamboo, and the money which he received for the tea shall be forfeited.

References

Adshead, S.A.M. 1988. *China in World History.* London: Macmillan Press.

Ball, Samuel. 1848. *An Account of the Cultivation and Manufacture of Tea in China.* London: Longmans, Brown, Green and Longmans.

Bawden, C.R. 1968. *The Modern History of Mongolia.* New York: Praeger.

Bell, Sir Charles. 1928. *The People of Tibet.* Oxford: Clarendon Press.

Cai, Hengsheng. 1982. Shangdui cha kaoshi (Research on caravan tea). *Lishi yanjiu* 6:117-33.

Cammann, Schuyler. 1951. *Trade through the Himalayas: The Early British Attempts to Open Tibet.* Princeton: Princeton University Press.

Chan, Fanzhou, and Chen Yishi. 1988. Dian-Zang maoyi lishi chutan (A preliminary exploration of the history of Yunnan-Tibetan trade). *Xizang yanjiu* 4:51-58.

Ch'en, Kuo-tung. 1989. Transaction Practices in China's Export Tea Trade, 1760-1833. Conference paper, Second Conference on Modern Chinese Economic History, Academia Sinica, Taibei, Taiwan.

Cheng, Zhenfang, Wang Datong, and Xu Gongsheng. 1984. Cong shijiu shiji de chaye maoyi kan Sha E dui woguo de jingji qinlue (Czarist Russian Economic aggression against China from the perspective of the nineteenth-century tea trade). *Qingshi yanjiuji* 3:319-33.

Chu, T. H. 1936. *Tea Trade in Central China.* Shanghai: Kelly and Walsh.

Ch'u, T'ung-tsu. 1969. *Local Government in China under the Ch'ing.* Stanford: Stanford University Press.

Cooper, T. T. 1871. *Travels of a Pioneer of Commerce.* London: John Murray.

Crawfurd, John. 1820. *History of the Indian Archipelago.* Edinburgh: Archibald Constable and Company. Vol. 3.

De Rosthorn, A. 1895. *On the Tea Cultivation in Western Ssuch'uan and the Tea Trade with Tibet via Tachienlu.* London: Luzac and Company.

Duncan, Marion H. 1964. *Customs and Superstitions of Tibetans.* London.

Esherick, Joseph W., and Mary Backus Rankin, eds. 1990. *Chinese Local Elites and Patterns of Dominance.* Berkeley: University of California Press.

Fletcher, Joseph. 1978. "Ch'ing Inner Asia ca. 1800." In *The Cambridge History of China, Vol. 10, Late Ch'ing, 1800-1911, Part 1,* ed. John K. Fairbank. Cambridge: Cambridge University Press.

Gardella, Robert P. 1988. "The Antebellum Canton Tea Trade: Recent Perspectives." *The American Neptune* 48, 4:261-70.

————. 1990. "The Min-Pei Tea Trade during the Late Ch'ien-lung and Chia-ch'ing Eras: Foreign Commerce and the Mid-Ch'ing Fukien Highlands." In *Development and Decline of Fukien Province in the 17th and 18th Centuries,* ed. E. B. Vermeer. Leiden: E. J. Brill.

Goldstein, Melvyn C. 1989. *A History of Modern Tibet, 1913-1951: The Demise of the Lamaist State.* Berkeley: University of California Press.

Grunfeld, A. Tom. 1987. *The Making of Modern Tibet.* Armonk, N.Y.: M. E. Sharpe.

Gu, Daquan, and Chen Yishi. 1988. *Sichuan chaye shi* (A history of the Sichuan tea industry). Chengdu: Bashu.

Hill, Ann Maxwell. 1989. Chinese Dominance of the Xishuangbanna Tea Trade: An Interregional Perspective. *Modern China* 15, 3:321-45.

Huang, Kangxian. 1972. Qingji Sichuan yu Xizang zhi jian de chaye maoyi (The tea trade between Sichuan and Tibet in the Qing). *Dalu zazhi* 45, 2:38-51.

Huang, Ray. 1974. *Taxation and Governmental Finance in Sixteenth Century Ming China.* New York: Cambridge University Press.

Hutchison, J. 1906. *Indian Brick Tea for Tibet: Report on a Mission to Ssu-chuan.* Calcutta.

Jagchid, Sechin, and Paul Hyer. 1979. *Mongolia's Culture and Society.* Boulder, Colorado: Westview Press.

Jagchid, Sechin, and Van Jay Symons. 1989. *Peace, War, and Trade along the Great Wall: Nomadic-Chinese Interaction through Two Millennia.* Bloomington: Indiana University Press.

Kano Naosada. 1963. Chama boeki no shumatsu (The end of the tea-horse trade). *Toyoshi kenkyu* 22, 3:73-93.

Klaproth, M. 1835. On the Use of Tea in China, and the Laws Respecting this Article of Commerce. *The Canton Register* 8, 11:43-44.

Lattimore, Owen. 1975. *Mongol Journeys.* New York: A.M.S. Press.

_____. 1984. *Wei Yuan and China's Rediscovery of the Maritime World.* Cambridge, Mass.: Council on East Asian Studies, Harvard University.

Leonard, Jane Kate. 1987. Ch'ing Perceptions of Political Reality in the 1820s. *The American Asian Review* 5, 2:63-97 (Summer).

_____. 1988. Geopolitical Reality and the Disappearance of the Maritime Frontier in Qing Times. *The American Neptune* 48, 4:230-36.

Li, Hua. 1987. Qingdai Hubei nongcun jingji zuowu de zhongzhi he difang shangren de huoye—Qingdai difang shangren yanjiu zhi wu (The activities of local merchants and the planting of economic crops in the rural economy of Qing Hubei—researches on Qing local merchants No. 5). *Zhongguo shehui jingjishi yanjiu* 2:50-60.

Liang, Tingnan. [1838] 1968. *Yue haiguan zhi* (Gazetteer of the Guangdong Maritime Customs). Vol. 3. Reprint. Taibei.

Lin, Yongguang. 1982. Qingdai de chama maoyi (The Qing tea-horse trade). *Qingshi luncong* 3:100-16.

Mann, Susan. 1987. *Local Merchants and the Chinese Bureaucracy, 1750-1950.* Stanford: Stanford University Press.

Martynov, A. S. 1981. "Notes on Trade in the Ming Era." In *China and Her Neighbors: From Ancient Times to the Middle Ages,* ed. S. L. Tikhvinsky. Moscow: Progress Publishers.

Murray, Dian. 1987. *Pirates of the South China Coast 1790-1810.* Stanford: Stanford University Press.

NMZ. Nei Menggu zhengxie wenshi ziliao yanjiu weiyuanhui. 1984. *LuMengshang Dashengkuai* (Travelling merchants in Mongolia, the Dashengkuai). N.p.: Nei Menggu wenshi shudian.

Ng, Chin-keong. 1983. *Trade and Society: The Amoy Network on the China Coast 1683-1735.* Singapore: Singapore University Press.

_____. 1990. "The South Fukienese Junk Trade at Amoy from the Seventeenth to Early Nineteenth Centuries." In *Development and Decline of Fukien Province in the 17th and 18th Centuries,* ed. E. B. Vermeer. Leiden: E. J. Brill.

Peng, Zeyi. 1986. Quantification Problems in the Study of Chinese Economic History. *Social Sciences in China* 7, 3:63-88.

Pozdneyev, Aleksei M. 1892. *Mongolia and the Mongols.* Ed. John R. Krueger. Bloomington: Indiana University Press. Vol. 1.

Ran, Guangrong. 1986. Lecture on local archival research in Sichuan and elsewhere in China at the East Asian Institute. Columbia University, New York.

Rockhill, William W. 1891. *The Land of the Lamas.* New York.

Rossabi, Morris. 1970. The Tea and Horse Trade with Inner Asia during the Ming. *Journal of Asian History* 2:136-68.1975.

_____. 1975. *China and Inner Asia: From 1368 to the Present Day.* New York: Pica Press.

_____. 1979. "Muslim and Central Asian Revolts." In *From Ming to Ch'ing: Conquest, Region, and Continuity in Seventeenth-Century China,* ed. Jonathan D. Spence and John E. Wills, Jr. New Haven: Yale University Press.

Rowe, William T. 1984. *Hankow: Commerce and Society in a Chinese City, 1796-1889.* Stanford: Stanford University Press.

Saeki Tomi. 1962. "Cha (Tea)." In *Ajia Rekishi Jiten* (Encyclopaedia of Asian history) 6:163-65. Tokyo: Heibonsha.

Sanjdorj, M. 1980. *Manchu Chinese Colonial Rule in Northern Mongolia.* Translated from the Mongolian and annotated by Urgunge Onon. New York: St. Martin's Press.

Shigeta Atsushi. 1962. Shinmatsu ni okeru Konan cha no shintenkai—Chugoku kindai sangyoshi no tame no dansho (New developments in Hunan tea in the late Qing: A brief study in the history of modern enterprises in China). *Ehime daigaku kiyo* 7, 1:47-62.

Smith, Paul. 1983. Taxing Heaven's Storehouse: The Szechwan Tea Monopoly and the Tsinghai Horse Trade, 1074-1224. Ph.D. diss., University of Pennsylvania.

Snellgrove, David and Hugh Richardson. 1986. *A Cultural History of Tibet.* Boston: Shambala.

Sun, E-tu Zen. 1962-63. The Board of Revenue in Nineteenth-Century China. *Harvard Journal of Asiatic Studies* 24:175-228.

Waldron, Arthur. 1990. *The Great Wall of China: From History to Myth.* Cambridge: Cambridge University Press.

Whitbeck, B. H. 1965. The Tea System of the Ch'ing Dynasty. Unpublished B.A. essay, Harvard University.

Wiest, Nailene Chou. 1984. "The Ming-Ch'ing Transition: Frontier History." In *Soviet Studies of Premodern China: Assessments of Recent Scholarship,* ed. Gilbert Rozman. Ann Arbor: Center for Chinese Studies, University of Michigan.

Wiley, Thomas W. 1986. Macro Exchanges: Tibetan Economics and the Roles of Politics and Religion. *The Tibet Journal* 10, 1:3-20.

Wills, John E., Jr. 1988. Tribute, Defensiveness, and Dependency: Uses and Limits of Some Basic Ideas about Mid-Qing Dynasty Foreign Relations. *The American Neptune* 48, 4:225-29.

Wu, Chengming. 1983. Lun Qingtai qianqi woguo guonei shichang (A discussion of early Qing domestic markets). *Lishi yanjiu* 1:96-106.

————. 1985. "Lun Mingdai guonei shichang he shangren ziben" (A discussion of Ming domestic markets and commercial capital). In *Zhongguo Zibenzhuyi yu guonei shichang* (Chinese capitalism and domestic markets), ed. Wu Chengming. Beijing: Zhongguo shehui kexue chubanshe.

Wu, Hui. 1990. Ming Qing (qian chi) caizheng jiegou bianhua de jiliang fenxi (A quantitative analysis of changes in financial structure in the Ming and early Qing). *Zhongguo shehui jingjishi yanjiu* 3:39-45, 56.

Wu, Juenong. 1990. *Zhongguo difangzhi chaye lishi ziliao xuanji* (Collected source materials on the history of tea in Chinese local gazetteers). Beijing: nongye chubanshe.

Zelin, Madeleine. 1984. *The Magistrate's Tael: Rationalizing Fiscal Reform in Eighteenth-Century Ch'ing China.* Berkeley: University of California Press.

7

Guarantors and Guarantees in Qing Government-Business Relations

Andrea McElderry

Guarantors (*baozheng ren*) have long been an important feature of Chinese business transactions. They are third parties to an agreement who vouch for the assets and character of an obligee in a contractual arrangement and who bear responsibility in cases of non-fulfillment of the terms. The importance of this practice in China contrasts with the West where the development of liability limiting institutions, such as joint-stock companies and insurance, obviated a central role for guarantors. In China, guarantors provided a measure of protection in a context where unlimited liability was the rule. Guarantors served to limit liability by guaranteeing the solvency and good faith of contractual parties whether in the exchange of goods and property, in labor arrangements, or in financial agreements. They served to facilitate impersonal transactions and hence reinforced the ties of kinship and regional association around which Chinese business organizations were built.

Guarantors were a crucial link in the relations between the Qing state and the private economy. This relationship was concerned principally with maintaining the fiscal system and enhancing economic stability throughout the empire, both of which were linked to security. The Qing state's dealings with the private economy centered on the collection of government revenues, regulation of the production, sale, and distribution of key commodities, and the maintenance of an orderly market place and monetary system. Private economic organizations were indispensable to the state's

119

performance of these functions because the regular bureaucracy was very thinly spread across the empire, and it had neither the mission nor the manpower to carry out those tasks that were planted, for the most part, in a sub-district setting.

This paper attempts to define and outline the pivotal role that guarantorship played in state-private undertakings from the early Qing to the Republican periods. It will highlight the role of guarantorship in changing institutions that the Qing state used to facilitate joint government-private undertakings. These include brokers (*yahang*) in local markets, head merchants in foreign trade and in government monopolies, native banks, and guilds. Throughout the Qing period, the government licensed private merchants as brokers. These brokers took on greater importance as the head merchant systems of the early Qing gave way to reliance on private merchants and guild organizations to perform many of the state's functions. Guarantorship was vital to all of these state-private arrangements. Its purpose was to insure that private individuals or organizations would fulfill their obligation to the state.

Brokers, Head Merchants, and Guarantors in the Early Qing Period

In local markets, few commercial transactions between strangers took place without going through a broker. In addition to bringing buyer and seller together, brokers guaranteed the satisfactory completion of the transaction including taking financial responsibility in cases of default (Mann 1987, 179-181; Watson 1972, 23-24). To do business legally, these intermediaries had to obtain licenses (*yatie*). Provincial governments, following Board of Revenue guidelines, set quotas on the number of brokers' licenses, and the local magistrate issued the license upon receiving approval from the provincial treasurer (QCWXTK 732:5148; Mann 1987, 45). The brokers were expected to maintain fair prices, insure correct weights and measures, and collect commercial taxes as well as guarantee transactions. They were to be a hedge against speculators and "scheming" merchants who might drive up prices or create a monopoly in a given market (DQHDSL 765:1; Ng 1983, 167; Mann 1987, 183).

To obtain a license, brokers had to have guarantors. Such a requirement was one way to insure that brokers would fulfill their obligation to the state. Guarantors might be prosperous merchants from the applicant's area or an established firm in the same trade. They vouched for the broker's solvency and his personal conduct (QCWXTK 32:5148; Mann 1987, 183).

Sometimes, the principle of mutual guarantee (*lianhuan baojie*) applied. For example, in the Shanghai silk trade, an applicant for a license had to have five established silk firms agree to take joint responsibility for paying his taxes regardless of malfeasance or losses (Mann 1977-78, 77). If an offense was committed, guarantors could be liable along with brokers. For example, a salt regulation from the Kangxi period stipulated that licensed merchants who bought and sold salt illegally would receive eighty blows. Brokers and guarantors would be punished one degree less (DQHDSL 762:5). However, the government might be more interested in restitution than in punishment. A 1740 edict from the Qianlong Emperor stipulated that brokers found guilty of deception would have their licenses and mutual guarantee revoked and be given a deadline to make restitution. In cases where a broker extorted from merchants, both the guilty broker and those brokers who had mutually guaranteed him could loose their licenses. If the guilty broker did not make restitution before the deadline, then the guarantors were proportionately liable. Guarantors who reported wrong-doing on the part of those they guaranteed could avoid punishment. On the other hand, officials who issued licenses illegally were to be impeached and punished while clerks implicated in such cases would be flogged (QCWXTK 732:5148-5149).

The fact that guarantors were most often from the same trade, region, or family as the obligee had both strengths and weaknesses. On one hand, close ties meant that social obligations reinforced economic commitments. On the other hand, the guarantor and obligee might more easily act together against state interests. For example, a Guizhou official reported corrupt practices in the acquisition of military rations and resultant general shortages. Sub-officials who had been sent to supervise the grain market were using false family names and collaborating with their relatives "to adjust arbitrarily the scales up and down for their own profit." The official concluded, "Although there are many people who have permits to receive grain and are guaranteed, there are many false names and it's hard to trust them" (YZZP 5, 29:48-49b).

Because of such problems, some officials attempted to reduce the state's reliance on brokers. One way to do so was to assert direct bureaucratic control over functions assigned to them. In 1731, Shi Lin, the governor-general of Shanxi, reported that Gao Yongzi, the new district magistrate at Lingchuan, had found that brokers and gentry were misappropriating taxes. As a result, the magistrate collected them directly, remitting the tax quota plus a surplus of over 169 *taels*. The governor-general concluded, "Now the brokers have no way to fleece the people" (YZZP 18, 110:244b-245).

Such action, however, was limited because the regular bureaucracy lacked sufficient personnel.

Another approach is illustrated by a 1735 proposal from Zhao Hong'en, the governor in Nanjing, who proposed that the government establish "people's brokers" (*minya*). Zhao reported that a commoner and a bannerman had been apprehended posing as fuel brokers, forcibly intercepting rural people who had come to sell fuel outside of the Huyang Gate. An investigation revealed that although the licensed brokers had been aware of the extortion, they had not reported it to the government. Zhao wrote, "If [the government] does not establish broker firms, [I] am really afraid that . . . prices will rise. If the bannermen use force to buy extortionately, then conflict could ensue." His solution was to "set up one 'people's broker' at each of Nanjing's four gates." He ordered local magistrates to select honest and well off (*xuanshi*) people to serve as brokers. Like other brokers, these people's brokers were to collect a small fee for the government. "These measures," Zhao concluded, "[will insure] security and harmony" (YZZP 18, 108:74-75b).

Frequently, however, official efforts centered on making the broker system work by strengthening the guarantor system. In 1745, the Hubei governor was concerned about the large number of marginally solvent brokers in Hankou. He ordered the brokers to produce an additional guarantor, a wealthy man recognized in the community. These guarantors had to sign a written bond and take a verbal oath before the Hanyang magistrate (Rowe 1984, 189). According to a 1740 decree from the Qianlong Emperor, local officials in Jiangsu were issuing more licenses than provincial quotas allowed. They either claimed that old markets were new ones or continued to appoint brokers after the provincial government had reduced the quotas. The decree, among other things, spelled out guarantor liability (QCWXTK 732:5149). This latter example suggests that some of the strains on the broker system were connected to economic growth and the resultant proliferation in markets. By this time, economic change also was placing strains on the head merchant systems.

The establishment of head merchants (*zongshang*) in the late seventeenth and early eighteenth centuries in certain trades was another way in which the government sought to insure that its interests were protected. Head merchants were mutually responsible for each other and also acted as guarantors for other merchants active in the trade. These principles are illustrated by examples from the salt and ginseng monopolies and from foreign trade. Early in the Kangxi period (1667), the Lianghuai salt administration appointed twenty-four wealthy head merchants to supervise and guarantee the shipping merchants. To ship in a particular year, a merchant had to obtain a license (*zhudan*) and be listed on a tax register at the Lianghuai headquarters under the name of the head merchant, who stood as his guarantor. The head merchants "were authorized by the state to guarantee the proper conduct of merchants and to enforce collective financial responsibility." This head merchant system remained in place until the 1830s (Metzger 1972, 25).

In the Yongzheng reign (1730), head merchants replaced Manchu and Mongolian bannermen in the administration of the Imperial Household's ginseng monopoly (Symons 1981, 10-11). These merchants, usually brewers who owned the large cauldrons necessary for processing ginseng, were held mutually responsible for each other's activities, for delivering the assigned quotas, and for the quality of the harvest (Symons 1981, 13-19, 21-23, 42-46). They also vouched for the reliability of the gatherers whom they had to recruit and provision. In return, the merchants received frontier trading privileges and could retain some of the ginseng collected.

The Yongzheng reign also saw the establishment of a head merchant system in maritime trade where mutual responsibility was already the rule. According to a 1707 regulation, every ten ships were to be mutually responsible for the others' conduct and activities while at sea, and each ship had to be guaranteed by an officially designated firm (Ng 1983, 154, 171). After the second trade ban was lifted in 1728, monopolies were granted to head merchants at Ningbo, Zhabu, and Shanghai to oversee the Japan trade and at Amoy and Canton to oversee the Nanyang trade. Head merchants soon were established in other ports in Jiangsu and Zhejiang (Shulman 1989, 177, 211-12; Viraphol 1977, 125; YZZP 18, 112:40-b). Mutually responsible for each other, these merchants enforced government regulations which included a ban on rice exports and a prohibition against Chinese remaining abroad. Head merchants were also charged with guarding against smugglers and pirates and insuring that foreign merchants paid the appropriate duties (Cushman 1975, 41). They stood at the top of a hierarchy of guarantees.

Sea-going merchants and vessels had to be guaranteed by a head merchant (YZZP 18, 112:40-b; Shulman 1989, 190-91). In addition, each ship had to be guaranteed by three firms in the same business, and these firms, in turn, had to have guarantors (GDYCZ 9:568-69; YZZP 14, 87:100-b; Viraphol 1977, 121). All vessels that traveled abroad had to file a report on each one of the men on board. These men first needed to have a family member vouch for the fact that they would not remain abroad. Then they had to obtain a written bond (*juyinjie*), including their finger-prints, from a local official (*difang guan*). Port officials checked these documents and registered the ages, descriptions, and native places of each individual, under the name of the sea-going vessel. They also examined the goods being exported and verified each merchant's license both at departure and return (YZZP 18, 112:40-b). Shipbuilding, likewise, required licenses and guarantors. A merchant had to have the headman of both the harbor and his native village as well as a neighbor testify to his reliability, both financial and otherwise (Cushman 1975, 58; Ng 1983, 153-54).

Problems attended the establishment of the system. It seems that it was easier to memorialize the emperor than to get merchants to return to their native places to obtain the necessary papers. The Fujian governor-general, Gao Qizhuo, memorialized in 1728 that, although he had publicized the new regulations for several months, some merchants had still not complied. He asked, "How can anyone not be informed of this and get a bond while waiting for the trade winds?" On one boat, he continued, "the captain and most of the sailors were from Quanzhang, not far away. I ordered them to [return to their native place] and obtain a bond before [I would] approve [their sailing]. I also issued an order that those returning . . . with their bond would have three days to have it approved" (GDYCC 9:568-69). Another official worried that if merchants failed to obtain the proper bonds from their native place before the wind direction changed, their sailing would be delayed (YZZP 4, 26:45).

The latter example illustrates the vested interest officials in the maritime provinces had in the overseas trade. It brought income to their official, and, in some cases, their personal treasuries. Officials could and did find ways to circumvent central government regulations. In Amoy, only the provincial treasurer's office was empowered to issue licenses to head merchants who dealt with foreign traders. However, authorities "could always ignore the regulation and appoint an ad hoc group from among the favoured and trusted merchants to handle the occasional visits by foreign ships" (Ng 1983, 173).

Merchants also found ways to circumvent the regulations. To trade directly with Southeast Asia or Japan, a ship needed to be guaranteed by a head merchant. But intracoastal vessels could and did transport goods to Canton from other ports for transshipment to Southeast Asia or for sale to foreign merchants. Shortly after the establishment of the head merchant guild (*yanghang*) at Amoy, commercial guilds (*shanghang*) sprang up to guarantee these intercoastal vessels (Viraphol 1977, 128). Merchants licensed to trade in Japan for copper often went to Southeast Asia first, delaying copper shipments for up to two years (Shulman 1989, 182).

In some cases, merchants falsified bonds and ship registers. Governor-general Gao Qizhuo reported in 1728 that merchants, shopkeepers, and sailors connected with an Amoy vessel "are working together hand in glove to deceive. . . . There are ten temporary sailors who have been hired to replace others for reason of death or illness. The origin of their bond is unclear, and their fingerprints do not match [those on the surety]. Moreover, the ship's register of merchants has many aboard who are from different prefectures and departments.'' He ordered the merchants and sailors to obtain proper bonds and told them that if even one registered person remained overseas, all would be punished severely (GDYCZ 9:568-69). In the same communication, Gao reported the seizure of a boat smuggling iron from the mainland to Taiwan. The would-be purchaser planned to sell it to a foreign boat captain. On investigation, Gao found that the mainland smuggler had been guaranteed properly by a broker in Amoy and approved by officials. But when the ship was seized, some unregistered merchants were aboard.

Guarantors were liable for criminal punishment in cases where maritime trade regulations were breached. In an eighteenth-century case involving the illegal export of rice, two guarantors were sentenced to flogging. Security concerns, fears that supplies might go to potential rebels overseas, and worry over domestic grain shortages, lay behind the prohibition. One of the offenders, a merchant in Amoy, had been assigned to stand surety for a ship carrying a government shipment to Taiwan. On the return, another merchant, based in Taiwan, guaranteed the same ship now carrying government rice. A storm blew the ship to Luzon where the ship's captain sold the government rice. Both security merchants were tried and sentenced to be punished by flogging (Ng 1983, 172).

Another eighteenth-century example indicates that at least the Yongzheng Emperor had questions about the efficacy of threatening criminal sanctions against guarantors. An official proposed arresting and questioning guarantors for overseas vessels if the number of people on board or their ages and descriptions did not tally with the register. The emperor commented that he feared that ''people from the interior who go overseas find all sorts of sternly worded regulations very, very laughable.'' He added, ''If they are collaborating with foreign barbarians in illicit activities and have something to hide, I assume that they will be prepared for [an investigation]'' (YZZP 14, 87:99b-100b). Here again a security issue was involved: the concern that people remaining overseas might join with foreigners to commit illegal acts.

On the other hand, having a proper bond could keep a merchant out of trouble. In 1728, a merchant's junk was mistakenly identified by the naval patrol as one involved in illegal activities. A broker in Kiaochow testified saying that the accused merchant was his old acquaintance and customer. Authorities also checked the personal description as recorded in his trading license and were satisfied that the merchant was properly registered (Ng 1983, 160).

Brokers, Guilds, and Guarantors in the Late Qing

After 1800, head merchant systems declined for a number of reasons: increased trade volume, commodity shortages, the rising price of silver, foreign pressure, and internal rebellion. One result was that the state placed greater reliance on brokers to achieve its economic objectives. At the same time, guilds took on greater importance as intermediaries between the state and private business. Guarantors, however, remained an essential feature of state-private relations in the late Qing.

Concern with the effectiveness of head merchant systems is evident as early as the Qianlong reign. Beginning in 1744, the court experimented with alternative arrangements in the ginseng monopoly and in the copper trade but eventually re-established head merchants. In 1744, the court replaced head merchants with direct bureaucratic control in the ginseng monopoly. Apparently it was becoming increasingly difficult for the head merchants to provide the "high ginseng quotas established by the government" (Symons 1981, 15). Officials were no more successful in fulfilling the quotas. Around 1800, the court once again placed the responsibility with merchants but this time with 400 merchants rather than a select few (Symons 1981, 19). In the copper trade with Japan, the government appointed head merchants in 1728 as part of the general policy for overseas trade. These merchants received government loans, but by the early Qianlong period, many of them had defaulted. As a result, the court replaced them with "private" merchants, men who supplied their own capital and were permitted to sell some copper in the open market (Shulman 1989, 187). Then in 1744, the same year that officials took responsibility for ginseng quotas, the court financed some "imperial" merchants to participate in the copper trade along with the private merchants. Eleven years later, in 1755, the Qianlong Emperor re-established a head merchant system that lasted until disruptions of the Taiping Rebellion brought it to an end (Shulman 1989, 190-91).

During the Taiping Rebellion, head merchants were replaced in other areas of the economy as well. Authorities in Hankou replaced head merchants in the salt trade with licensed brokers. These firms had to "enter into a security bond (*hubao*) whereby financial responsibility for any impropriety would be shared equally by all" (Rowe 1984, 117). Earlier, in the 1830s, the Lianghuai Salt Administration had been faced with the fact that salt tax increases and the rising price of silver relative to copper had driven up salt prices and decreased economic incentives for the head merchants. The solution was to switch to a system of issuing certificates to small-scale traders (Metzger 1972, 20, 42). Presumably these traders needed guarantors to obtain the salt certificates. In foreign trade, the Treaty of Nanking (1842) brought an end to the head merchant system only to see new forms of guarantorship appear. Western firms required guarantors and bonds for their compradores who, in turn, guaranteed their Chinese staffs. In Shanghai, compradores also guaranteed the *qianzhuang*, or native banks, which received loans from foreign companies (Hao 1970, 156-77; McElderry 1976, 91). The *qianzhuang* themselves formed guilds that took on importance as regulators of the money market. By the late nineteenth century, guilds were common not only in banking but in other trades as well.

The development of guilds in the late eighteenth and nineteenth centuries created a new link in relations between the Qing state and the private economy. Guilds took over broker functions. They insured the use of correct weights and measures and of the correct currency, regulated the prices and quality of goods in their particular trade, and insured the payment of commercial taxes. In addition, they enforced their own rules and guaranteed their own members.

In Prasenji Duara's terminology, guilds may be viewed as "protective brokerages" whereas licensed brokers or *yahang* may be seen as "entrepreneurial brokerages." In his study of rural administration and tax collection in the Republican period, Duara describes protective brokerages as organizations seeking "to circumvent the predatory activities of tax farmers and state brokers by choosing collectively a representative of their own to deal with the task at hand" (Duara 1988, 52). Entrepreneurial brokerage was the system of sub-administrative personnel, such as clerks, who performed official functions in return for collecting fees. Because protective brokerages were organizations that developed within the marketing structure rather than being imposed from without, they could exercise "legitimate leadership in the nexus." For this reason, Duara suggests that the state preferred protective brokerages to entrepreneurial brokerages in administration (1988, 55).

Guild formation was, in part, a response to state reliance on brokers. In some cases, brokers themselves founded guilds. For example, in Shanghai in 1860, silk brokers formed a guild as a result of a solicitation of funds from the Zhejiang governor. After its establishment, the guild stipulated the procedures that potential silk merchants had to follow to obtain brokers' licenses (Mann 1977-78, 77-78). Other guilds formed for protection against brokers (Xu and Wu 1985, 293). According to an inscription from Beijing's indigo guild in the Qianlong period, "brokers were swindling [indigo dealers], bringing false charges, and causing litigation." The indigo dealers appointed their own agents to act as brokers. With the surplus fees collected, the indigo guild was founded in 1810 (Xu and Wu 1985, 293; Niida 1976, 2:362-63). The author of a history of Beijing's oil guild, written in the Republican period, comments, "After our oil guild was established [in the Kangxi reign] we were no longer bothered by [brokers and middlemen]" (Niida 1976, 2:182-83). In another example from Beijing, a member of the Hedong (Shanxi) tobacco guild enlisted the guild's support to get a broker to treat him fairly, and was successful. In 1753, apparently with guild backing, a *tong* oil dealer gained the support of a local official against a swindling broker (Xu and Wu 1985, 293).

In the nineteenth century, the government increasingly looked to guilds to maintain an orderly market place and collect revenue. Guilds took over certain government functions, such as stipulating procedures for obtaining brokers' licenses and enforcing "fair trade" rules. And they policed their own membership. In effect, they stood as guarantors to the government for their members. These functions are reflected in guild rules. Guilds sought to guarantee their members' solvency and integrity but invoked sanctions against members who breached guild rules.

Formal guarantors were not required universally for guild membership, but prospective guild members did have to be "introduced" by a member in good standing, as a kind of informal surety. Evidence suggests that the use of formal guarantors had become more common by the Republican period. Wider marketing networks and weaker government could account for such a development. In the early Republican period, the "five clans" (*wuzu*) controlled the Beijing oil market and, apparently, people associated with these clans could open shops without presenting guarantors. However, prospective oil shop operators from outside the city as well as oil processing and hemp oil firms, needed guarantors to set up business (Niida 1976, 2:174). It is not clear whether this guarantor requirement was new or a revision of an earlier requirement. It does indicate that guarantors were more likely to be required when close family and regional ties within a trade became diluted.

When guarantors did not insure the smooth functioning of the market place, guilds invoked sanctions. Penalties specified in guild rules reflect guilds' regulatory and administrative functions. Regulatory concerns included use of correct weights and measures, and deception in this area carried some of the heavier sanctions. An 1828 document from a Beijing dyemakers' guild bemoans the fact that "the moral standards in our society have greatly deteriorated. . . . Of late, people have become cunning. There has been a great deal of exchange of *tong* oil, but no one has reported the exact amount of this to our guild. It is beneath our dignity to audit the amount of member transactions." Nonetheless, the document specifies that if guild merchants fail to disclose correct amounts, they would be "assessed a fine to pay for an entire theatrical performance to be presented before our deities replete with a large banquet" (Chen and Myers 1978, 25; Niida 1976, 2:323). A 1904 set of sugar guild rules from Tainan began with similar concern about society's morals. Penalties ranged from a simple fine for not paying a commission due a seller, to being fined and then charged in court or turned over to local officials for employing containers of a heavier weight than specified by the guild. The use of product weights other than those specified by the guild meant paying for a theatrical performance (Chen and Myers 1978, 22-24). In late nineteenth-century Wenchou, the druggists' guild required mediation if one member was in debt to another and transferred his business to a third party. The guild would bring the three parties together, and the debtor would not be allowed to trade with the third party until he settled his debt with the second (Macgowan 1882-83, 145).

The severest sanction was expulsion from the guild which could effectively deny a man's livelihood, given guild power in the market place (Burgess [1928], 200; Jamieson [1921], 114-15). In effect, guilds had their own courts. The Tainan sugar guild regulations provided that sanctions for irregularities not mentioned specifically would be taken up for discussion by all guild members to decide on the kind of punishment (Chen and Myers 1978, 24). Burgess reported that, in most Beijing guilds, "at the time of the annual meeting, the respected elders of experience are appointed to be judges of persons reported to have broken the guild rules" ([1928], 200). Lack of jurisdiction over non-members, however, limited how far guilds could replace government intervention in the market place.

The financial market in the late nineteenth and early twentieth centuries exemplifies the interactions between the state and private business and the continued importance of guarantors in the late nineteenth century. Increased trade volume in this period led to the proliferation of native banks in commercial centers throughout the empire: *qianpu* in Beijing, *piaohao* or Shanxi banks in North China, *qianzhuang* in Shanghai and Hankou, and *yinhao* in Tianjin. Guilds formed by each of these financial institutions served as intermediaries between the government and the money market. They oversaw the financial market, enforced guild and government rules, and guaranteed their members. However, with continued economic growth, these guilds were either unwilling or unable to monitor the opening of undercaptialized banks and insure sufficient reserves against banknotes. Hence government officials often had to intervene in the money market.

Various agencies of the Qing government licensed financial institutions; and to receive a license, these banks needed guarantors. Their respective guilds oversaw these guarantor requirements. Historically, the government had taken greater regulatory interest in the Beijing *qianpu* and the Shanxi *piaohao* because of its own fiscal interests. The Shanxi banks held and transferred government funds. To open a *piaohao*, a prospective banker had to obtain a Board of Revenue license, and to get a license, he needed a guarantee from an established bank. In other words, he needed a guarantee from a member of one of the Shanxi bank guilds. But these banks withheld guarantees from anyone but fellow Shanxi provincials (Chen 1937, 148-49). State concern with the Beijing *qianpu* dated back to the early days of Manchu rule and was related closely to attempts to regulate the price of copper in the capital (Shulman 1989, 259-61). The banks needed government approval to open; and to gain approval, they needed guarantors. If the *qianpu* failed, its owners had one year to make restitution, and if full restitution had not been completed in three years, the guarantors had to make good on the amount (Yang 1962, 157; Zhongguo renmin yinhang 1960, 16).

In late nineteenth-century Hankou, a bank had to have guild endorsement before the local magistrate approved its petition for issuing credit. To obtain guild endorsement, a prospective banker had to present a joint security bond (*lianming baozheng*) with the signatures of a minimum of five guild members as guarantors (Rowe 1984, 172-74). The dominant Shanghai *qianzhuang* developed in the International Concession and were hence beyond direct imperial regulation. However, their guild did institute a guarantor requirement although exactly when is not clear. Republican regulations required a guild member guarantor who was responsible for any bad debts of the new member for an indefinite period (McElderry 1976, 34; Kuo 1933, 814). Both the Shanghai and Shanxi banks required guarantors for their employees. The Shanxi banks virtually held branch manager's families as hostages (Jernigan 1905, 283; Wei 1939, 316).

Despite these regulatory procedures, a number of financial crises in the late nineteenth century necessitated official intervention. At one point, in Hankou, a high rate of business failure and particularly a high rate of default on banknotes prompted an official to try unsuccessfully to prohibit the circulation of banknotes. After this, local administrators left supervision of credit to the financial guild that instituted the guarantor requirements described above. In Shanghai, the local magistrate (*daotai*) became involved in successive money market crises between 1883 and 1910. Because of the jurisdictional complications of extraterritoriality, his role was limited largely to bailing out insolvent banks (McElderry 1976, 83-130). The government had more leverage in the cases of the Shanxi banks and Beijing *qianpu*.

The 1883 Shanghai crisis was part of a larger problem caused by the devastating failure of Hu Guangyong's banking network. This crisis focused the Board of Revenue's attention on "private" remittance banks or unlicensed *piaohao*. Many of the proprietors of private remittance banks in the late nineteenth century, such as Hu Guangyong, were not Shanxi men. Hence, in the Board of Revenue's eyes, they lacked a proper guarantee from an established banker. According to an 1884 Board of Revenue memorial, since these banks were called *piaohao*, depositors might believe they were handling government funds. Rather, the memorial asserted, they were "clip joints" set up by "scheming merchants" to fleece the people. The proposal called for local officials to investigate whether the proprietor of a *piaohao* was "a wealthy man" and to insure that he had a guarantee from another bank. A yearly investigation in every province was to verify the banker's name, native place, the location of the bank, and the name of the guarantor. In addition, each bank had to pay an annual tax of 600 *taels*. Only then would the Board of Revenue issue a license (Chen 1937, 149).

The Boxer Rebellion brought widespread failure among Beijing *qianpu*. As a result of the fighting, only twenty-plus out of a total of 511 *qianpu* in the capital and its environs remained. Most of these banks had been unable to redeem their insufficiently backed notes at face value. The reckless issue of notes, local officials concluded, lay ultimately in the weakness of the guarantor system. A memorial from two Beijing officials reviewed the situation:

> As time went on, local magistrates and *yamen* clerks stopped strictly overseeing the finances of new *qianpu*. [Officials and clerks] did as they wished and searched for guarantors at their convenience. *Qianpu* with guarantors made out false documents which were not investigated. As a result, the number of unbacked banks increased significantly. If one failed, . . . they would settle by discounting 10-20 percent of the cash value [of the notes they issued]. And because the waste paper guarantors had a three-year limit [to make restitution], their compliance was very leisurely. Besides this, every amount

which is not paid in full causes . . . great distress for the masses (JDZD, section 1).

The officials' proposal, approved by the emperor, specified that henceforth prospective *qianpu* proprietors would need three guarantors rather than one. Two of these had to be prosperous *qianpu*. The third could be "a gold shop, assay shop, a *piaohao* (Shanxi bank), foreign goods shop, piece goods shop, oil and wine firm, tea firm, an official salt merchant, a large dried fruit shop, a silk goods shop, or any well-known and prosperous firm." Detailed regulations specified procedures for registering with the *yamen* (JDZD, section 3).

Guarantor liability also was spelled out. One of the two guarantor *qianpu* had responsibility to investigate the accounts of the bank they guaranteed and report the issuance of any unbacked banknotes to the appropriate official. The regulations stipulated:

If the designated guarantor is lax and doesn't investigate, allowing the *qianpu* with the deficit to fail and [its proprietors] to abscond, then the manager of the *qianpu* [standing surety] will be pre-emptorily arrested. . . . If the [proprietor of the failed *qianpu*] absconds and is not caught or if he is caught and doesn't have the means to make restitution, then each guarantor firm will be responsible to make restitution according to their apportioned amounts. They must not be allowed to shirk their duty in the slightest way (JDZD, section 1).

In 1904, another memorial reported that the *yamen* "has been assidious in investigating guarantors, and few firms have failed. The people commend this, and the corrupt think of ways [to get around the regulations]. They set up outside the gate and issue notes. This practice is spreading day by day. At the end of 1903, I again ordered the businessmen to return to the old rules and to increase each shop's guarantors by one. Still there are very few conforming to the regulations" (JDZD, section 4).

Epilogue

Was it reasonable for officials in 1904 to expect businessmen to return to the old rules in the changed economic and political context of the early twentieth century? To stabilize the market place in 1903-1904, the Beijing officials proposed a solution similar to their eighteenth-century predecessors. They sought to strengthen the guarantor system. The "modern" alternative to guarantors would have been to set minimum levels of cash and security reserves against banknote issue. Cash deposits were hardly unknown in the Qing. By the nineteenth century, such deposits had become common in rental of agricultural land (Zelin 1986, 504, 508; Perdue 1987, 154-56). Shanxi bank guilds and some other guilds required deposits from their members (Jernigan 1905, 285). By the turn of the twentieth century, foreign firms usually required their compradores' sureties to post substantial bonds (Hao 1970, 157-60). In some instances, the Qing government required cash deposits. Ginseng merchants in the nineteenth century had to make a cash deposit with the court which was forfeited if the diggers they guaranteed absconded (Symons 1981, 22). However, the institutional structure to require reserves and cash and security bonding was only beginning to develop in the first decade of the twentieth century.

Republican governments had different institutional options and showed a tendency to prefer cash bonding over guarantors in regulating markets. For instance, the Produce Exchange Law adopted in 1921 specified that before opening for business, the exchange had to deposit a business bond amounting to one-third of its capital with the Ministry of Agriculture and Commerce (Fong 1934, 65). The 1931 bank law (not enforced until 1935) set minimal capital requirements and mandated that banks register their capital and place reserves in the Central Bank (McElderry 1976, 177-78; Zhongguo renmin yinhang 1960, 212-16).

Alternative ways of limiting liability, however, did not supplant guarantorship in government-business relations nor in private business. Republican governments continued to rely on guaranteed brokers and on business associations, guilds, and Chambers of Commerce, to perform government functions (Mann 1987, 179-81). Traditional business organizations continued to require employees to have guarantors, and modern enterprises, such as factories, banks, and department stores, adopted the practice (Hershatter 1986, 145; Yao 1967, 29; SASS 258-59). After World War II, the Nationalist government specified that investors who wished to open a bank had to have a letter of guarantee from a bankers' association or a chamber of commerce (Zhongguo renmin yinhang 1960, 353).

The continued use of guarantors in the Republican period can be attributed, at least partially, to the level of development of liability-limiting institutions. The disruptions of war and inflation curtailed the development of institutional alternatives to guarantorship. It is probably no accident that the post-war bank law of the Nationalist government required guarantors, whereas the 1931 bank law simply required registration of capital and reserves in the Central Bank. People may have been more dependable than cash. As in the Qing period, limited central authority perpetuated reliance on semi-official groups, such as brokers and guilds, and on their already established guarantor systems.

The establishment of the People's Republic in 1949 brought a strong central authority and major economic changes. With the introduction of central planning in the early 1950s, the government took over unlimited liability for the economy. The state became, in effect, both the guarantor and manager of the economy. Socialist agencies took over the functions of liability limiting institutions in a capitalist economy. Since 1978 with the economic reforms, the state has been attempting to limit its liability (McElderry 1990-91, 45). Guarantors have reappeared in some government-private arrangements as one way of limiting the state's liability. For instance, some city governments now lease small- and medium-sized municipally owned enterprises to private managers who, among other sureties, have to provide guarantors (Han 1988, 26; Wang 1988, 27-28).

While the role of guarantors *per se* is apparently limited, the concept of guarantorship has been central to the economic reforms. In the "Factory Managers' Responsibility System," various organizations from the Commmunist Party committees to labor unions are deemed *inter alia* guarantors of production, of the factory director's authority, of the implementation of party policy, and of workers' welfare (JPRS 12:37-41; Chamberlain 1987). Such language suggests that although the development of modern institutions may obviate a central role for guarantors, it does not necessarily eliminate guarantorship as a concept in economic organization. This concept of guarantorship in the People's Republic is all the more significant because of its historical roots in the Qing period.

References

Burgess, John Stewart. [1928] 1966. *The Guilds of Peking*. Taibei: Ch'eng-wen.

Chamberlain, Heath. 1987. Party-Management Relations in Chinese Industries: Some Political Dimensions of Economic Reform. *The China Quarterly* 112:631-61.

Chen, Fu-mei Chang, and Ramon Myers. 1978. Customary Law and the Economic Growth of China during the Ch'ing Period. *Ch'ing-shih wen-t'i* 3, 10:4-27.

Chen, Qitian. 1937. *Shanxi piaozhuang kaolue* (A Short history of Shanxi banks). N.p.

Cushman, Jennifer. 1975. Fields from the Sea: Chinese Junk Trade with Siam during the Late Eighteenth and Early Nineteenth Centuries. Ph.D. diss., Cornell.

DQHDSL. *Da Qing huidian shili* (Collected statutes and sub-statutes of the Qing). [1899] 1963. Reprint. Taibei.

Duara, Prasenjit. 1988. *Culture, Power, and the State, Rural North China, 1900-1942.* Stanford: Stanford University Press.

Fong, H. D. 1934. *Grain Trade and Milling in Tientsin.* Peking: Sanyu Press.

GDYCZ. *Gongzhong dang Yongzheng chao zouzhe* (Secret palace memorials of the Yongzheng period). 1977-80. Taibei: National Palace Museum. Vols. 9, 17.

Han, Baocheng. 1988. Wuhan: Enterprises Compete and Thrive. *Beijing Review* 31, 3:24-27.

Hao, Yen-p'ing. 1970. *The Comprador in Nineteenth Century China: Bridge between East and West.* Cambridge, Mass.: Harvard University Press.

Hershatter, Gail. 1986. *The Workers of Tianjin, 1900-1949.* Stanford: Stanford University Press.

Jamieson, George. [1921] 1970. *Chinese Family and Commercial Law.* Reprint. Hong Kong: Vetch and Lee.

Jernigan, Thomas R. 1905. *China in Law and Commerce.* New York: MacMillan.

JDZD. *Jingdu zhengdun qianshang piantong zhangcheng* (Revised regulations for Beijing native bank business). N.d. Tokyo: Tokyo University Oriental Institute Library.

JPRS. Joint Publications Research Service: China Reports, Economic Affairs. [1984] 1985. Translation of "Chuangzhoushi guoying qiye shixing changzhang fuzezhi de janxing guiding" (Provisional regulations for the implementation of the factory director responsibility system in the state enterprises in Changzhou). *Jingji guanli* (Economic management) 12:37-41.

Kuo, Xiaoxian. 1933. Shanghai de qianzhuang (Shanghai native banks). *Shanghai shi zongzhi guan qikan* (Journal of the Shanghai historical society) 1:803-47.

Macgowan, Daniel J. 1882-83. Chinese Guilds and Their Rules. *China Review* (Shanghai) 12:144-48.

[Mann] Jones, Susan. 1978-79. The Organization of Trade at the County Level: Brokerage and Tax Farming in the Republican Period. *Select Papers from the Center for Far Eastern Studies,* no. 3. Chicago: University of Chicago.

Mann, Susan L. 1987. *Local Merchants and the Chinese Bureaucracy, 1750-1950*. Stanford: Stanford University Press.

McElderry, Andrea L. 1976. *Shanghai Old-style Banks (Ch'ien-chuang), 1800-1935*. Ann Arbor: Center for Chinese Studies, The University of Michigan.

————. 1990-91. Guarantors and Guarantees in Chinese Economic Reforms. *The Journal of Intercultural Studies* (Kansai University of Foreign Studies, Japan), nos. 17 and 18.

Metzger, Thomas A. 1972. "The Organizational Capabilities of the Ch'ing State in the Field of Commerce: The Liang-huai Salt Monopoly, 1740-1880." In *Economic Organization in Chinese Society*, ed. William E. Willmott. Stanford: Stanford University Press, 18-45.

Ng, Chin-keong. 1983. *Trade and Society, the Amoy Network on the China Coast, 1683-1735*. Singapore: Singapore University Press.

Niida, Noboru, comp. 1976. *Pekin kosho girudo shiryoshu* (A collection of materials on Beijing trade and merchant guilds). Tokyo.

Perdue, Peter C. 1987. *Exhausting the Earth, State and Peasant in Hunan, 1500-1850*. Cambridge, Mass.: Council on East Asian Studies, Harvard University.

QCWXTK. *Qingchao wenxian tongkao* (Comprehensive selection of documentary records from the Qing dynasty). 1936. Shanghai.

Rowe, William T. 1984. *Hankow: Commerce and Society in a Chinese City, 1796-1889*. Stanford: Stanford University Press.

SASS. Shanghai shehui kexue yuan, jingji yanjiu bu (The Shanghai Academy of Social Sciences, Economics Institute), et al., comps. 1988. *Shanghai jindai baihuo shangye shi* (A history of modern Shanghai department store business). Shanghai: Shanghai shehui kexue yuan chuban she.

Shulman, Anna See Ping Leon. 1989. Copper, Copper Cash, and Government Controls in Ch'ing China (1644-1795). Ph.D. diss., University of Maryland.

Symons, Jay Van. 1981. *Ch'ing Ginseng Management: Ch'ing Monopolies in Microcosm*. Tempe: Center for Asian Studies, Arizona State University.

Viraphol, Sarasin. 1977. *Tribute and Profit: Sino-Siamese Trade, 1652-1853*. Cambridge, Mass.: Council on East Asian Studies, Harvard University.

Wang, Yongfu. 1988. Famous Lessee on Leasing System. *Beijing Review* 31, 5:26-28.

Watson, Andrew, trans. 1972. *Transport in Transition: the Evolution of Traditional Shipping in China.* Ann Arbor: Center for Chinese Studies, The University of Michigan.

Wei, Jixian. 1939. *Shanxi piaozhuang* (Shanxi banks). Xinju: Shuowen she shushe.

Xu, Dixin and Wu Chengming. 1985. *Zhongguo ziben ahuyi di mengya* (Sprouts of Chinese capitalism). Beijing: Renmin chuban she.

Yang, Duanliu. 1962. *Qingdai huobi jinrong shi* (A history of money and finance in China). Beijing.

Yao, Songling. 1967. Zhonghang fuwu ji (A record of service in the Bank of China). *Zhuangji wenxue* (Biographical literature) 1, 6:27-33.

YZZP. *Yongzheng zhupi yuzhi* (Imperially endorsed memorials of the Yongzheng reign). 1965. 10 vols. Taibei.

Zelin, Madeleine. 1986. The Rights of Tenants in Mid-Qing Sichuan: A Study of Land-related Lawsuits in the Baxian Archives. *Journal of Asian Studies* 45, 3:499-526.

Zhongguo renmin yinhang, Shanghai shi fenhang (The People's Bank of China, Shanghai branch), ed. 1960. *Shanghai qianzhuang shiliao* (Historical materials on Shanghai native banks). Shanghai: Shanghai renmin chuban she.

8

The Qing State and Merchant Enterprise: The China Merchants' Company, 1872-1902

Chi-kong Lai

Introduction

Since the late 1950s, China scholars have examined the Qing state's involvement in late nineteenth-century Chinese business enterprises (Chan 1977, 1980; Feuerwerker 1958; Hao 1971, 1986; Liu 1959, 1964; Zhang 1979; Xia 1985). The general purport of these works is to emphasize the severe limitations of government-sponsored Chinese enterprises, especially in comparison with developments taking place in Meiji Japan, casting China's early modernization efforts in a dim light.

Another theme running through the literature is the negative role of the state. Albert Feuerwerker (1958) argues that bureaucratic capitalism was one of the basic reasons for China's failure to industrialize. Duan Benluo contends that "when private capital was invested in an enterprise 'operated by merchants under government supervision,' it was as if it had fallen into a trap" (1982, 14-18). Scholars have insisted that the extraction of funds by state officials seriously hindered the development of modern enterprises (Balazs 1964). Wellington Chan (1977, 1980) claims that because politics took precedence over economics, poor economic decisions were made. Other scholars would argue that in China the critical link between the role of the state and economic development was negative (Coble 1980).

Recent studies, however, have made a more systematic reevaluation of the nature of the modern Chinese economy. Works by William Rowe (1984), Yen-p'ing Hao (1986), Thomas Rawski (1989), Loren Brandt (1989), and David Faure (1989) have challenged the conventional view that the late nineteenth and early twentieth centuries constituted a period of stagnation or decline. Rawski sees significant growth in the modern sector of manufacturing, commercial banking, and land and sea transport. Furthermore, he does not see the state as an obstacle to China's economic development. On the contrary, he argues that the state had little impact, either negative or positive. A similar view is shared by both Dwight Perkins (1967) and Marie-Claire Bergere (1989) who believe that the Chinese state was unable to give help to industrial development.

The main trouble with the state extraction argument is that the scholars making it have not traced the changes of actual state policy over time, nor have they put the enterprises involved in historical context. However, newly available material now enables us to arrive at a better understanding of these historical complexities in the new environment created by foreign competition and the rise of commercial nationalism in the mid-nineteenth century.

The present study examines a particular case of state involvement in the development of one of China's earliest modern enterprises, the China Merchants' Steam Navigation Company (Lunchuan Zhaoshangju) or CMC. The CMC was a unique, hybrid experiment, undertaken by Qing officials and Chinese merchants to counter the inroads of Western steam shipping in China's coastal trade. The CMC was China's first joint-stock company (*gongsi*) and its use of this organizational structure marked a new departure in Chinese business practice. Yet government-merchant cooperation in the creation and development of this enterprise followed earlier well-established patterns of Qing government cooperation with private merchant groups to achieve mutually advantageous goals (Leonard 1991; Kelley 1986). In such cases, the government recruited (*zhaoshang, zhaolai*) private human, organizational, and material resources to launch various kinds of joint ventures that used different approaches to "government supervision and merchant operation" (*guandu shangban*).

From 1872 to 1884, the CMC struggled to weld together old patterns of government-business cooperation with its new joint-stock structure during a period of challenging and rapidly changing political and economic conditions. In the end, the company failed. But the experiment showed that, from 1872 to 1884, when the operational management of the company was left in the hands of merchants and simultaneously received government support in the form of subsidies and the exclusive right to ship the grain tribute tax to the capital, it prospered. However, when government involvement in the actual management of the firm increased from 1885, the CMC failed.

This paper will analyze the role of government in the CMC from its origins in 1872 to its demise in 1902, and it will highlight the different approaches of Qing officials, especially that of Li Hongzhang, to company management.

The CMC as a Joint-Stock Enterprise

The CMC was planned in 1872 and officially formed on January 14, 1873 (Xu 1985, 68-83) to transport government grain tax, or tribute rice, from the lower Yangzi to Tianjin and compete with foreign steamship lines in coastal freight service. The company's business results in the first decade of its operation (1873-1884) were excellent. This remarkable achievement was largely attributable to the CMC's managerial practice and official protection (Lai 1990).

The CMC was neither a state enterprise nor a family firm, but the first indigenous joint-stock company sponsored by the Chinese state. The joint-stock enterprise model was first introduced into China's treaty ports by foreign traders around the time of the Tongzhi Restoration (1862-74). The Shanghai Steam Navigation Company, managed by the American firm of Russell and Company, was founded in 1862 and grew rapidly during the ensuing decade (Liu 1962). The Hong Kong and Shanghai Banking Corporation was another major foreign joint-stock company. As early as 1865, the Hong Kong Bank issued 20,000 shares, and the total paid-up capital was 2.5 million H.K. dollars (King 1987, 7). In nineteenth-century Europe and the United States, a joint-stock company was seen as a legal entity, whose characteristics, such as legal personhood and existence beyond the life of its members, made it more advantageous than partnerships. From the very beginning, Chinese joint-stock companies operated in a different political environment from their European and American counterparts, inasmuch as government promotion and regulation played a key role in the development of Chinese companies as business entities.

There are at least two reasons for this course of development. First, mid-nineteenth century Chinese merchants needed state support to develop indigenous joint-stock companies to compete with foreign firms (Zheng 1982, 635-38). Second, a number of Chinese officials themselves, including Ding Richang and Li Hongzhang, recognized the value of the joint-stock company as the vehicle by which the large amounts of capital necessary for industrialization could be raised. Ding and Li encouraged the formation of Chinese joint-stock companies by offering state support, despite the absence of domestic legal codes concerning joint-stock companies at that time. Merchants were to invest funds in a modern firm, yet the latter was to exist under the state's protective umbrella. Its management structure diverged substantially from Western joint-stock companies, from the private family firms of Qing China, and from indigenous state-sponsored enterprises of the past.

The Founding of the Company

When he founded the CMC, Li Hongzhang's principal motive was, as he put it, "to get a share of the foreigners' profits." In his letter of 11 December 1872 to Zhang Shusheng, the Liangjiang governor-general, Li stressed:

> The use of steamships for the transport of tribute rice by sea route is but a minor consideration. The project will open up new prospects for the dignity of the state, for commerce, for revenue, and for military strength for China for hundreds of years to come (LWZG:BH 12:31).

Therefore Li Hongzhang's goal was to build a competitive enterprise which would divert the profit of the foreign enterprises in China back to the Chinese themselves, and it expressed a kind of commercial nationalism.

Li considered three different proposals regarding the company's ownership: (1) state ownership, (2) joint-ownership between state and merchant, and (3) merchant ownership (LWZG:ZG 20:32b; Wang Jingyu 1983, 38-39). Zhu Qi'ang, commissioner of sea transport for Zhejiang province, drafted two proposals for the company (HFD 3:910-12; 921-23). Zhu's first proposal suggested joint-ownership between state and merchant. He proposed that the company's steamships be purchased from government shipyards; and, if the merchants did not have enough capital to buy the steamships, the government could regard the ships as its stock subscriptions. Although the project was designed to serve state interests, Li Hongzhang rejected Zhu's early plan on joint-ownership, preferring instead a private joint-stock company. Li had no objection to committing government resources, but he believed the funds should take the form of a loan, rather than of a stock subscription. He felt that a joint-stock venture had greater potential for mobilizing private capital and that its private investors should shoulder the entire responsibility for the company's management.

Li was able to secure government loans and other subsidies to modern enterprise, but he realized that the resources of the state alone were inadequate to sustain industrialization. Li decided that the company should be owned solely by Chinese merchants. Merchant capital, i.e., non-bureaucratic private capital, would have to be mobilized. At the same time, Li realized that it was "difficult to recruit merchants" to join innovative enterprises of this kind. With his letters to the Zongli Yamen dated 2 June 1872, Li enclosed a memorandum from Wu Dating, a former Taiwan *daotai*, which noted:

> In China wealthy and reliable merchants usually have their own businesses. They will not offer funds to a business that they do not know well. Merchants would refuse to join the project, perhaps even to consider it. Moreover, some merchants are in business with foreign firms; they have been dealing with foreigners for a long time. Knowing that government regulation cannot be enforced against the foreigners, they [the merchants] may not be pleased with this plan. . . . These are the difficulties (HFD 1:904).

Chinese merchants in the treaty ports would invest in a government-sponsored enterprise only when they were guaranteed a large measure of independence, yet such enterprises needed government support to get started. The key questions are: (1) how did Li "invite merchants" (*zhaoshang*) to invest in modern enterprise? (2) how did he secure government support for such an enterprise? and (3) what impact did such policies have upon economic innovation?

In the planning stage, he considered a range of proposals regarding the composition, ownership, and regulation of the steamship enterprise. Beginning in early 1872, Lin Shiji, a deputy of the Tianjin native customs, proposed to recruit Cantonese merchants, who already had invested in many foreign steamship companies, to undertake the new project. He proposed that the government arrange a loan of 300,000 *taels* and appoint a "merchant-chief" to receive it and supervise the company's affairs (LWZG:BH 12:4). In April, Sheng Xuanhuai, a member of Li's staff of advisers, proposed a different plan which outlined six points: establish a company, centralize administrative authority, recruit sufficient merchant capital, acquire steamships from the government shipyard, fix the rate of rent for these ships, and give them a share in transporting tribute rice.

Sheng argued that investors should shoulder the entire responsibility for profit and loss and that government should remain uninvolved in this issue. In order to strengthen the competitive power of the joint-stock company, however, Sheng also suggested that the government arrange a loan of 100,000 *taels* to the company on the understanding that the latter would ship approximately 400,000 *piculs* of tribute rice each year (SXH, CMC regulations, 1872). Although the proposals of Lin and Sheng were not officially adopted, they were analogous to the guidelines Li later used in his steamship project.

In October 1872, Li ordered Zhu Qi'ang to establish just such a bureau in Shanghai, and the latter was appointed commissioner in charge of the new steamship project. Li wanted to recruit Chinese merchants who previously had invested in the coastal trade or in foreign firms in China. To attract capital, investors were guaranteed a generous annual official dividend of 10 percent on their investment. Li appropriated 135,000 *taels* of Zhili military funds as a government loan to the company in late 1872. However, despite these measures, Chinese merchants were not willing to invest in the company. As of April 1873, merchants were said to have pledged share capital totaling more than one hundred thousand *taels*, but only ten thousand in cash had been paid up. Two prominent figures of the Shanghai Chinese mercantile community, the banker and silk merchant Hu Guangyong and the tea merchant Li Zhengyu, had declined to take any subscriptions.

Zhu proved to be totally incompetent in his effort to raise capital; and in June 1873, he was replaced as director of shipping operations, but continued to be in charge of grain tribute shipping. The joint-stock organization was reorganized under the management of two comprador-merchants, Tang Jingxing and Xu Run, who became the actual administrators between 1873 and 1884. Tang and Xu were the largest shareholders, and the merchant directors of branch establishments were also shareholders. Under the leadership of Tang and Xu, the paid-up share capital increased to 476,000 *taels* by the fall of 1874, and the amount reached one million in 1880 and two million in 1882.

Guandu Shangban in Practice: Organizational Innovation in the CMC

Since the company's rules and regulations were approved by Li Hong-zhang, they embodied his intentions. In recruiting Tang and Xu to undertake the shipping enterprise in June 1873, Li succeeded in mobilizing new technology and management as well as capital. Tang and Xu reorganized the CMC on the model of a Western joint-stock company, not unlike the American and British steamship companies in China (Liu 1959; 1962). When Tang took charge and commenced the reorganization of the company in 1873, certain rules (*juqui*) and regulations (*zhangcheng*) were drafted according to which the affairs of the company were to be carried out on sound business principles (JTSHZB 2:143-46).

Although Li Hongzhang regularly gave instructions to the company (at least 400 instructions by him on the daily affairs of the company are still on file), and he appointed the CMC's top administrators, he nonetheless approved of Tang and Xu's reorganization. The company was meant to be an enterprise operating strictly on a commercial footing. According to the adopted regulations, no officials were to be appointed to the company. No *yamen* clerks or runners were to be employed; the company was exempted from the custom of making formal official reports and forwarding accounts for official inspection. Even though government-sponsored, the company was to be owned and administrated privately by risk-taking shareholders.

Yet the CMC had to rely on government loans in order to supplement merchant capital. Li Hongzhang accepted the necessity of such loans and regarded them as an important part of his approach to the *guandu shangban* model. Thanks to Li and his influence with top officials in Jiangsu, Zhejiang, Jiangxi and Hubei, as well as the customs' *daotais* of Tianjin and Shanghai, public loans were, at different dates, deposited in the company to the extent of 1,903,868 *taels*. At least eighteen official loans were arranged before 1885 (see Table 1). With the government loans, the company was able to repay the short-term high-interest loans made by native banks, and the company could purchase the American-managed Shanghai Steam Navigation Company in 1877.

Before 1882, the total of the government loans to the company was much larger than its total paid-up share capital. These loans represented around 50 to 60 percent of the company's total debts, or 2.2 times more than the maximum paid-up capital between 1876 and 1880. They were guaranteed an interest of only 7 to 10 percent per annum, a lower rate than the shareholder's annual 10 percent guaranteed dividend. In 1877 Li obtained imperial permission to suspend payment of interest on the company's government loans for three years, and to allow the company five years for the repayment of the principal of these loans. Actually, no interest was paid on these loans between 1877 and 1885. The suspended interest totalled more than 900,000 *taels* over those eight years. This amounted to about half of the paid-up share capital of the company in the period 1882-93. In other words, the Qing state gave a few hundred thousand *taels* to subsidize the enterprise during this period.

Table 1[a]
Government Loans to the CMC, 1872-1883 (in Shanghai *taels*).

Sources	Year	Amount of loan	Annual Interest Rate (%)
Tianjin military funds	1872	120,000	7
Wood *likin* of Nanjing	1875	100,000	8
Zhejiang public funds	1875	100,000	8
Coastal defense funds	1876	100,000	8
Yangzhou commissary	1876	100,000	8
Zhili military funds	1876	50,000	10
Baoding military funds	1876	50,000	8
Chefoo customs	1876	100,000	8
Nanjing prov. treasury	1877	100,000	10
Jiangan commissary	1877	200,000	10
Shanghai customs	1877	200,000	10
Zhejiang silk revenue	1877	200,000	10
Jiangxi treasury	1877	200,000	10
Hubei treasury	1877	100,000	10
Coast-defense funds	1878	150,000	
Coast-defense funds	1878-81	100,000	
Diplomatic missions	1881	80,000	
Tianjin coast-defense	1883	200,000	

[a]Source: Lai 1988, 21.

Good government connections were also important for subsidizing the company's business through preferential shipping arrangements. Part of the CMC success during its first decade of operation resulted from the fact that Li left the management to the experts—the merchants—and used his enormous power to create favorable conditions for its operation. He influenced provincial officials to consign to the company a part of their annual shipment of tribute rice. For shipping tribute rice, the company was paid at the same rate of freight as that enjoyed by the seagoing junks, as much as 0.6 *taels* per *picul* before 1879 or 0.531 *taels* per *picul* between 1880 and 1884. These rates were two to three times higher than the average rate charged by foreign steamship companies for ordinary freight. As Table 2 indicates, the company received an average of 500,000 *piculs* of tribute rice freight per year.

Table 2[a]
Tribute Grain Shipped by the CMC.

Year Shipped	Tribute Grain (*Piculs*)	Rate of Freight	Total Earning[b] (Shanghai *taels*)
June 1873	170,000	0.600	102,000
1873-74	250,000	0.600	150,000
1874-75	300,000	0.600	180,000
1875-76	450,000	0.600	270,000
1876-77	290,000	0.600	174,000
1877-78	523,000	0.600	313,800
1978-79	520,000	0.600	312,000
1879-80	570,000	0.600	342,000
1880-81	475,415	0.531	252,445
1881-82	557,000	0.531	295,767
1882-83	580,000	0.531	307,980
1883-84	390,000	0.531	207,090
1884-85	470,000	0.531	249,570

[a]Source: Lai 1988, 20.
[b](Tribute Grain Shipped) × (Rate of Freight).

The Nationalization Plan and
Merchant Disenchantment, 1877-1885

As the company expanded and was making a profit, many officials proposed that the government take over the ownership of the company. Such proposals were made in 1877 by Shen Baozhen, governor-general of Liangjiang, in 1879 by Ye Tingjuan, a tribute-grain manager of the company, and in 1881 by Liu Kunyi, then governor-general of Liangjiang. Liu's proposal posed an especially serious threat (Lai 1988).

Ye Tingjuan, who was the Shanghai *daotai* at one time, suggested in a letter to Li Hongzhang that the government should expend about 2,000,000 *taels* of public funds to take over the CMC although he did not use the modern term "nationalization" (*guoyouhua*). Ye noted that the take-over action would save interest totalling 200,000 *taels* due the native banks and dividends to the shareholders amounting to 70,000 *taels* annually. Ye believed that the government would get full returns from the 2,000,000-*tael* investment within ten years. However, Li did not accept this proposal. In fact, he removed Ye from the company's management.

Liu Kunyi suggested converting government loans into government shares, making the state the largest single shareholder of the company. In his letter to Li Zhaotang, dated 15 February 1881, Liu said, "The suspended interest [on government loans to the company] was more than 700,000 *taels,* so the total amount of government loan was over 1,500,000 *taels* which I proposed to put in the CMC as government shares" (Liu Kunyi 1909, 8:17).

The company's shareholders immediately interpreted Liu's proposal as a strategy to introduce government control over the company's management. As already mentioned, the company's directors were the largest share-holders, and the managers of branch offices were also shareholders. The total number of shares the CMC had issued amounted to 800,600 *taels* in 1878-1879. Tang and his close relatives owned around 80,000 *taels*, and Tang's other relatives subscribed to 200,000 *taels*. Xu Run and his relatives controlled as many shares as Tang and his relatives. More than half of the shares were thus under the control of the two merchant managers. From their standpoint, there was no need for official inspection. If the managers were to act dishonestly in any way, they reasoned, "How could the majority of the shareholders who were friends or relations of the managers and live so near each other fail to detect these acts?" The merchants should thus be responsible for their own investment. When the CMC was under heavy criticism from the censors in Beijing, Tang and Xu had declared in a letter:

> In order to repay the loans to the government, we could [if necessary] sell all the ships and wharves. We could also close the company and establish another one. Since profit and loss are entirely the responsibility of the merchants and do not involve the government, the government does not need to investigate the company's accounts (Sheng Archives, cited in Liu N.d., ms.).

Thanks to Li Hongzhang's objections, Liu Kunyi's plan was not realized. In his letter to Wang Xianqian, Liu ruefully acknowledged the success of Li's efforts: "Li Hongzhang memorialzed the court that the funds [which were borrowed from the public funds] should be returned in five years and that later all the profit would belong to the CMC, and not to the government. In the future the administration of the company will belong to merchants, not the government!''

Li tried his best to protect the autonomy of the company, stressing that "all matters of profit and loss affect shareholders only; the government has nothing to do with them." But when Li's subordinates wanted to convert public funds into their private shares, Li allowed them to do that (CMC 468/82). This act of Li's was detrimental to the autonomy of the company and merchant investment.

What conclusions are to be drawn from the early history of the CMC? From 1877 on, a number of officials suggested that the court take over the ownership of the CMC. It was Li Hongzhang who protected the autonomy of the company's management and encouraged the merchants to invest in the enterprise. However, Li's policy could not escape criticism and interference from conservative officials, both in Beijing and in the lower Yangzi area. The failure of the court of the Empress Dowager Cixi (1835-1908) to provide for the increasing needs of China's defense efforts, as well as the 1883 financial crisis in Shanghai (Quan 1972, 777-94; Hao 1986, 323-34; Liu 1990, 571-93), caused partly by the Sino-French tension over Vietnam, made it very difficult to continue further state support of the shipping company (Eastman 1967). In fact, the Qing state now strove to extract more resources from Chinese corporations. In 1883-85, the CMC's merchant managers were replaced by officials, and the company's capacity for growth declined. It is clear that the comparative success of the CMC during its first decade was the result of a balance between government financial support and the autonomy of the company's merchant management. When government support was replaced by bureaucratic control, the formula changed.

The Decline of the CMC, 1885-1902

During the crisis of China's foreign relations in the 1880s, Li was unable to maintain his earlier policy of protecting the merchants' interests. As a result, bureaucratic intervention increased, and merchants, on their part, reduced their support for these enterprises (Chan 1977; Hao 1986; Xia 1985; Zheng 1982, 611). The success of such government-sponsored undertakings, therefore, was cut short. After 1885, the original *guandu shangban* formula no longer worked. Because Li's own political position was weakened, his ability to help the company declined. During the Sino-French War and peace negotiations, Li was criticized heavily, especially by the "Purity party" (Qingliu dang), for military setbacks and the proposed concessions to France.

Because of China's defeat in the Sino-French War and because of Japan's threat to Korea, more government military spending was necessary. This was when Li Hongzhang was building up the Beiyang navy. When available funds were heavily allocated to national defense and to the Empress Dowager's construction of pleasure palaces, government support for private enterprises suffered. The Qing government was able to give the CMC strong support in the first decade, but after 1880 it was no longer able to support similar enterprises on the same scale, nor to offer the CMC itself sustained support. When the military needs for coastal defence mounted, Li decided to divert resources from the CMC to the Beiyang navy (CMC 468/81) and to his other projects (CMC 468/68, 113:1). In August 1885, Li even transferred shipping personnel from the CMC to the Beiyang navy (CMC 468/81). Weaknesses in China's modernization effort must be attributed to China's military needs and to fiscal limitations. However, to these weaknesses must be added the shortcomings of bureaucratic government.

Following the financial crisis in Shanghai in 1883, Li ordered the reorganization of the company. In 1885, he appointed Sheng Xuanhuai as its director-general (*duban*). Former merchant directors were removed, partly because they had lost their capital during the financial crisis. Sheng had meanwhile been buying the company's shares and was the largest shareholder in 1885. During his directorship, between 1885 and 1902, Sheng continued to hold such official posts as customs *daotai* in Chefoo or Tianjin, and he controlled the company's affairs from a distance. He appointed his favorites as top administrators of the company, regardless of the amounts of their share-holding. Bureaucratic control in the company increased. Most of the top administrators were of official background, lacking modern business experience (Lai 1990).

Despite the advantages that the CMC once enjoyed, profits were not reinvested in technological improvements after the Sino-French War of 1884-85. To be sure, the company was paying off its debts, donating large amounts of funds to the hard-pressed government, and investing in other enterprises in this second period (1885-1902). But capital investment stagnated, and the tonnage of the fleet remained constant. In 1877, the company owned thirty steamships and had the highest tonnage among steamship companies in China. Between 1878 and 1883, the company purchased nine new ships and completed a large investment in wharves and warehouses in the company's well-located frontage area. By 1893, however, the CMC had a fleet of only twenty-six ships, while the shipping tonnages of foreign steamship companies in Chinese waters had grown rapidly. Finally, the loss of mercantile control of the CMC led to a more general disenchantment among Chinese merchants regarding government-sponsored enterprises, and it dampened their willingness to invest in other modern enterprises.

In seeking an explanation for the company's stagnation, one must conclude that bureaucratic interference in the company's management was the foremost factor, along with Li Hongzhang's diminished political influence and his dwindling fiscal resources. The question to be examined further is whether the short duration of Li's successful policy indicates that it was an anomaly within the context of late Qing institutions, or whether it was a basically viable policy which simply fell victim to unfortunate accidents of history.

Conclusion

The most important finding from this brief history of the first thirty years of the CMC is that the Qing state had a positive impact on China's industrialization when it pursued an appropriate policy. The initial success of China's modern enterprises, such as the CMC, was due to a balance between government financial support (which ensured profits) and enterprise autonomy (which guaranteed sound management). Government support led later to direct bureaucratic control of the company's affairs, and undermined managerial autonomy, upsetting the balance. Especially after the 1883 financial crisis, the government changed its policies in ways that severely impaired the quality of management and discouraged subsequent investment. Merchant reluctance was in part a reluctance to engage in an enterprise over which the merchants themselves had no personal control. Their belief was that an enterprise was something from which they could not retrieve their resources readily.

In a well-known analysis of the CMC and other late Qing *guandu shangban* enterprises, Albert Feuerwerker depicts the company as fundamentally flawed by bureaucratism, inefficiency and corruption (1958). That image does not accord with the objectives of the CMC's founder Li Hongzhang, nor with the record of the company's initial decade of operation from 1873-84. While flaws became evident in the *guandu shangban* model from the mid-1880s onward, the subsequent history of the CMC should not prejudice the reassessment of its origins and early growth based on newly available sources.

In trying to explain why government protection was needed in the development of China's first indigenous joint-stock company, we have examined the interaction between the officials and merchants involved. The fundamental problem lay in the fact that merchants were extremely reluctant to invest in an indigenous joint-stock company. Most potential investors were not motivated by economic nationalism alone; they needed a concrete demonstration that the new Chinese-owned joint-stock company could work well and make a good profit. At the same time, some government officials, notably Li Hongzhang, believed that the modern corporate or joint-stock form of organization was essential to the development of modern transport and industry. With state support, merchants were willing to commit their resources to these undertakings. This was the positive side of the *guandu shangban* model.

The company's early success was partly due to interaction between Li Hongzhang's astute policies and the initiative and skill of merchant managers. However, the importance of Li's personal role in China's early industrial modernization also highlights the difficult question of the stability and reliability of state policy and the environment for investment. The political context in which modern enterprises operated could never be discounted in late Qing China, as the shift in CMC fortunes after 1885 demonstrates. This government-sponsored company existed within a given political framework. Its rise and decline thus depended as much on political as on economic circumstances. In brief, the CMC foundered not in the ebb and flow of the market, but in the unpredictable winds of late nineteenth-century Chinese politics.

References

Balazs, Étienne. 1964. *Chinese Civilization and Bureaucracy*. New Haven: Yale University Press.

Bergere, Marie-Claire. 1989. *The Golden Age of the Chinese Bourgeoisie, 1911-1937*. Cambridge: Cambridge University Press.

Brandt, Loren. 1989. *Commercialization and Agricultural Development: Central and Eastern China, 1870-1937* Cambridge: Cambridge University Press.

Chan, Wellington K. K. 1977. *Merchants, Mandarins, and Modern Enterprise in Late Ch'ing China*. Cambridge, Mass.: Harvard University Press.

_____. 1980. "Government, Merchants and Industry to 1911." In *The Cambridge History of China, Vol. 11, Late Ch'ing, 1800-1911, Part*

2, ed. John. K. Fairbank and Kwang-ching Liu. Cambridge: Cambridge University Press.

CMC. The China Merchants' Steam Navigation Company Archives. Nanjing: the Second Historical Archives of China.

Coble, Parks M., Jr. 1980. *The Shanghai Capitalists and the Nationalist Government, 1927-1937*. Cambridge, Mass.: Harvard University Press.

Duan, Benluo. 1982. Jianlun guandu shangban dui minzu zibenjuyi fazhan di zuzhi zuoyong ("Government supervision and merchant operation" system as an obstacle to the developmnt of national capitalism). *Lishi jiaoxue* 10:14-18.

Eastman, Lloyd E. 1967. *Throne and Mandarins: China's Search For a Policy During the Sino-French Controversy, 1889-1885*. Cambridge, Mass.: Harvard University Press.

Faure, David. 1989. *The Rural Economy of Pre-Liberation China: Trade Expansion and Livelihood in Jiangsu and Guangdong, 1870-1937*. Hong Kong: Oxford University Press.

Feuerwerker, Albert. 1958. *China's Early Industrialization: Sheng Hsuan-huai, 1844-1916 and Mandarin Enterprise*. Cambridge, Mass.: Harvard University Press.

HFD. *Haifangdang* (Archives on maritime defense). 1957. Photo-offset reproduction of Zongli Yamen papers. Taibei: Institute of Modern History of Academia Sinica.

Hao, Yen-p'ing. 1971. *The Comprador in Nineteenth Century China: Bridge between East and West*. Cambridge, Mass.: Harvard University Press.

_____. 1986. *The Commercial Revolution in Nineteenth-Century China: The Rise of Sino-Western Mercantile Capitalism*. Berkeley: University of California Press.

JTSHZB. *Jiaotongshi: hangzhengbian* (History of communications: shipping). 1931. Comp. by a committee jointly sponsored by the ministries of communications and railways. Nanjing.

Kelley, David E. 1986. Sect and Society: The Evolution of the Luo Sect among Qing Dynasty Grain Tribute Boatmen, 1700-1850. Ph.D. diss., Harvard University.

King, Frank H. H. 1987. *The Hong Kong Bank in Late Imperial China, 1864-1902*. Cambridge: Cambridge University Press.

Lai, Chi-kong. 1988. Lunchuan zhaoshangju guoyou wenti, 1878-1881 (The proposal to nationalize the China Merchants' Steam Navigation Company, 1878-1881). *Bulletin of the Institute of Modern History, Academia Sinica* (Taipei)17:15-40.

_____. 1990. Lunchuan zhaoshangju jingyin guanli wenti, 1872-1901 (Enterprise management of the China Steam Navigation Company 1872-1901). *Bulletin of the Institute of Modern History, Academia Sinica* (Taibei) 19:67-108.

Leonard, Jane Kate. 1991. "Controlling from afar": The Daoguang Emperor's Management of the Grand Canal , 1824-1826. Unpublished manuscript.

Liu, Kunyi. 1909. *Liu zhongcheng gong yiji* (Collected papers of the late Liu Kunyi). Reprint. Taibei: Wenhai.

Liu, Kwang-ching. 1959. Steamship Enterprise In Nineteenth-Century China. *The Journal of Asian Studies* 18, 4:435-55.

_____. 1962. *Anglo-American Steamship Rivalry in China, 1862-1874.* Cambridge, Mass.: Harvard University Press.

_____. 1964. "British-Chinese Steamship Rivalry in China, 1873-1885." In *Economic Development of China and Japan: Studies in Economic History and Political Economy,* ed. C. D. Cowan. London: Allen and Unwin.

_____. 1990. *Jingshi yu ziqiang* (Statecraft and Self-Strengthening). Taibei: Lianjing.

_____. N.d. Cong Lunchuan zhaoshangju zaoqi lishi kan guandu shangban di liangge xingtai (The early history of the CMC and the two different patterns of the *guandu shangban* system). Unpublished ms.

LWZG. Li Hongzhang. [1905] 1921. *Li Wenzhonggong chuanji* (A complete collection of Li Hongzhang's papers). Reproduction of the original edition (Nanjing). Shanghai.

LWZG: BH. Bengliao han'gao (Letters to friends and colleagues.

LWZG: ZG. Zougao (Memorials).

Perkins, Dwight H. 1967. Government as an obstacle to Industrialization: The Case of Nineteenth-Century China. *Journal of Economic History* 27, 7:478-92.

Quan, Hansheng. 1972. *Zhongguo jingjishi luncong* (Collected essays on Chinese economic history). Hong Kong: Xinya Yanjiusuo.

Rawski, Thomas G. 1989. *Economic Growth in Prewar China.* Berkeley: University of California Press.

Rowe, William T. 1984. *Hankow: Commerce and Society in a Chinese City, 1796-1889.* Stanford: Stanford University Press.

Shenbao (Shanghai news). [1873-1884] 1965. Reprint. Taibei: Xuesheng shuju.

SXH. Sheng Xuanhuai Archives. Hong Kong: Chinese University of Hong Kong.

Wang, Jingyu. 1983. ''Shijiu shiji waiguo qingua qi-ye zhong di huashang fugu huodong'' (The activities of Chinese merchants in subscribing to capital shares in the aggressive foreign enterprises in China during the nineteenth century). In *Shijiu shiji xifang cibenzhuyi dui Zhongguo di jingji qinluan* (The encroachment of Western capitalism on the Chinese economy in the nineteenth century). Beijing: Renmin.

Xia, Dongyuan. 1985. *Wan Qing yangwu yundng yanjiu* (Studies on Self-strengthening Movement in late Qing China). Szechwan: Renmin.

Xu, Run. [1927] 1977. *Xu Yuzhai zixu nianpu, fu Shanghai zaji* (Autobiographical chronicle by Xu Yuzhai, together with miscellaneous notes on Shanghai). Reprint. Taibei: Shihuo chubanshe.

Zhang, Guohui. 1979. *Yangwu yundong yu Zhongguo jindai qiye* (The Westernization movement and modern Chinese enterprise). Beijing: Zhongguo shehui kexue.

Zhang, Houquan, ed. 1988. *Zhaoshangju shi* (A history of the China Merchants' Steam Navigation Company). Beijing: Renmin jiaotong.

Zheng, Guanying. 1982. *Zheng Guanying Ji* (Collected Zheng Guanying). Shanghai: Renmin.

9

Business-Government Cooperation in Late Qing Korean Policy

Louis T. Sigel

Introduction

Late Qing foreign policy in Korea represents a distinctive pattern of business-government relations, compared to the other studies in this volume. In those instances, the formulation of policy and the initiative for merchant involvement generally came from government officials who were attempting either to control and restrict, or to encourage and stimulate private individuals from the commercial, transport, or industrial sectors to act in ways that would promote the administrators' objectives. Pragmatic Qing statesmen generally recognized their reliance on prosperous businessmen for assistance in successful policy implementation. They were aware of the problems involved in trying to enlist merchant participation coercively, so they often resorted to trying to convince Chinese businessmen of the identity of their interests with those of the state (Metzger 1966, 4-10; 1970, 23-46). Whether in its negative or passive aspects or its more positive and activist modes of behavior, however, the perspective remained one of a paternalistic interaction of the state with the economy.

The case of late Qing Korean policy, on the other hand, stands at the other end of the spectrum of state interaction with the economy. Chinese businessmen from the modern commercial community were far more active in devising the strategy that responsible Qing officials should adopt, and they exerted influence in determining the character of Qing involvement in

Korean affairs. Prominent Chinese from the modern business community also worked to secure formal government sanction and support for achieving their commercial ends and in convincing officialdom of the complementarity of the interests of the state with their private interests. In this sense, business-government cooperation in late Qing Korean policy represents more of a mutual collaboration for mutual benefits than is the case in any of the other studies.

This uniqueness is, in large part, a function of the time and place of this policy in the historical context of late Qing China. The late Qing period witnessed the beginnings of modern Chinese nationalism, and the modern commercial community, concentrated in the treaty ports, played a prominent part in this cultural transformation. One important aspect of the special circumstances of the late Qing was the growing menace to China's national security posed by foreign encroachment on the frontiers. The perception of this threat and the need for a more active response to confront these external pressures was an essential component of early nationalist thinking. For these reasons, members of China's modern commercial community assumed pivotal roles in conceiving, gaining adoption of, and carrying out a new, more nationalistic and more aggressive approach to dealing with the foreign powers.

The modern commercial community which emerged in the treaty ports along the coast and on the Yangzi River was composed primarily of businessmen involved in foreign maritime trade. The treaty-port Christian community and those who gained a better understanding of the West through involvement with the missionary movement formed another important component of this community. A third major element in the modern commercial community came from the leading gentry families from the regions linked economically and socially with the treaty-port economies.

Influential spokesmen from the modern business sector called for far-reaching reforms. They argued for the abolition of extraterritoriality and for the recovery of national economic privileges, such as tariff autonomy and the exclusion of foreign vessels from domestic shipping. These businessmen stressed the promotion of industrial development and advocated "waging commercial warfare" to prevent foreigners from monopolizing the benefits at the expense of Chinese national interests.

This community brought a more aggressive, modern-oriented, outward-looking world view to the perception of foreign threats to the Qing empire. They aimed at reasserting China's national rights, both political and economic, and generated demands for extensive reform to regain China's legitimate prerogatives. A key facet of their outlook was their perception of the dynamism and significance of commerce and industry as the source of wealth and power in the West (Sigel 1985, 223-33). Their distinctive brand of mercantile nationalism was a critical factor in their involvement in Korean policy in the 1880s and 1890s.

Qing Korean Policy in the 1870s

During the last three decades of the nineteenth century, the more limited foreign encroachment on China's national sovereignty and territorial integrity by the treaty powers, characteristic of the 1840s and 1850s, was replaced gradually by more ominous imperialist incursions on the Chinese world order. The autonomous kingdoms on China's frontiers which functioned as buffer states, came under persistent pressure from foreign colonial expansion. In the end, almost all of these countries succumbed to these external assaults, leaving China itself increasingly exposed.

The tributary system which defined a pattern of diplomatic relations between the Qing empire and countries on China's periphery reinforced the dynastic claim to the Mandate of Heaven, but the primary function was political. Qing officials were concerned with the security of the border-lands, and the tributary states fulfilled the vital task of fending off possible foreign threats to the empire. Ritual etiquette aside, the feudal ties between the emperor and his tributary vassals were essentially of a strategic character.

Korea, as the most culturally sinicized and politically reliable of the states within the Chinese world order, was the model Qing tributary. Unlike the more troublesome relationship with Vietnam, where both Ming and Qing authorities had felt obliged to intervene to maintain the appropriate orientation of subservience to China (Lo 1969, 41-42), Korea had sought Ming aid against the Japanese invasions of the late sixteenth century and had remained closely aligned with China. The tributary ties with Korea could be maintained without requiring the Qing to interfere in Korea's internal affairs.

Korean rulers viewed their link to China as a bolster to their power and status, and they scrupulously observed the regulations regarding embassies to and from the Qing emperors (Chun 1968, 90-111). The closeness and significance of the Sino-Korean relationship is most clearly illustrated by the metaphor commonly used to describe it: "lips and teeth." Korea was seen as the lips which safeguarded the Chinese teeth; without the lips, the teeth would be exposed and unprotected (Tsiang 1933, 53).

In the 1870s, leading Chinese statesmen reached the conclusion that Japan posed the greatest threat to China's security. The Zongli Yamen repeatedly warned the Korean court that Japan was the major danger and that, like China, Korea should assure her future protection through the use of Western diplomatic practice. The Korean authorities, however, citing French and later American naval expeditions aimed at forcing the opening of Korean ports, saw the West with its Christian missionaries as the main cause for alarm. The Koreans wanted Chinese assistance in preserving their isolation but judged Japanese intentions as peaceful (Tsiang 1933, 54-63).

As governor-general of Zhili and commissioner of the northern ports after 1870, Li Hongzhang assumed the leading role in dealing with the perils as well as the possibilities the international situation represented to Chinese interests. He was one of the foremost proponents and practitioners of the mainstream approach to diplomacy characteristic of the Self-strengthening reformers of the late nineteenth century. The dominant element in their pragmatic outlook was rigid compliance with treaty stipulations in order to minimize incidents that the treaty powers might exploit to force further concessions. With responsibiltiy for guarding the capital and protecting the most strategically important region of China, Li perceived Korea as the first line of defense in resisting any threats to the empire. Korea thus posed unique problems in attempting to handle foreign affairs.

The defensive and dilatory style of the mainstream approach sought to utilize international agreements and Western diplomatic conventions to forestall menacing foreign aggression. With both Russian and Japanese pressure impinging directly on Korea, however, Li tried to pursue a two-pronged policy. On the surface, he seemed to work for the preservation of Korean autonomy with respect to the foreign treaty powers, but covertly he worked to transform Korea's traditional relationship with China into one of greater dependence and subservience. In this way, he could prudently confront imperialist encroachment on the northeast and ultimately on North China.

In dealing with the problems posed by the foreign threats to China, Qing statesmen, like Li Hongzhang, had to rely to an inordinate degree upon the modern commercial community for the personnel to advise and assist them. This business sector emerged as a direct consequence of the growth of foreign trade after 1842, and the success of these compradors, merchants, and entrepreneurs was dependent upon their mastery of Western techniques and foreign languages. They were far more receptive to the idea of adopting Western institutions and had a different perspective on the need to promote "wealth and power" compared to that of the Self-strengtheners they served.

On the important issue of foreign political and economic penetration of China's tributaries, modern Chinese businessmen favored a skillful but aggressive response. They argued in favor of converting the traditional tribute system into a Chinese colonial empire along Western lines, through the extension of Chinese authority and the adoption of the techniques of foreign imperialism. This policy was elaborated most clearly in the writings of Zheng Guanying, one of the most influential of the reform publicists of the late nineteenth century and the most articulate of China's treaty-port merchants. His writings brought the ideas of the modern commercial community with its greater understanding of Western knowledge to a wider elite audience.

In his earliest essays on reform, *Yiyan* (Facile words), which he started writing in the early 1870s and published in 1880, Zheng Guanying advocated that the policy of non-interference in the domestic affairs of tribute states be drastically altered. He asserted that China should take the lead in advising these countries on how to achieve wealth and power and that this assistance should serve as a means by which China could gain control over their internal administration rather than as an end in itself. As examples, Zheng specifically pointed out:

> Korea and Vietnam have hitherto been submissive, relying upon China to serve as a screen for their countries. It is appropriate to select carefully high officials to go there to assess their strengths and weaknesses and to ascertain the conditions there, for example, about commercial conditions and the development of mining. If there are things which will assist them in achieving wealth and power, these officials should direct these countries in the actions that must be taken. If there is great skepticism because the plan would be too difficult to . . . carry . . . out, China should take the initiative in providing financing which is to be repaid on an annual basis. . . . By having them accept our assistance, we can make them dependent upon us. In the beginning, it will not be easy to carry this plan out. We must have quick-witted officials to whom to entrust this task and have them devote themselves to it thoroughly. They should speak in terms of the long-standing, long-established policy but act according to this strategy. . . . The foreign powers will have to comply with it. In a few years, the results will be observable (Liu 1970, 386-87; Lee 1969, 1-9).

The adoption and implementation of this more modern and nationalistic stance depended, in large part, on the influence that individuals from the modern business sector could exert on Li Hongzhang and the other Self-strengtheners. The reformist governors-general relied upon entrepreneurs, advisers, and administrators from the treaty-port business community to propose, establish, and operate the new Self-strengthening enterprises. These businessmen served largely as private consultants within Li Hongzhang's *mufu* (secretariat), and their effect on policy was limited to the pressure they could exert on him through personal and informal persuasion. The relationship of these treaty-port Chinese businessmen to the Self-strengtheners was described by Tang Tingshu, the former Jardine, Matheson comprador, in a comment on his influence with Li Hongzhang, as: "The viceroy leads, but I am the man that pushes" (Martin 1896, 351).

Qing Korean Policy in the 1880s

Because of his ranking of strategic priorities, Li Hongzhang was not prepared to be pushed into supporting a more active stance against French aggression in Vietnam (Sigel 1975, 79-105; 1976, 272-81); but for the same reason, he viewed the escalating Japanese involvement in Korea with concern. On their part, the treaty-port business sector actively cooperated in the effort to transform Korea into a colonial protectorate of China as the means of safeguarding Korea from Japan and Russia. Their proposals and activities reflected a commitment to use Western concepts of international relations in the assertion of Chinese national rights rather than as a mere restriction on foreign intervention. Their approach and their actions, however, were also indicative of their belief in the interdependence of commerce and the national interest. As reflected in Tang Tingshu's Charles Wilson-like comment in 1883 regarding China's southern frontier, he saw the prospects of his company as intimately intertwined with the fate of China. Tang noted:

> I hope that before this reaches you the Vietnamese situation will have proceeded in due course [to a solution] because the good fortunes of China and Vietnam are also the good fortune of the China Merchants' Steam Navigation Company (ZFYN, doc. 532, app. 2:1080).

Li Hongzhang could exert considerable, though indirect, influence on Qing Korean policy through his advice to the Zongli Yamen in his capacity as commissioner of the northern ports in the 1870s. After the Japanese forced the Treaty of Kanghwa upon the reluctant Koreans in 1876, Li's apprehensions about Japanese involvement in the peninsula increased. However, when Japan took the king of the Ryukyus and his heir-apparent into custody, prevented them from sending their regular tribute mission to China, and proceeded to annex these islands, Li Hongzhang was stunned into action as he witnessed his worst fears and suspicions being realized. He advised the Zongli Yamen:

> As the Ryukyus have been annexed, Korea is in a position of imminent danger. In view of this and of the growing interest of the Western powers in Korea, we can no longer refrain from devising ways and means for the security of Korea (Lin 1935, 219).

In 1880, the Zongli Yamen transferred full responsibility for Qing Korean policy directly to Li Hongzhang, and Li resolved that China should become more vigorous in protecting Korea and preserving her close relationship with China. He abandoned the policy of abstaining from interfering in Korean internal affairs and patiently advising the hesitant Korean authorities about Self-strengthening reform and diplomacy because he believed China's vital interests were now directly threatened. Li decided to bring Korea into the international community of foreign diplomacy as a first step in thwarting Japanese involvement there. He selected the United States, a country whose representatives already had expressed an interest in Korea but a country without territorial designs in the region, as the best place to start for introducing the protection of international law and the international balance of interests. He sought to persuade the Koreans to conclude a treaty with the United States and served as intermediary for Commodore R. W. Shufeldt, who was commissioned to establish American diplomatic relations with Korea (Deuchler 1977, 114-20; Kim and Kim 1967, 17-25).

Although the Treaty of Amity and Commerce between the United States and Korea was formally signed in Inch'on in May 1882, the negotiations for it were conducted in Tianjin by Li Hongzhang and his principal adviser in handling Korean affairs, Ma Jianzhong. Ma was largely responsible for the original draft submitted by Li to Shufeldt and was present at the bargaining sessions to work out the final details of the agreement. Ma also was dispatched to Korea at the conclusion of the treaty negotiations to deal with any political problems that might be encountered, and he was in attendance at the signing ceremony as Li's representative (Deuchler 1977, 20-21).

Ma Jianzhong and his elder brother Ma Liang were among the most outstanding examples of the Chinese Christians in the modern commercial community. The Ma family of Zhenjiang in Jiangsu province had been early converts to Catholicism in the late Ming, and both of the Ma brothers had received formal training in Jesuit schools in Shanghai. Ma Jianzhong had been sent to France in 1877 under Li Hongzhang's patronage, and he was the first Chinese to receive the baccalaureate degree and to be awarded the licentiate. Because of his foreign language proficiency and his familiarity with international law, Ma Jianzhong emerged as one of Li's most valued foreign affairs experts in the 1880s (Cohen 1974, 250-52).

In light of the urgency for Korean security, Li Hongzhang and Ma Jianzhong not only ignored Korean demands for the inclusion of a ban on missionaries in the American treaty, but they were also willing to compromise on the inclusion of a statement of Korean vassalage and Chinese suzerainty (Lee 1976, 19-26). The final version of the treaty omitted an acknowledgment of Korean dependence on China that Li had originally hoped it would contain. With this initial opening of Korea to the West, Li arranged for Britain, France, and Germany to conclude treaties with Korea in rapid succession (Deuchler 1974, 122-27).

Commercial Aspects of Qing Korean Policy

Chinese merchants actively participated in the policy of dominating Korea politically and economically in the 1880s and 1890s. Qing officials, with origins in the treaty-port business community, attempted to assist Chinese merchants in their competition for Korean markets as a means of bolstering China's position. The opening of expanded trading relations between China and Korea began in 1882 with the signing of the Regulations for Maritime and Overland Trade between Chinese and Korean Subjects. This agreement ended the long-standing prohibition on maritime intercourse between the two countries and placed Chinese and Korean merchants on equal terms with foreigners in being allowed to reside and trade in each other's opened ports. The terms of this document were negotiated by Li Hongzhang with the Korean emissaries sent to discuss the American treaty with Commodore Shufeldt. Again, the more specific details of the wording were handled by Ma Jianzhong, who was careful to find means of asserting Chinese prerogatives. The preamble of the agreement stipulated that special privileges were being conceded by both sides in view of their unique tributary relationship and that other powers could not make any claims to these advantages under the most-favored-nation clause. Among these special concessions was that of Article 5, which allowed Chinese and Korean merchants to trade at ports on the Yalu and Tumen Rivers that were closed to other traders (Deuchler 1974, 122-27).

Business participation in the more active Chinese supervision of Korean affairs became much more significant after September 1882, when Li and Ma became concerned with the political consequences of the loan agreements that the Japanese minister to Korea, Hanabusa Yoshitada, was trying to finalize. Prominent Korean officials—Kim Hong-jip and Cho Yong-ha —were worried that the Japanese were deliberately over-extending credit in order to put Korea so deeply in debt that Japan could extract harsh terms

Map 5. Korean Cities Opened to Chinese Trade, 1870-1895.

to ensure repayment. Commenting on these fears, Li stressed China's obligation "to shelter with humaneness and be kind to the weak," arguing that otherwise Korea would fall into the clutches of the Japanese. In the end, he agreed to a secret scheme put forward by Tang Tingshu and Ma Jianzhong, the principal members of Li's *mufu* from the modern commercial community. They proposed a loan to Korea to be negotiated with rich Chinese merchants who would underwrite it jointly; and as security for repayment, they agreed to accept customs revenue and the opportunity to develop Korean mineral wealth (ZRH 910).

Subsequently, in early October 1882, Tang Tingshu arranged a loan of 500,000 *taels* for Korea out of the funds at his disposal as director-general of the China Merchants' Steam Navigation Company and of the Kaiping Mining Company. The preliminary contract stipulated that Korea would permit the Kaiping Mining Company to conduct surveys in the interior. After sites for development had been selected, Tang could request approval to commence mining operations from the Korean government and negotiate regulations on the basis of Sino-Western precedents. If the Koreans preferred to undertake mining development on their own, they were to employ experts from the Kaiping Mining Company. Or, Koreans could choose the option of establishing mining enterprises jointly with the China Merchants' Steam Navigation Company and the Kaiping Mining Company. The loan was to be used to establish a customs service and to carry out other reform measures (ZRH 968-70).

Taking advantage of Korea's plight and the anxieties that had led to the appeal for Chinese assistance, Li Hongzhang took further measures to secure Chinese control over the domestic and foreign affairs of Korea. Under Li's supervision, Korea consented to Chinese guidance in the administration of the T'ongni Amun, an institution similar to the Zongli Yamen, which Korea had set up for handling international relations. Its staff was to be instructed in diplomatic practice and foreign languages by Chinese teachers. Li also urged the Koreans to set up a customs service similar to China's but under the separate jurisdiction of the king of Korea and the Chinese commissioner of the northern ports—at the time, Li himself. The Korean Customs Service subsequently was organized on terms that allowed foreigners only temporary employment and with the stipulation that Koreans eventually would replace them. Not surprisingly, these stipulations corresponded with the objections the modern commercial community had to the Imperial Maritime Customs Service in China.

Li selected Paul Georg von Mollendorff, the German consul in Tientsin, to serve as inspector-general of the Korean Customs Service and as adviser to the Korean government on reform and foreign policy. Although appointed in response to the Korean application to the Qing Emperor, von Mollendorff was engaged as a subordinate within Li Hongzhang's bureaucratic network. He was hired by Li and was responsible to him, not to the king of Korea. In a move that was later to prove very ironic, Li attempted to maintain the separate identity of the Korean customs and restrict the authority of Sir Robert Hart, the inspector-general of the Imperial Maritime Customs Service. At the time, Hart reported sarcastically:

> Li has paid me the compliment of sending von Mollendorff to open the Customs in Corea just as he selected Richtofen's bankrupt Belgian valet to join the Chia-yu-Kwan Taotai [*sic*] on the Kansuh (Russian) frontier. This, of course, is a part of the German progress and plan, and as it also chimes in with what the Chinese like (and Li in particular) viz. to have low-class men who will obey orders rather than better-class men who will give advice, it is done. I am spared a deal of trouble by being out of both jobs, but I feel chiefly sorry over it because I see in it the proof that China is very far from being anything more than "the sick man of the Far East" yet! (Fairbank et al. 1975, no. 392: 17 December 1882)

In accepting this assignment, von Mollendorff requested that six of the students from the Chinese Educational Mission recently recalled from the United States be assigned to his staff. They would be able to serve instead of foreigners in establishing and operating the Korean customs service and in teaching English to Korean officials in the customs and foreign services (von Mollendorff 1930, 39). These American-educated assistants, who served their apprenticeships in Seoul from 1883 to 1885 in the conduct of international affairs under von Mollendorff, inevitably came from the comprador-merchant sector. During the early 1870s when these Chinese students were sent abroad, interest in Western learning and projects for overseas studies was concentrated in and largely confined to this group. Jong Hong [Yung Wing] had proposed and largely administered this mission in the Connecticut River Valley, but Tang Tingshu and Xu Run, the most influential of the Cantonese compradors in Shanghai, were in charge of selecting students and arranging the logistics for the Chinese Educational Mission. The students were essentially the second generation of the modern commercial community: the sons, nephews, and other younger relatives of the comprador-merchants. Included in the group of six students assigned to Korea in 1882 were Tang Tingshu's junior clansman Tang Shaoyi, Tang

Shaoyi's first cousin Liang Ruhao, and Xu Run's brother-in-law Cai Shaoji (La Fargue 1942, 116).

In December of 1882, Tang Tingshu accompanied von Mollendorff and his three Cantonese subordinates to Korea. On arrival, Tang rode into the interior with an English mining engineer named Burnett to survey mining sites. Tang subsequently submitted a report advising the promotion of industrial development beginning with mines and railways, but he stipulated that China should obtain a monopoly interest in these projects. When the Sino-Korean loan negotiations later took place in Shanghai, Tang demanded strict control over the expenditure and wanted to provide funds only on the guarantee of the Chinese government. Because von Mollendorff refused to consent to such close supervision, the payment of the first installment of the loan funds raised by the China Merchants' Steam Navigation Company was delayed until the end of January of 1883 (F.O. 405, no. 33, 25 November 1882; 7 April 1883).

The abortive pro-Japanese *coup* of December 1884, marked the end of von Mollendorff's tenure as a Chinese agent and signalled the beginning of a more concerted drive to establish Chinese supremacy in Korea. Yuan Shikai, the commander of the Chinese garrison in Seoul, succeeded in crushing the attempted takeover, and the conspirators were forced to flee to Japan. Von Mollendorff sought to preserve Korean independence by introducing Russian influence as a counter to renewed pressure from China and Japan. In response to von Mollendorff's initiatives, Sir Robert Hart self-righteously commented:

> Li is so confident of his own superior knowledge and so easily captured by flattery that he will let anybody lead him into giving an order. He will then reproach himself for doing so and after buying and paying for the thing ordered will throw it into a ditch to rot. And when another man comes along, he will do the same thing over again. I, by nature, cannot flatter, and I cannot, seeing Li so rarely, hold my own against his visitors, except in Customs' matter. On my own ground I have the right to be heard, and as long as I am in the right, no one can upset me. In naval affairs a fit of the blues will at any moment tempt Li to say to me, "Mind your own business. This does not concern you!" He did so in the Corean Customs' affair (practically) when he appointed von Mollendorff, and now von M. appears to have achieved his independence. . . . I hear Li is inwardly wild over this, but

outwardly says it's what he intended! (Fairbank et al. 1975, no. 443: 6 November 1883)

When the Chinese and Japanese authorities learned of von Mollendorff's secret approach to St. Petersburg, they jointly agreed on removing him from the scene. With his departure, his former responsibilities were divided between two Americans: Henry Merrill, who became head of the customs service, and Owen Denny, who served as adviser to the Korean government on reform and diplomacy (Guo 1963, 781-87, 784-85, 789).

Merchant-Official Collaboration in Korea

In September of 1885, Yuan Shikai was appointed to the post of Trade and Diplomatic Resident in Korea, and he assumed responsibility for implementing Chinese policy in November. From that time until his ignominious flight from Seoul in 1894, Yuan exercised effective authority over Korea's internal affairs, and he utilized various means to gain foreign acknowledgment of China's special status. Since the foreign powers all had formal treaties that explicitly recognized Korean independence, Yuan required skillful handling of the diplomatic problems, so he recruited some of the alumni of the Chinese Educational Mission with prior Korean experience under von Mollendorff's tutelage. The most noteworthy of this younger, better-trained generation was Tang Tingshu's clansman, Tang Shaoyi, who joined Yuan's service at this time (NCH, 9 December 1885, 655; La Fargue 1942, 108, 133).

The major economic objective of Qing Korean policy during Yuan's residency was the promotion of Korea's dependence on China. The principal means adopted to obtain this goal were the encouragement of Chinese commercial expansion into the Korean market, the securing of Chinese primacy in the provision of loans to the Korean government, and the establishment of Chinese supervisory control over official economic activities. In all three aspects of the policy, the expertise, outlook, and connections of Tang Shaoyi, Liang Ruhao, and Cai Shaoji were valuable in coping with the difficulties that arose in converting Korea into a Chinese protectorate.

In the matter of the Korean customs, it was ironically Li Hongzhang's failure that assured greater Chinese control. With the ouster of von Mollendorff, the appointment to positions in the Korean Customs Service came under the authority of Sir Robert Hart and were treated the same as appointments in the Imperial Maritime Customs Service.   As Hart concluded in 1888:

> Corea is on the brink of a decision. The King is either to turn out all my men, or will let them stay on and thereby acknowledge and recognize China's . . . control of the Customs affairs of Corea's . . . Treaty ports (Fairbank et al. 1975, no. 669, 7 October 1888).

Hart continued to express doubts about the king of Korea's treatment of his nominees until 1892, despite the lack of grounds to support these fears (Fairbank et al. 1975, no. 719, 29 September 1889; no. 720, 6 October 1889; no. 832, 10 April 1892).

In similar fashion, the Chinese issued new procedures in 1889 for the handling of Korean exports to Chinese ports.   As evaluated by Charles Denny, the American Minister to China:

> In short, China by this regulation has applied the identical regulations which control the shipment of goods from one treaty port in China to another treaty port in China. The result is that for Customs purposes China has incorporated Corea into itself as one of its provinces (Palmer 1963, 2:18).

In addition to these more direct administrative measures, the political position of Chinese authorities in Korea was reinforced substantially by the steady Chinese penetration of Korean import markets during the years of Chinese hegemony.   Chinese merchants achieved rapid and significant success in destroying the virtual monopoly that Japanese merchants had enjoyed in the late 1870s, after the Treaty of Kanghwa. This remarkable reversal of fortunes can be seen in Table 3.

These statistics, in fact, demonstrate the growing share of the Korean import trade in Chinese hands in the three ports opened to international trade in compliance with the treaties concluded with the foreign powers: Inch'on, Pusan and Wonsan. This was not, however, the full extent of Korean foreign trade. In addition, there was a substantial commercial exchange in the prosperous provinces of P'yongan and Hwanghae to the north of Seoul. According to the assessment of F. H. Morsel in his review of Korean trade in 1891:

> The outlet for the former province is the Yaloo and the head of the Pyongyang Inlet, also the Taitong river which empties

into the Inlet. The Ouel River is the outlet for the Hoanghai province. At these points a brisk trade is carried on so long as the ice does not prevent navigation. . . . Here then we see is a northern trade carried on, which if under proper control would be beneficial to merchants in general, instead of being confined to a few Chinese from the Shantung province (Morsel 1892, 189-93).

Table 3[a]
Commodity Imports Into Korea.

Year	China (%)	Japan (%)	Russia (%)
1885	18.0	81.9	0.1
1886	17.8	81.7	0.6
1887	26.0	73.6	0.4
1888	27.8	71.5	0.7
1889	32.1	67.6	0.2
1890	34.9	64.9	0.1
1891	38.9	60.9	0.2
1892	44.6	55.3	0.1
1893	49.1	50.2	0.7

[a]Based on: China, Imperial Maritime Customs. *Trade Returns and Reports*. 1885-1893.

As long as this technically illicit trade was tolerated, no customs duties were collected. Chinese merchants could monopolize this trade without competition from Japanese or other traders as long as it was not officially opened. According to Morsel's report:

Steps were taken in 1887 toward the opening of Pyeng-yang[*sic*] to Foreign Commerce by Mr. Merrill, the chief of the Customs, with Sir Robert Hart's permission. His efforts in this direction were fruitless. The Chinese government (Li Hung Chang's government) objected. . . . It is hoped that some steps will be taken in the near future towards opening this province as it is really important to commerce in general, no matter what may be the objections of the Chinese government whose main objection is based on a political point of view (Morsel 1892, 189-93).

In line with this policy of encouraging the Chinese mercantile penetration of Korea, Yuan Shikai and Tang Shaoyi resisted any Korean efforts to restrict the activities of Chinese businessmen. In January of 1890, for example, the Korean merchants in Seoul suspended trade for five days in protest against foreign competition, seeking to have all Chinese and Japanese merchants removed from the capital. They petitioned the Korean court for these Chinese and Japanese firms to be ordered to move to Yangsan, five kilometers away. Yuan Shikai strongly opposed this plea, and the Korean authorities refused to act. In December of the following year, the mayor of Seoul prohibited the sale of real estate to Chinese merchants. This time, Tang Shaoyi forcefully intervened and insisted that this proclamation be retracted (ZRH, 2734-2740, 2942-2944).

The Chinese authorities played a significant role in enhancing the competitive standing of the Chinese businessmen operating in Korea. By the terms of the 1882 trade regulations governing Sino-Korean trade, the Korean government was obligated to sudsidize the cost of a steamship to run on a fixed date each month between Korea and China. In 1888, the China Merchants' Steam Navigation Company inaugurated a monthly service between Inch'on and Shanghai via Yantai. This line had the support of the Chinese commercial community in Korea, which pledged to guarantee the shipping company against any losses. Since both the Chinese and Japanese traders were vying to handle the import of British cotton goods for the Korean market and both acquired their inventory on the Shanghai market, the Chinese now enjoyed a big advantage. Unlike the Japanese who had to route their Shanghai purchases through Japanese ports, the Chinese could benefit from this shorter, quicker, and cheaper shipping service (Kim and Kim 1967, 69-70).

While promoting the interests of Chinese commercial firms in the Korean import market, Yuan Shikai intervened in the Korean export trade in ways that seriously undermined the position of the Japanese firms that dominated it. The Chinese trading companies operating in the three open ports never played a significant role in this export market. The Chinese share of exports in the period 1885-1893 fluctuated between a maximum of 8.9 percent in 1889 to a low of 1.9 percent in 1890, with an annual average of 5.0 percent over the nine-year period. The Japanese on the other hand, accounted for over 90 percent of Korean exports, with a maximum share of 97.9 percent in 1890 (China, Imperial Maritime Customs 1885-1893).

The staples of the Korean export trade were beans and rice which were exported to Japan to meet any shortfalls in its own domestic harvest. During the early 1890s, Korean provincial authorities frequently acted to prohibit the export of beans or rice when the Korean crop seemed to be threatened. Although this type of restriction was allowed under these circumstances according to the treaty stipulations, the Japanese diplomats in Seoul strongly protested this action and demanded compensation for the heavy losses incurred by Japanese firms. According to the American Minister to Korea in 1893:

> The prohibition of exports mentioned in my Nos. 472, Oct. 18, & 481, Nov. 7, is now known to be the work of Mr. Yuan, and he admitted as much to Mr. Frandin. When this decree was announced, the conditions were such that the Government had a perfect right to make the prohibition—according to treaty. . . . Mr. Otori, the Japanese minister, expresses himself as satisfied with the present condition, while the banks of his countrymen here are on the point of failure, and hundreds of Japanese merchants are desperate with fear of ruin. . . . His countrymen . . . say that the present interference is an attempt on the part of China to drive Korean commerce out of their hands into the hands of the Chinese (Palmer 1963, 2:291).

The following month, H. N. Allen, the American Minister reported:

> To Japanese trade the export question is one of life or death. . . . And while they are contesting the matter strongly, it has long been known that the Chinese used the prospective famine to get in a master stroke against Japanese trade, for, while it was soon known that Mr. Yuan proposed the prohibition, any further evidence as to his action in the matter that might be needed, is furnished by the fact that the Korean people are about to erect a memorial tablet to him in the market space; on which will be inscribed characters praising him for "prohibiting the export of rice and saving the country." I hear that the Foreign Office is very anxious to prevent the erection of this stone, lest the Foreign Representative resent it, but it will probably be erected.

Chinese policy here is well illustrated in this incident, showing as it does that while China rules here with a rod of iron when necessary, she yet manages to make the people kiss the hand that smites them. The Japanese on the contrary make themselves positively hated (Palmer 1963, 2:329-30).

One of the reasons for the popularity of Yuan's actions in the "bean controversy," as this confrontation came to be known, was that the Japanese commercial agents who controlled the export trade often contracted to purchase the grain harvest prior to the end of the growing season. In return for cash advances, provided at high interest rates to facilitate peasant purchases of imported goods, these Japanese buyers could contract to obtain the cereal crop at low prices. The disruption of this exploitative system jeopardized the commercial interests of Japan (Kim and Kim 1967, 71).

Another important aspect of Chinese economic imperialism in Korea was the exclusive position Chinese firms gained as a source of loans for the impoverished Korean government. Chinese enterprises cooperated with the Qing authorities in the execution of this strategy. At the same time, Chinese government officials and diplomats were actively discouraging alternative sources of financial assistance. Yuan Shikai, in particular, frequently clashed with foreign advisers and diplomats in Korea who were attempting to preserve Korean independence in the face of Chinese domination.

Owen Denny, for example, like his predecessor von Mollendorff, sought to procure Russian and American aid in order to prevent the Chinese takeover. When this failed, he wrote a book denouncing China's high-handed, illegal, and unjust attempt to subvert Korean sovereignty. In June of 1889, Denny tried to persuade the king of Korea to negotiate a loan from France to repay the funds owed to China. He also urged the Korean monarch to redeem the Korean telegraph lines which were held as security against the loan for their construction. These telegraph lines would otherwise remain under Chinese control until the loan was repaid. This and subsequent attempts to borrow elsewhere, however, were successfully blocked by the Chinese (Denny 1888, 655; ZRH 2601-2603).

As part of this Chinese campaign of interference, the Chinese legation in Washington sent a warning to the American Secretary of State:

> It having been brought to the attention of the Imperial Government that it is proposed to seek the negotiation of a foreign loan or loans on behalf of Korea, my Government has instructed me to represent to you, and through you, to the capitalists or bankers of your country that the Imperial Government regards such a step as unwise and likely to involve those who should participate in such loans in serious trouble and financial losses. It should be borne in mind that Korea is a poor country inclined to be extravagant in its expenditures, and with small resources out of which to repay

a foreign loan. This is shown by the fact that it has not been able to repay to the Imperial Government a considerable sum of money which a number of years ago my Government in view of the tributary condition of Korea and out of a benevolent desire to relieve it from foreign embarrassment, advanced to the King of that country.

It should be made known that the Imperial Government will not guarantee the repayment of loans made in behalf of Korea, nor will it permit the customs revenue of Korea to be seized for liquidating any indebtedness contracted on behalf of that country (Palmer 1963, 19).

The firm most prominent in working with Yuan Shikai and Tang Shaoyi in promoting Qing Korean policy was the Tongshuntai Company, headed by Tan Yishi, Director of the Guangdong League in Korea, and his clansman Tan Jiesheng, Chairman of the Guangdong Guildhall (*huiguan*) in Seoul. Tongshuntai was the family enterprise of the Tan clan of Gaoyao county, Guangdong, and had affiliated branches at Wonsan and Inch'on in Korea, at Nagasaki in Japan, as well as at Shanghai, Guangzhou, and Hong Kong on the China coast (ZRH, 3038-3040).

The Chinese commercial community in Korea was organized into three groupings according to the provincial origins of its members. The Northern League, comprised of Chinese from Shandong and Hebei, was the largest association and exerted the greatest economic influence in Korea. It was concentrated in Inch'on and maintained a steamship line between Inch'on and the Chinese mainland. The Southern League was composed of Chinese from Jiangsu, Zhejiang, Hunan, Hubei, and Anhui; and the Guangdong League was the third group (Lu 1956, 17-18).

It can be surmised that the close involvement of the Tongshuntai and members of the Tan clan in Qing Korean policy was based upon the Cantonese connection with Tang Shaoyi. Tang became Yuan's leading adviser and foreign affairs expert and was part of China's most prominent commercial family. It would have been natural for Tang, a Cantonese, to turn to the head of the Guangdong guildhall, Tan Jiesheng, for cooperation in implementing the plans he believed would be mutually beneficial.

In the spring of 1892, Yuan Shikai advised the king of Korea that he should repay all Japanese debts as soon as possible and that in the future he should rely exclusively on China. When the head of the Korean Foreign Office came to Yuan in August of that year with a request for a loan of one hundred thousand *taels* for the purchase of a steamship, Yuan felt obliged to honor his pledge to arrange any necessary financing. The solution was provided through the Cantonese commercial connections of Tang Shaoyi (ZRH, 3038-3040, 3042-3043).

A formal loan agreement was concluded between the Tongshuntai Company and the Korean Transport Bureau on October 9, 1892, with Yuan Shikai and the director of the Korean Foreign Office as witnessing signatories. The customs *daotai* in Shanghai, Nie Qigui, was instructed to transfer funds to the Hong Kong & Shanghai Banking Corporation to assist the private Chinese firm in fulfilling its obligations to the Koreans (ZRH, 3044-3056). Repayment of this loan was to be made by the Korean customs in Inch'on and "should the Customs fail to make the stipulated payments punctually, the amount of interest due increases at the rate of 100 percent daily and such overdue installments are to be recovered finally from the customs dues paid into the customs by the Chinese retail merchants in Korea" (Agreement . . . *Korean Repository* 1892, 1:375-76).

Subsequently, on November 24, an additional agreement was concluded between Tan Yishi of Tongshuntai and the Korean Transport Bureau for a supplementary loan of one hundred thousand *taels*. The contract for this loan stipulated that the Tongshuntai Company was authorized to launch a Sino-Korean joint-stock shipping venture. The accords governing this enterprise were signed the same day and stated that the Tongshuntai could issue shares restricted to Chinese and Korean merchants for the construction of two shallow-water steamships of forty- to fifty-ton capacity. This steam navigation line was to operate between Inch'on and Seoul on the Han River. It would be granted the franchise to transport Korean government rice and would be under the management of the Tongshuntai Company (ZRH, 3066-3071).

The establishment of this transport link had the added advantage of destroying the monopoly the Japanese had enjoyed on this important route up until this time. This move represented the interdependence of commercial enterprise and national interest that had been demonstrated previously by Tang Tingshu when he extended the shipping lines of the China Merchants' Steam Navigation Company to encompass Korea. By the Sino-Korean Trade Regulations of 1882, moreover, the Koreans had even been persuaded to provide a subsidy for the monthly round-trip between China and Inch'on (Chien 1967, 119).

Business Involvement in the Late 1890s

The privileged position China enjoyed in Korea came to an abrupt end in 1894, when the Japanese used the dispatch of Chinese troops against the

Tonghak rebels as a pretext for armed invasion. With the armistice and the signing of the Treaty of Shimonoseki, it was the Chinese merchant community in Korea that took the initiative in petitioning their government to resume diplomatic representation in Korea. In November of 1895, they urged the new commissioner of the northern ports, Wang Wenshao, to send a consular official to negotiate the normalization of trade relations, particularly with regard to concession areas in the treaty ports. They also desired the appointment of a diplomat to reside in Korea to handle commercial matters and to safeguard their interests. In response, Wang proposed sending Tang Shaoyi back to Korea to cope with all outstanding Korean problems, including customs, loan repayment, and related business concerns once the unsettled situation in Korea stabilized (ZRH, 4516-4517, 4563).

Tang Shaoyi returned to Korea in June of 1896 as director-general of Korean trade affairs. During his five-month stay, he used his expertise in international law to forestall the emergence of any semblance of equality in standing between China and her former tributary. He twice succeeded in delaying the departure of a Korean diplomatic mission to China. Meanwhile, Tang reported to Wang that despite his temporary achievements in fulfilling his instructions, he felt that Waeber, the Russian Minister in whose legation the king of Korea was residing, and the other diplomats from the treaty powers would soon resolve any doubts the king might have. Tang warned that China could not legitimately cite any international law to refuse the Korean approach and cautioned that there could not be any means of resolving Korean affairs if China clung to anachronistic statutes. Tang advised Wang to discuss revisions in the handling of Korean relations with the Zongli Yamen as a matter of urgency, noting that China's national interests should be borne uppermost in mind (*The Independent* 27 June 1896; ZRH, 4872-4873).

Tang informed the Zongli Yamen directly that it was essential to make changes in Sino-Korean relations. He noted that while he could provide short-term expedients for the Beijing authorities unwilling to conclude an agreement based on equality, it was in China's own interest to adopt Western practices and seize the initiative before confronted with a Korean envoy in Beijing. He indicated that, without the exchange of envoys, England and Germany had consuls-general resident in Seoul, had negotiated customs regulations, and had consuls stationed in the various Korean treaty ports (ZRH, 4958-4959).

Tang presented the Zongli Yamen with the alternatives of passively following the German and British examples to avoid receiving an envoy from the king of Korea or pursuing a more positive foreign policy by formally recognizing the independence of Korea in accordance with Article I of the Treaty of Shimonoseki. China, in his view, could still make effective use of the members of the powerful pro-Chinese faction and exert considerable political influence in Seoul. He argued that the policy he advocated could best be carried out if China were represented in Seoul by a fully accredited minister-resident rather than by a consul-general (F.O. 405, no. 73, 25 August 1897).

The Zongli Yamen, which hitherto had rejected a treaty based upon equality, the dispatch of a Chinese diplomat to Korea, and the exchange of diplomatic credentials, dramatically altered its Korean policy after the death of Prince Gong in May of 1898. Tang's requests for an accredited diplomat and a treaty to resolve the Korean problem finally were viewed in a favorable light by the Zongli Yamen. In the end, his appeals led to the appointment of Xu Shoupeng as imperial commissioner to Korea with second-level rank (ZRH, 5135).

Conclusion

Qing Korean policy, in the late nineteenth century, marks a crucial turning point in the emergence of members of the modern commercial community to positions of power and influence in the development and execution of Chinese foreign policy. The critical state of Chinese security after 1895 led to a wider reception of their ideas and views by more classically oriented reformist gentry. The importance of preserving China's economic rights and promoting industry came to be accepted aspects of national policy. This new nationalistic spirit raised the social standing and political importance of merchants and capitalists as part of the Chinese elite.

China's modern commercial community brought a transformed perspective to late Qing Korean policy based on an awareness of the need to recover national prestige and regain sovereign rights. They devised measures to increase Chinese power and influence, gained acceptance for these proposals, and provided the personnel for putting them into effect. They also made their activities and resources available to support the plans they were advocating.

In late Qing Korean policy, a considerable alteration in business-state relations is evident. The initiative for change came from the business community. These merchants sought to convince Qing officials that Chinese interests were best served by safeguarding and promoting their economic interests. They gained official encouragement and patronage for their enterprise and effectively recruited government support for them to "wage commercial warfare" in China's interest.

References

Agreement Concerning a Loan of *Taels* 100,000. 1892. *The Korean Repository* 1:375-76.

Chien, Frederick Foo. 1967. *The Opening of Korea.* Hamden, CT: Shoestring Press.

China, Imperial Maritime Customs. 1885-1893. *Trade Returns and Reports.* Shanghai: Statistical Department of the Inspectorate-General of Customs.

Chun, Hae-jong. 1968. "Sino-Korean Tributary Relations in the Ch'ing Period." In *The Chinese World Order*, ed. John K. Fairbank. Cambridge, Mass.: Harvard University Press.

Cohen, Paul A. 1974. *Between Tradition and Modernity: Wang T'ao and Reform in Late Ch'ing China.* Cambridge, Mass.: Harvard University Press.

Denny, O. N. 1888. *China and Korea.* Shanghai: Kelly and Walsh.

Deuchler, Martina. 1977. *Confucian Gentlemen and Barbarian Envoys. The Opening of Korea, 1875-1885.* Seattle: University of Washington Press.

Fairbank, John K., et al. 1975. *The I.G. in Peking.* Cambridge, Mass.: Harvard University Press.

F. O. Great Britain, Foreign Office. 1883 and 1897. F. O. 405, Confidential Prints on China and Korea: No. 33, Affairs of Corea 1883 and No. 73, Affairs of Corea 1897. London: Foreign Office.

Guo, Tingyi. 1963. *Jindai Zhongguo shishi rizhi* (Daily record of events in modern Chinese history). Taibei: Institute of Modern History, Academia Sinica.

The Independent. 1896. Seoul.

Kim, C. I. Eugene and Kim Han-Kyo. 1967. *Korea and the Politics of Imperialism,1876-1910.* Berkeley: University of California Press.

La Fargue, Thomas E. 1942. *China's First Hundred.* Pullman, Wash.: Washington State University Press.

Lee, Kwang-rin. 1969. 'I-yen' and the Ideas of Enlightenment in Korea. *Bulletin of the Korean Research Center, Journal of Social Sciences and Humanities* 31:1-9 (December).

_____. 1976. Progressive Views on Protestantism (1). *Korea Journal* 16, 2:19-26 (February).

Lin, T. C.   1935.   Li Hung-chang: His Korea Policies, 1870-1885. *Chinese Social and Political Science Review* 19:202-33.

Liu, Guangjing (Liu Kwang-ching).   1970.   Zheng Guanying *Yiyan*: Guangxu chunian zhi bianfa sixiang (Zheng Guanying's *Yiyan*: reform thought of the early Guangxu period). *Tsing Hua Journal of Chinese Studies*, New Series 8, 1-2:373-425 (August).

Lo, Jung-pang.   1969.   "Policy Formulation and Decision-Making on Issues Respecting Peace and War." In *Chinese Government in Ming Times*, ed. Charles O. Hucker. New York: Columbia University Press.

Lu, Guanqun.   1956.   *Hanguo Huaqiao jingji* (The economy of the overseas Chinese in Korea). Taibei.

Martin, W.A.P.   1896.   *A Cycle of Cathay*. London: Harper and Brothers.

Metzger, Thomas A.   1966.   Ch'ing Commercial Policy, *Ch'ing-shih wen-t'i* 1, 3:4-10 (February).

_____.   1970.   The State and Commerce in Imperial China. *Asian and African Studies* (Jerusalem) 6:23-46.

Morsel, F. H.   1892.   "Review of the trade of Corea for 1891 in comparison with that of 1890." *The Korean Repository* 1:189-93.

NCH.   *North China Herald*.   1885.   Shanghai.

Palmer, Spencer J.   1963.   *Korean-American Relations*. 2 vols. Berkeley: University of California Press.

QZRH *Qingji ZhongRiHan guanxi shiliao* (Historical materials dealing with Sino-Japanese-Korean foreign relations in the Qing period).   1971. Taibei: Institute of Modern History, Academia Sinica.

Sigel, Louis T.   1975.   The Treaty Port Community and Chinese Foreign Policy in the 1880s. *Papers on Far Eastern History* (Canberra)11:79-105 (March).

_____.   1976.   "Foreign Policy Interests and Activities of the Treaty-Port Chinese Community." In *Reform in Nineteenth Century China*, ed. Paul A. Cohen and John E. Schrecker. Cambridge, Mass.: Harvard East Asian Papers.

_____.   1985.   "The Diplomacy of Chinese Nationalism, 1900-1911." In *Ideal and Reality. Social and Political Change in Modern China 1960-1949*, ed. David Pong and Edmund S. K. Fung. Lanham, Maryland: University Press of America.

Tsiang, T. F.   1933.   Sino-Japanese Diplomatic Relations, 1870-1894. *Chinese Social and Political Science Review* 17:1-105.

von Mollendorff, Rosalie.   1930.   *P. G. von Mollendorff, ein Lebensbild*. Leipzig: Otto Harrassowitz.

ZFYN. *ZhongFaYuenan jiaoshedang* (Diplomatic documents concerning Sino-French-Vietnamese relations). 1962. Taibei: Institute of Modern History, Academia Sinica.

ZRH. *Qingji ZhongRiHan guanxi shiliao* (Historical materials on Chinese-Japanese-Korean relations). 1971. Comp. by Institute of Modern History, Academia Sinica. Taibei.

Glossary

Ba *xian* 巴县

Balikun (Barkol) 巴里坤

Batang 巴塘

baojie 保結

baolan 包攬

baoren 保人

baozhengren 保證人

Bei 邶

Beilu 邶路

benseyin 本色銀

benwu 本務

benye 本業

Bi Yuan 畢沅

Biancha Gufen Youxian Gongsi 边茶股分有限公司

bianyin 边引

bingtun 兵屯

bochuan 剝船

boke 伯克

"Bu bai ying shu" 布帛贏縮

buxiao 不孝

chafa 茶法

183

chaguan 茶館

chamasi 茶馬司

chama yushi 茶馬御使

Changshu 常熟

Chen Hongmou 陳宏謀

Dajianlu 打箭炉

Dashengkuai 大盛魁

daotai 道台

difang guan 地方官

fangju 紡局

"Fangzhi zhi li" 紡織之利

feimei 肥美

fu dao 婦道

fu geng fu yan 夫耕婦餘

fuyin 腹引

fu zi xieli 婦子協力

Gao Jin 高晋

guoji minsheng 國計民生

Gujin tushu jicheng 古今圖書集成

Gu Yanwu 顧炎武

guandu shangban 官督商辦

guan shougongye 官手工業

Guo Qiyuan 郭起元

hengchan 恆產

hubao 互保

Hubu 戶部

Huang Liuhong 黃六鴻

Huangqi 黃溪

huiguan 會館

Jiading 嘉定

jiangjun 將軍

Jiangnan 江南

Jiang Yuxian 蔣攸銛

jin 斤

jinli qinjian 筋力勤健

juyinjie 具印結

juanna 捐納

junxian 郡縣

junzi 君子

ka'er 卡倫

kalun 卡倫

kaizhong 開中

kanjing 坎井

ke 科

kenwu 墾務

kuailao qiangjia 拐逃搶嫁

Lei Zu 嫘祖

Li Ba 李拔

Litang 里塘

lianhuan baojie 連環保結

lianhuan hubao 連環互保

lianming baozhen 連名保証

"Mianhua tu" 棉花圖

minya 民牙

Ming shi 明史

mo 末

mu 畝

nan geng nu zhi 男耕女織

Nanzhu 南柱

"Nong shu" 農書

nongsang 農桑

nugong 女紅

panba jieyun 盤霸接運

piaohao 票號

Puyuan 濮院

qiaijiming 戒雞鳴

qianpu 錢鋪

qianzhuang 錢莊

Qinding shouyi guangxun 欽定授衣廣訓

quanqie 權且

shanghang 商行

shengke 升科

Shengze 盛澤

shi 石

shibozhou 矢柏舟

Shiji 史記

shu ren 殊人

Shuanglin 双林

shui 稅

Songjiang 松江

Songpan 松潘

Song Rulin 朱如林

Subei 蘇北

Tang Zhen 唐甄

Tianshan beilu 天山北路

Tianshan nanlu 天山南路

Tongxiang 桐鄉

tou'an 偷安

tuyin   土引

tuntian   屯田

Wangjiangjing   王江泾

Wuyi   武惫

wuzu   五族

Xibang   西帮

Xilu   西路

xiansan   閒散

xiangmin   鄉民

Xiangyang   襄陽

xiaomin wei li shi tu   小民惟利是圖

Xinghua   兴化

xiuwu zhi xin   羞惡之心

yahang   牙行

yatie   牙帖

yanghang   洋行

"Yangmin sizheng"   養民四政

yencha daotai   鹽茶道台

yibian yangbian   以邊養邊

yishan   驛站

Yiyan   易言

yin   引

yinhao 銀號

yongzhe 永折

Yuzhi gengzhi tu 御製耕織圖

zafu 雜賦

za gengyu 雜耕耦

zhasako 扎薩克

Zhangjiakou 張家口

Zhang Luxiang 張履祥

Zhao Erfeng 趙爾豐

zhaolai 招徠

zhaoshang 招商

zhecao 折漕

zhejian 摘尖

zhese 折色

Zhenze 震泽

zhengxiang 正項

Zhou Kai 周凱

zhudan 硃單

zongshang 總商

zulin 族隣

zushi 足食

CORNELL EAST ASIA SERIES

For ordering information, please contact:

Cornell East Asia Series
East Asia Program
Cornell University
140 Uris Hall
Ithaca, NY 14853-7601
USA
(607) 255-6222.

2-93/.6M/BB